Ronit Plotnik, Ph.D

GROWING UP DIFFERENTLY

Ronit Plotnik, Ph.D

GROWING UP DIFFERENTLY

Senior Editors & Producers: Contento De Semrik

English Edition: Barak Milner
English Edit: BookMasters Group
Cover Design: Yael Rosen | www.yds.co.il

ISBN: 978-965-550-059-2

International sole distributor:
Contento De Semrik
22 Isserles, 67014 Tel-Aviv, Israel
Semrik10@gmail.com
www.Semrik.com

Ronit Plotnik, Ph.D

GROWING UP DIFFERENTLY

THE EMOTIONAL AND SOCIAL WORLD OF
CHILDREN WITH LEARNING DISABILITIES
AND ATTENTION-DEFICIT DISORDER

A NEW LANGUAGE FOR PARENTS AND EDUCATORS

Contento De Semrik

To my daugthers, Brit and Tair

and the memory of Yahel, RIP

Table of Contents

Introduction

Learning Disability and Attention Deficit Disorder belong to a group of disorders that anyone who comes into contact with children, young people, and adults these days notices is increasingly prevalent. From the history of the disorders' diagnosis and from the various conceptualizations of them over the years, we have come to know the various aspects and emphases chosen in the attempt to account for the origins and characteristics of this group of disorders. However, it is agreed beyond any dispute and definition differences, that both disabilities interfere and create difficulty for these children in various areas of life as they develop, especially in the modern era - when they are required to fit into both formal and non-formal educational, social, and academic systems.

Nowadays when one assembles the large body of work accumulated on the clinical and diagnostic aspects, some typical components present in, and characteristic of the disabilities emerge.

First, it should be emphasized that the disorder in question has as its underlying basis a central nervous system dysfunction pertaining to several brain regions, causing functional and biochemical changes. It is manifested by the individual's failure to accomplish achievements that are standard and normative for his or her age such as acquiring basic skills (reading, writing, arithmetic) despite having normal intellectual ability, i.e., a learning disability; and by the individual's inability to acquire habits and behavioral norms - and to develop normally - emotionally and psychologically; and by his or her inability to be organized and regulated according to life's requirements, i.e., with an **Attention Deficit Disorder**.

Attention Deficit Disorder stems from an individual's inability to focus on and invest in the particular stimuli and information he or she is required to at a certain moment. This individual, therefore, tends to be distracted or more invested in other stimuli that attract his or her attention.

A hereditary component seems to be involved in most cases, and a large proportion of children who are diagnosed with the disability have a family relative who suffers from similar disorders.

Most researchers who pursue the study, diagnosis, and treatment of the disorders, differentiate between the disorder defined as a "learning disability" and that which pertains to attention and concentration. They point out that each of the disorders can be accompanied by additional difficulties such as hyperactivity, rebelliousness, distractibility, Tourette Syndrome and more, and that it is possible for both to appear together or separately. However, this book mainly refers to what is common to the totality of these disorders;

as it is intended to shed light particularly on the emotional–psychological aspect of the disabilities.

The definition of the difficulties as a learning, attention, or concentration disability tends by itself to focus attention on the years of life parallel to the formal education age - pre-school and school - and thus, information concerning the possible existence of the disorder already at the embryonic phase, and concerning the disorder's implications for the growing child's emotional, psychological, and behavioral development is omitted. For the same reason, to this day, an unforgivable separation has been created between the academic characteristics of the disabilities - difficulties in acquiring academic skills - and the characteristics pertaining to the children's psychological and emotional and/or behavioral and interpersonal course of life. This separation does not benefit the children and their parents at all, because one cannot talk about the existence of the disability at all without considering the psychological and emotional components. Worse still, this is an attempt to define psychological, social, and behavioral development as a separate process from intellectual development.

The uniqueness of this book is in presenting the interested reader - a parent and a professional practitioner - with an integrative model that does not differentiate between the types of neurological disorders, but rather, emphasizes the complex developmental course occurring in the psyche of a child born with one or more aspects of the disorder. It is intended to show that while the newborn, infant, toddler, child, or adolescent is suffering from this or that disability, one cannot talk about ordinary psychological, emotional, and behavioral development.

Furthermore, children's mental health is determined not only by innate potential (genetic and constitutional), but also by the ongoing contact with their familial environment, and later on - with their social and educational environments. And when the people close to them in the various environments are not aware of what it means to grow up with a learning and attention disability, they continue to address the child as a neurologically-normal "entity," and continue to interpret his or her difficulties as unrelated, or worse still - separate from; or even more severe - secondary to the disability itself. And so, due to lack of knowledge, a heavy and dark shadow is cast on the children's lives, and a heavy burden of feelings of guilt and failure is laid on their parents.

As time goes by, an escalating cycle forms, where every child and his or her parents are simultaneously faced with three fronts: the front of the disability and its implications - the psychological-emotional-life front, and the environmental (educational and social) front. The fact that consolidating all the fronts as one totality is not worthwhile not only diminishes from the correctness of the diagnosis, but it also interferes with the ability to assist and help.

Many research studies show that every disability's aspects stem from different components in the individual's development, and that each child or adult has a unique profile of these, alongside the common characteristics. Due to the multiplicity of causes and characteristics of each of the disabilities, one can relate to the phenomenon as a **multi-disciplinary syndrome,** hence the need for simultaneous intervention of a multi-disciplinary team that includes experts from several disciplines - both in diagnosis methods and manners of intervention.

1. "The Transparent Disability"

Contrary to other innate disorders among infants and children, learning- attention-and concentration-disabilities appear in children whose external bodily appearance seems to be completely normal. There is hardly any overt manifestation, visibly recognizable by everyone, that can "transmit" the information "I suffer from a neurological disability" for the sake of the child or parents". Therefore, until an accurate diagnosis is performed, the child will grow up with functional difficulties while accumulating "titles" and criticism, interpreted as a normal child but…"impatient, sleepy, disruptive, disturbed, lazy, does not apply himself," and often "does not learn the lesson" from his or her own mistakes.

Underlying normal development from infancy, processes termed "learning- attention-and concentration" pertain to all of the individual's aspects of life. When a disruption exists in one or more components of these processes, this has immediate implications (even if hidden from the eye at first) for all aspects of life.

My purpose in this book is to serve as the mouthpiece of all those children and parents, to tell their story from infancy and write the multi-disciplinary developmental story for them, And I am doing this to raise awareness and alertness to as-early-as-possible diagnosis, to light up the hidden areas that create a twisted stigma, and mainly to enable the structuring of a better educational and clinical environment. The book is intended to contribute to raising the level of empathy in the environment toward the difficulty and burden imposed on the child and his or her family's life.

The parents of children with the disabilities are required - every single day and every single hour - to deal with various aspects of the syndrome, sometimes not knowing, or not being aware, over many years, that their child suffers from the syndrome, and that therefore, his or her development course is different, and generally speaking, more difficult than that of siblings and other children in his or her environment. In this respect, the parents too, are victims of the same blindness with which many others are afflicted.

2. Learning & AD(H)D Disabilities as a Multi-Dimensional Model

As mentioned, a learning disability, with or without Attention Deficit and Hyperactivity Disorders, is a comprehensive, multi-disciplinary developmental syndrome requiring the intervention of professionals from various disciplines. Although children and teenagers suffering from this syndrome have a variety of specific symptoms, creating a unique profile for each individual, they all share a common fundamental clinical picture. Some of them have additional disorders in the motor-sensory areas, some of them have Attention Deficit Disorder with or without Hyperactivity/impulsivity, and in others, these come alongside other disabilities such as a hearing impairment, C.P (Cerebral Palsy) and more.

Every child suffering from a learning disability is part of a familial system, in which there are parents and siblings, and the genetic component has extra weight in the family's life: Some of them have one or two parents with similar disabilities, a brother or a sister with disabilities, and relatives from the expanded circle possessing the disabilities. Life alongside a learning-disabled child is subject to stresses and difficulties stemming from the disability, in and of itself, and from its presence in the child's emotional, behavioral, and social life.

The approach differentiating between the aspects of the disability itself and the emotional-familial, behavioral, and social aspects is still widespread among theoreticians and clinicians. This approach creates difficulty in understanding the child with the disability and viewing him or her as a whole entity with diverse difficulties and needs. What is worse, this approach casts heavy guilt on the child's parents, who are incapable of coping with the child's special needs in an educational–normative manner.

New research and clinical approaches enable a broader examination of the subject - a multi-disciplinary perspective and an ability to integrate the syndrome's aspects with their implications for the child's course of development over his or her years of growth.

According to these developmental approaches (Barkley, 1997; Stern, 1985; Thomas, Chess & Birch, 1970; Fonagy, Gergely, Jurist & Target, 2002; Brown, 2000; Greenspan, 1998; and more) signs of the syndrome can already be seen from the embryonic phase. The syndrome's influence on the child's course of development is already apparent from early infancy. The involvement of key neurological processes in functions related to the memory system, sensory-motor development, to the development of language and regulation ability, creates an infrastructure for developmental changes as early as the primary attachment processes, and later on - during emotional development. And if to this we add the involvement of non-formal learning (e.g., learning by modeling), and non-verbal as well as verbal learning in the development of interpersonal relations, and the involvement of emotional relations in the ability to develop social skills, we can see the basis of the developmental disorder on the behavioral, interpersonal plane as well.

It follows then, that the learning-attention-concentration disability syndrome tends to exist at varying intensities in all areas of the child's life - as a primary and secondary factor - and hence stems the consolidation of the book's rationale: It (the syndrome) should be examined with a multi-disciplinary approach!

The integrative reference model identifies four key areas of difficulty that are typical of the disability and are revealed at varying intensities and extents among all children afflicted with it:

A. Neurological Developmental Difficulties

- Temperament difficulties - self-regulation, stimuli perception threshold, distractedness, reaction intensity, activity level and more.
- Impairment of Executive Functions
- Disruptions in memory processes, the various senses, and attention
- Persistence difficulties (distractedness, tendency to perseverations and more).
- Difficulties in constructing the inhibitory mechanism

B. Disorders in Sensory-Motor and Perceptual Capability Development

- Impaired muscle tone
- Sensory disorders
- Intersensory integration difficulties
- Impaired motor planning
- Difficulties in sequence execution
- Deficiency in the visual/auditory channel including its various components
- Impaired midline and spatial perception
- Difficulty in fine motor skills, impaired visumotor and grapho-motor coordination

C. Difficulties in Cognitive and Linguistic Functions

- Deficient temporal processing (rapid sequential processing of stimuli)
- Difficulty organizing simultaneous information
- Difficulties in memory system components, including

Working Memory
- Difficulties in automation processes (ability of automatic execution without the involvement of cognitive awareness of the various learning processes)
- Sorting difficulties, difficulty differentiating between the most important thing and that which is of secondary importance, in controlled use of associative thinking; difficulties in normal transition from the Egocentric phase to the Operational phase
- Difficulties in perception of and distinction between the auditory components of language
- Difficulties in innate language structures
- Delayed expressive language due to motor or structural changes
- Difficulty in getting organized verbally
- Difficulties in verbal memory and construction of Inner Language
- Difficulty in quantity, number perception; deficient serial processing
- Damage to high-level thought processes (generalization, abstraction, analysis, and synthesis)
- Difficulty creating multi-area contexts

D. Difficulties in Emotional and Social Development - Learning & AD(H)D Disabilities as a Unique State of Mind

Emotional development, continued by interpersonal development, mostly depends on overall developmental normality. Except in cases of severe pathology in the primary caregiving figure (the parent), or a sick psychological constitution of the newborn (innate disorders such as mental retardation, autism, and more), emotional development depends on complex interactions between the newborn and its parents and later on - between the child and his or her parents. Innate damage or difficulty in any one of the components of development, and its presence as a neurological constitution in the child means disruption in the emotional and interpersonal systems. As a result, the child with the learning-attention disability can be viewed as having a Unique State of Mind present in all stages of development:

- Disruption in perception of parental schema and establishing object relations (Piaget, 1972<<; Winnicott, 1988, 1998; Klein, in Segal, 1979; Klein, 2002).
- Disruption in course of attachment formation - tendency to Type-C (ambivalent) attachment (Ainsworth, 1963, 1991)
- Difficulties in separation and individuation stages (Mahler, Bergman & Pine, 1975 Fixation at the Phallic-Egocentric stage (Freud, in Muuss, 1982; Piaget and Inhalder, 1969)
- Difficulties in internalizing the parental figure during the transition from the Oedipal-Conflictual Stage to the post-Oedipal stage
- Difficulties in constructing socialization processes
- Anxious mental constitution
- Difficulties in social learning
- Living under the shadow of experiences of shame, guilt, inferiority (Erikson, 1951)

-   Identity Diffusion and difficulty in Identity
    Achievement at adolescence (Erikson, 1951)

3. Parenting Children Who Suffer from Learning & AD(H)D Disabilities

Parenting children who suffer from a learning disability is a unique parenthood and is predominantly painful and difficult. In contemporary society, the opinion that the child's overt behavior, including his or her performance and academic accomplishments, are a sign of and a score for the parents' parenting quality, is still widespread. Therefore, not only are parents of learning-disabled children required to cope with a complex and difficult problem, but in most cases, they are also judged by the environment as "not good enough parents." who supposedly find it hard to set limits and to provide proper upbringing, are neglectful, violent, and more.

Parenthood in general is a complex and multi-faceted occurrence. It is a combination of overt, concrete behavior and covert psychological aspects. Parenthood can be defined as a psychological developmental occurrence, constructed anew with every decision to give birth to a new child, and it has tangential aspects to the child's life stages. The Parental Voice Model (Plotnik R., 2006) - as shown in this book - presents each parenthood as a unique, one-time occurrence, specific to each parent-child composition.

The Parental Voice and the psychological parental being

of parents of learning- and attention-disabled children are characterized by their own components, specific to this population.

Parenthood Characteristics of Parents to Children Afflicted with the Syndrome

1. Parenthood overshadowed by a constant hunger for a satisfying, total parenthood (Anthony & Benedek, 1970) and by the lack of secure Basic Trust within the child (Erikson, 1951), while having a continuous experience of damage to the parent-child Object Relations (Klein, M, 2002; Winnicott, 1998).
2. Separation Anxiety and difficulty providing separation and autonomy (Mahler, Bergman & Pine, 1975)
3. Constant struggle with regulation/arousal facing the Phallic and Oedipal child (Freud, in Muuss, 1982).
4. The difficulty of letting the child out.
5. Parenthood under a load of experiences of shame, guilt, and inferiority (Erikson, 1951).
6. Parenthood with a constant struggle over limits (Blank & Fuchs-Shabtai, 2004).

The intervention plan for the sake of these parents assists in providing unique tools for "parenthood by remedial teaching" according to the following principles:

a. Constant and protective presence
b. Advance preparation and mediation when faced with assignments and changes
c. Timeline axis intervention: before and not after

d.   Verbalization of emotions and behaviors

e.   Creating a supportive familial set-up of a routine, limits/boundaries, preparation before a change, maintaining the constant things

4. The Educational and Cultural Environment's Place

According to the educational thought accepted in the Western world today, including the State of Israel, a learning- attention- and concentration-disabled child is in most cases an individual in a regular classroom. and since the percentage of those afflicted with the syndrome, which nowadays is under debate, ranges between 10–20 percent of children and adults, one can conclude that there are probably two to five children possessing various disability characteristics present in every kindergarten or classroom. The lion's share of dealing with these children falls, then, to the ordinary educator (lacking the relevant training and knowledge) and the children in the class. Within public schools, some help is provided by the school psychologist/counselor or Special Education specialists in dedicated help centers.

Private Special Education specialists in specific disabilities (reading, writing arithmetic etc.,) paid by the parents to help their children, are also present on the ground, but despite their contribution to problem solving, they are at the same time increasing confusion in the field.

Alongside the educators, a diverse non-governmental

support system has been developed - both in terms of means and resources. It is comprised of various professional bodies, private and non-profit, providing treatment services outside the educational system, such as CHADD; ADA, the Federation for Children with Special Needs; and others, including private, specialized clinics.

Operating in separate and burdensome systems, the issue of diagnosis as well, is still at the center of a conceptual and practical debate: from the didactic diagnostician (a teacher trained to perform diagnosis) through the educational psychologist, the physician who is a neurologist/psychiatrist, to the paramedical professions (mainly occupational therapists and speech therapists) and expressive art therapists.

The existence of these various professional bodies is indicative of the deep split existing in the system with regard to treatment agencies and methods.

Nowadays, the emphasis in the educational field is suited to disruptions in academic functioning, originating from neu-rological, perceptual-cognitive, and linguistic difficulties; however, the emotional aspects are mostly handed over to the separate treatment of mental health professionals, pre-dominantly outside the educational field, of whom only a minority are a supportive profession from within the edu-cational field.

This reality creates distortions in the understanding of the syndrome and difficulty in treating it with an integrative, multi-disciplinary perspective, as it exists within every child and his or her world. In addition, there is an erroneous approach regarding the family's place and ways it should be involved in treating the child and his or her difficulties. This split between the professions reflects an outdated approach that differentiates between the disorder in the learning domain (the correction of which is defined as the main objective of the school, with the aid of the didactic diagnosis and remedial teaching) and the other domains of the disorder that are diagnosed and treated separately. This situation makes it difficult for both the child and the family, as well as the school and its educators, and mainly causes lack of efficiency, and rigidity with respect to a new understanding of the syndrome.

Cross-cultural studies show different conceptualizations of the syndrome, its presence and intensity. In several countries in Europe (France, for instance) there is a tendency to completely ignore the difficulties and view them as an individual continuum of varied abilities in each child. By contrast, the health and education authorities in the United States have been working diligently for many years on developing measurement and evaluation tools, as well as treatment and intervention tools, and constructing definitions and characteristics. In a few countries the problem is completely ignored and viewed as an educational issue only, related to interpersonal differences, and in others, there is adherence to the psychiatric definition books because the disability is perceived as a type of sickness. Changing attitudes of the environment in this or other location might exacerbate or facilitate the experience of dealing with the syndrome, both from the child's point of view and certainly from the family's.

The age-related changes in the conditions of the social milieu and the academic requirements, as reflected from developmental models, also affect the extent of difficulty or weakness exhibited by learning-disabled children in the adaptation and coping processes. The educational conditions required in kindergarten are not the same as those required in high school. The required increase in the level of attention and concentration, the great number of assignments, the extent of the learning material, the acquisition of behavioral norms and more - all these only increase pressure on the children as they grow older. Further, since the educational environment is built on a cumulative process of acquiring knowledge, behavioral patterns, academic skills and more, then a cumulative lack of abilities in these areas in the learning-attention and concentration-disabled child might leave him or her far behind, while his or her peers go full speed ahead.

The frequent entry of diverse and complex demands into the lives of adolescents and young adults in modern Western society expands the disability's definition and the duration of its presence to an extent unknown in the Old World. Changing priorities and new cultural definitions of concepts related to success, self-realization, professional actualization and more, might turn a young person with a learning- attention- and concentration-disability into a person on an endless journey of difficulties and coping, with which, 20 or two hundred years ago, a similar young person was not familiar.

These changing conditions require us to have intervention performed sooner during the early childhood years and to "stretch" it further into the years in which the mature personality is shaped.

Every learning- and attention-disabled child bears his or her own personal and typical scale of the syndrome's components and intensity of their presence. In order to draft this integrated model for understanding the syndrome, all aspects should be examined, but one should bear in mind that their presence in each child is different and unique in intensity.

The mental health of each individual is redefined by the founding father of the Ecological Psychology stream, Bronfenbrenner (Bronfenbrenner, 1979, 1986), as stemming from circular interaction between three environmental factors: the familial environment, the educational environment, and the cultural-political environment (which defines the values, behavioral norms and priorities for the individual). Furthermore, in every society or culture, a somewhat different role division exists between the tasks imposed only on parents as opposed to those that are the educational system's responsibility and those that are shared by both. It is the shared ones that frequently create the difficulties and conflicts.

To this day, an enormous difference exists between societies. For example, between those that emphasize that the infant should remain for a prolonged period with one of its parents (usually the mother), at least until the age of 2 or 3, and those that allow, encourage, and sometimes require putting the child at an early age into a daycare center or kindergarten. The majority of Western society maintains a compulsory education law that requires behavioral norms and a role division from the parent that are different from those in a society without schools. Desire for achievement, measured by the realization of values, imposes a different role on the parent and educator in a society that prefers material accomplishment over that which emphasizes academic-professional accomplishment.

This environmental ecology directly influences the child and his or her parents' abilities to meet the demands of society; and the more the syndrome's characteristics are contradictory to what is required of the child, the more difficulties and tension increase.

The early entry of social bodies into the family's life (through "social" laws, such as: prevention of minor abuse, prevention of family violence and more) expands the potential circle of those intervening and limiting the parents' parenthood, as well as quickly labeling a few of them as dangerous to their children and increasing the tension. An increasing sense of invasiveness in the lives of learning- attention- and concentration-disabled parents and children stems from impaired judgment by society and from a lack of understanding and knowledge about raising these children.

5. Summary

This book is intended to provide a response to the need for presenting a multi-dimensional and multi-disciplinary developmental model that emphasizes both "covert" and overt aspects in the lives of learning- attention- and concentration-disabled children and parents.

While the majority of the literature, research, and knowledge has been devoted to the domain of learning and its meanings, the psychological, behavioral, social, and familial aspects have been neglected. Further, they have been described as secondary to the syndrome and have been handed over to other professions for treatment and evaluation. Thus, a confusing and harsh reality has been created for children and parents.

Before us is an attempt to describe the syndrome with a multi-faceted developmental perspective: from infancy to maturity and in all areas of life.

That is why the book has been constructed in such a manner that enables the deconstruction of the whole into its elements, into sub-aspects, while every element or aspect receives proper clarification and emphasis. Out of the deconstruction, the picture of the whole with all its components will be reconstructed, restoring for the child and his or her parents the experience of integration that is so lacking in the reality of their lives.

Learning & AD(H)D Disabilities as a Multi-Disciplinary and Multi-Dimensional Developmental Model

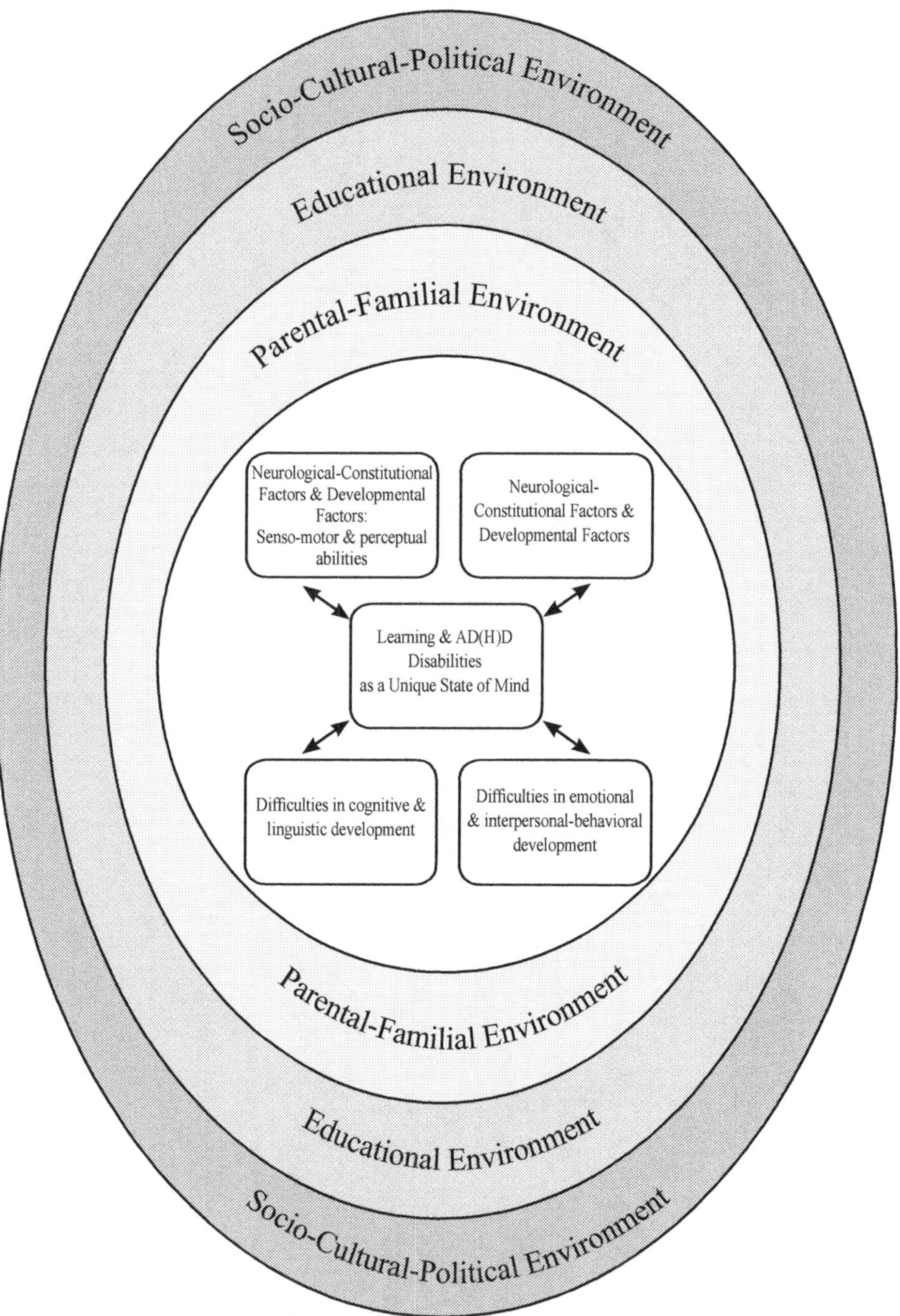

CHAPTER ONE

Learning & AD(H)D Disabilities

A Shared Journey of Parents and Children

1.

Aspects in Infancy and Toddlerhood

A. Concept of Temperament and its Meaning

Infants come into the world equipped with a temperament that is unique to each of them. This important and meaningful information is the fruit of prolonged research by the researcher duo Thomas, Chess and Birch (1970). In multi-year longitudinal follow-ups, they discovered that each infant emerging from its mother's womb has its own temperament, spread over nine dimensions. It is this temperament that is the innate cause factor of the newborn's ability to "achieve" proper adaptation to and coping with the world into which it emerges.

The nine temperament characteristics include various components that can be grouped into four main categories:

- Characteristics related to biological regulation (Activity Level, Rhythmicity (regularity of biological functions))
- Characteristics related to emotional/affective regulation (Approach or withdrawal when confronted with a new stimulus, Adaptability to the changing environment, Quality of Mood)

- Characteristics related to attention regulation (Threshold of Responsiveness, Attention Span and Persistence, Distractibility)
- Characteristics related to reaction regulation (Intensity of Reaction and its duration)

The temperament characteristics are spread out over a continuum with quantitative and qualitative measures at its ends such as: considerably-minimally, high-low, regular-irregular. When an infant is followed during a period beyond a specific stimulus, certain event, or age, it can be characterized with its profile of coping and adapting to the physical and human environment in which it lives.

The importance of the concept of temperament is that by using it we have an ability to evaluate and predict interpersonal differences stemming from an innate constitution, and to form a general picture of different infants. During the research, the researchers obtained a more complex picture of infants and their temperaments and divided them into three main groups:

The Easy Child - those whose adaptation course is pleasant and comfortable (parents of infants suffering from disabilities will often look at them jealously, and other parents will talk about them as the "next-door neighbor's children... but never my own...") (Rapoport & Ismond, 1996, Greenspan 1994,1998; Greenspan & Wieder, 1995).

The Slow-to-Warm-Up Child - those who will reach their destination, but their pace is relatively slower and lower than the norm. They are often evaluated by their parents in their first year of life as an "angelic baby" - does not demand much from the environment, enables the parent a sense of calm and many side-pursuits alongside its rearing. The "price" of the slow pace will only be discovered at a later stage, and will sometimes cause emotional turmoil in the parent over his or her lack of alertness.

The Difficult Child - a stormy group of newborns and infants whose reaction character, demandingness, lack of biological regularity in their daily and developmental life cycles (sleeping and waking times, hunger and satiation, activeness, and so forth) create a feeling of suffocation, exhaustion, and anxiety in the parent regarding her/his parental quality.

In an important study on temperament as predictive of future difficulties, and especially the dimension of regulation and attention, Stanley Greenspan (Greenspan, 1992, 1994; Greenspan & Wieder, 1993, 1994), found that many children who later in life would be diagnosed as suffering from a learning- attention- and concentration-disability were Difficult or Slow-to-Warm-Up as infants. And indeed, these two temperament groups are at the focus of our discussion because of the power of their implications: A Slow or Difficult infant is not only a focal source of difficulty for the parents in its rearing process, but also experiences psychological difficulties of its own. The experiences it gathers with regard to the world as a safe, reassuring, and trustworthy place, are different and of lesser quality than those of the infant with the Easy temperament. Biological irregularity, impacting waking and sleep patterns, difficulties in regulating hunger and satiation, difficulty adapting to changes in the environment and more, all gradually contribute to the sense of difficulty and distress that might accumulate in this infant.

Infants are not the only ones with their own personal temperament; the unique temperament accompanies the person until his or her maturity and later forms a central component of the person's own parenthood.

Daniel Stern (Stern, 1985, 1995; Stern, Bruchweiler-Stern & Freeland 1998), in his books on newborns and their parents, emphasizes the importance of the experience of matching and goodness of fit between the parent and child's temperaments, and views this experience as a significant factor in the infant and parent's quality of psychological life. The ability of every parent - mother or father - to build a close relationship with their infant, based on security, trust and emotional experiences of satisfaction, is founded on the goodness of fit between the parent and the infant. When the parent has a temperament that is unmistakably different from that of the child, a disturbance in the so essential dyadic relationship may develop, which Stern would call "lack of fit." This disturbance might over time damage the parental psychological development - create feelings of frustration, profound emotional injury of rejection or insult, parental inferiority and more - similarly to the infantile psychological development: a sustained sense of distrust, dissatisfaction, and insecurity.

If we continue along the lines of Stern's conceptualization, we will see that for a wide group of children, who in the future will be diagnosed as having disabilities, the initial course of life is characterized by difficulties stemming from an uneasy or slow temperament and lack of fit between their own and their parents' temperaments. A lack of matching between the child and its physical and human environment increases the risk of developing abnormal attachment, followed by a difficulty in developing efficient adaptation to the environment in which it lives.

Moreover, many studies (Fonagy, 2001, Fonagy, Gergely, Jurist & Target, 2002; Kranowitz, 2005) are nowadays indicative of the early connection between infants' regulation difficulties (in one or more areas: sensory, motor, emotional, and attentional) and temperament difficulties, and later on - adaptation difficulties in the various stages of development.

A regulation disorder that is already diagnosable at the infancy stage will create adaptation and behavioral difficulties in the child's daily functioning in his or her familial, educational, and social worlds.

When the issue of the development of the psychological life of children suffering from a learning- attention- and concentration-disability is discussed, one can see how the initial disruption in one of the primary and basic landmarks colors the course of their lives differently.

The high prevalence of a history of being Difficult- or Slow-to-Warm-Up infants with regulation difficulties among the children diagnosed with the disability, strengthens the assumption that a **learning & AD(H)D disability is also characterized by a different psychological development,**

sometimes having a negative shade. The temperament with the regulation difficulties from infancy has affected the disruption of the child's adaptation processes or the other disruption in the development of the relationship with the parents.

The concept of temperament is therefore of immense diagnostic and therapeutic value, not only theoretically but also practically speaking.

Many parents of infants with non-easy temperaments tend to share with the close and healthcare environments - the nurse and physician from the Center for Family Health, for example - the difficult feelings developed by them during the first months and sometimes even first weeks, mainly because of the difficulty to do good for, satisfy, and calm their infants. Professionals, like family members and others, still tend to react to this information in a judgmental and unilateral manner: "Look how tense you are," says the nurse to the mother who is exhausted from lack of sleep and the continuous difficulty to calm her child, "If you relax, then he (the infant) will also relax." With this short, decisive sentence, the nurse puts all the responsibility, and unilaterally, on the exhausted mother's shoulders and does not see the concept of bidirectional interaction and the **innate causing factor brought by the infant into creating the experience of difficulty.** The miserable mother is now not only tired and exhausted but also guilty. "And how the hell," she will say, "can I relax when he is awake at night, demands food all the time…cannot be calmed down in any reasonable way, and it seems like nearly everything arouses distress in him…?"

A more correct analysis of the situation as a **relationship disorder due to temperament and regulation difficulties** could not only have relieved her guilty feelings but also equipped her with insights and tools for better coping with her infant's special temperament. Sometimes, just knowing that the disruptive cause is not solely her own behavior and emotions is the first step toward experiencing a certain relief.

From the beginning of their journey with their child, parents will be exposed to a set of blame and they will be held responsible repeatedly, without being able to contain and cope with the responsibility.

B. Disruptions During Development and Their Implications for Psychological Life

Alongside the topic of temperament, there is an additional array of studies and clinical observations related to the developmental course of infants that are later on defined as suffering from learning- attention- and concentration-disabilities (Amir, Rapin & Branski, 1991; Piontelli ,1992 ; Bonshtein & Weintraub, 2006):

- **Difficulties during childbirth**

Among the children diagnosed with disabilities, a relatively large group of children have been found to have had an irregular course of birth (breech birth, forceps delivery, vacuum extraction, mother being rushed to the operating room for a caesarean section, strangulation by the umbilical cord, hypoxia[insufficient oxygen] and more), or born preterm and defined as premature.

In the past, these mishaps (hypoxia, head pressure, and more) have been perceived as an additional causative factor responsible for the appearance of the disability. However, lately a hypothesis has been raised that some of the mishaps are a direct result of the presence of the disability in the embryo's life even prior to its birth and it is this that will cause a mismatch in transferring information between the embryo and the mother's womb, leading to an abnormal course of birth.

- **"Health" difficulties of the newborn**

An additional group of disorders in early infancy, prevalent among newborns that later on are defined as learning- and attention-disabled, relates to continuous ear infections, liquids in the ears, respiratory asthma problems, and later on, skin asthma. These are all "medical" phenomena, some of which may signal to the parent that the child is "prone" to be diagnosed in the future as suffering from the disability, thereby directly and indirectly contributing to the child's and parents' poorer quality of psychological life.

- **Disruptions in sensory-motor development**

Other difficulties in infancy in high prevalence among children later diagnosed with learning- and attention-disabilities are associated with disruptions in the senso-motor developmental system (sensory, tactile, and muscle tonus).

These are newborns with disorders in the external or deep

sensory systems, with difficulties in the system responsible for balance, who show adaptation difficulties (and regulation difficulties) from the first moment they come into contact with water (or to the water's temperature), certain types of cloth and textures, difficulty in arranging a pleasant position for them to be touched while being hugged or rocked, intensive opposition to getting water on the face (washing the hair), having nails cut, lack of flexibility when transitioning from a stomach to back position, slowness in achieving the landmarks of gross motor development or skipping stages (standing up prior to crawling, or a short term of crawling and an accelerated attempt to walk), looseness in the mouth when transitioning from suckling to eating solid food, and more.

When these or some of these difficulties arouse the parent's suspicion, she/he will turn to the medical or paramedical (physiotherapy, occupational therapy, speech therapy) systems for help. Early treatment may not only assist a better course of development but also in building the dyadic parent-child relations. Associating these difficulties with a fear of learning and attention difficulties necessitates continued follow-up of the child and enables extremely early intervention. Nevertheless, it is appropriate to emphasize, that in part, the phenomena may be disassociated from the syndrome of "learning and attention disability" and they should not be viewed as an undoubted or determining factor. The appropriate approach here is to be alert and be satisfied with an initial suspicion only.

The presence of these or some of these difficulties might

"make a contribution in and of itself" to the disruption of early parent-infant relations. Parents who have experienced an infant who finds it hard to calm down from crying for no apparent reason, who is frightened when it is undressed, screams and resists bath time, reacts with great unrest to the feel of certain clothing or cloth, has difficulty finding a calming position for itself in the parents' hands (difficulty cradling or hugging it) or in bed, and so on - these parents experience themselves as "not good enough" for their child, and are also restless, because there is no way to "correctly care" for their infant. They experience the infant as oppositional to them, as one who views them as parents who do not calm and unknowingly return treatment that is laden with mental stress that gradually becomes tension in their relationship.

Instead of a relationship characterized by a good fit, a relationship develops within an experience of a lack of fit. This situation might create prolonged damage in both the parent and infant - in building their relations of trust between them.

C. Primary Objectives in Infant-Parent Relations: Basic Trust, Internalization of Object Relations and Total Parenthood

| Basic Objectives in Parent-Infant Relations

The first year of life of each infant and its parents is predominantly devoted to achieving a key objective in the lives of the two sides: mutual acquaintance and falling in love, while the main objective is building and internalizing relations of trust.

Parents and children go on the journey of attachment while being only partially familiar with each other. Innovative studies describe the ability of embryos to develop a multi-sensory, non-verbal memory store that is accumulated during their lives in the womb, enabling them to have a preliminary, partial familiarity with their mothers after birth (Stern, 1985; Piontelli, A., 1992). Stimuli such as heart beat rate, the murmur of the intestines, body odor, touch, and sweat are the infant's preliminary landmarks for identifying its mother when meeting her for the first time after birth. These are sensory signs telling the infant about their closeness and familiarity. Having experienced the movements, heart beat rate, and presence of her infant in the womb (and nowadays its "image" too, thanks to ultrasound and pre-birth screening) the mother as well, looks for the familiar characteristics in the image of the new and foreign infant. This mutual familiarity that comes alongside discovering the new characteristics of each figure, to a certain extent, reduces the distance between the two and the need to get to know each other.

The newborn and mother's reactions immediately after birth require a certain degree of drawing away from each other to moderate the excitement accompanying the birth, reorganizing in the world, and processing the birth experience. Termed by the literature as "developmental autism" in the infant (Mahler, Pine & Bergman 1975) and "normative post-partum depression" in the mother (Anthony & Benedek), this temporary remoteness serves as an intermediate station for recuperating and reorganizing; however, this disconnection is absolutely temporary and cannot continue for too long. The infant who is needy of its mother to have its existential caregiving needs (feeding, drinking, body warmth, dryness, and cleanliness) met, and who wishes for itself a constant state of harmony and restfulness (homeostasis: Freud, in Muuss, 1982) reacts immediately when its basic needs emerge and disrupt its peacefulness. These distress signals are registered by the mother, and despite her need for protective disconnection, she is driven to instinctively react to them. The quick reaction stems from the fact that post-partum mothers are dependent on, and in need of their infants no less than the infants are in need of them.

The woman's post-partum physiological recuperation processes include a need for comforting touch with the infant, which slowly influences her hormonal and emotional regulation and enables the gradual release of milk. The suckling by the infant prevents inflammation and infections that might have developed due to the congestion in the breast had there not been suckling. This mutual neediness brings the two together while they are simultaneously preoccupied with themselves. This meeting is considered successful when the mother recognizes the infant's signals, interprets them correctly and provides a calming response. The infant's return to calmness is experienced by the mother as an experience of satisfaction and thus the primary relationship pattern between them is formed:

Disconnection → emergence of a need (impulse) on the part of the infant → the infant gives off distress signals through crying (disruption of homeostasis) → the mother registers and prepares to react → the mother makes a correct interpretation of her infant's needs → the mother reacts with a satisfying response → calm infant (return to homeostasis) → satisfied mother.

Repeating itself in many different and diverse ways, this pattern starts engraving and setting a mutual memory of pleasantness and satisfaction with each other. As soon as a few weeks old, the infant is already capable of constructing an inner schema (Piaget, in Muuss 1982) for itself of familiarity with some of the mother's prominent characteristics such as the facial form, the sound of her walk, the sound of her voice, her body odor, and more. These characteristics are added to the characteristics remembered from the womb and gradually construct a full picture of the mother's image. In good mutual relations between the two, a positive sensation of pleasantness and satisfaction accompanies the image. The mother, on her part, also "learns" to be familiar with her infant's characteristics and constructs for herself an internal picture of it, based on the concrete image. She internalizes who her infant is and what it tells her in its distress, movements etc. In this manner, the identification of the infant's needs becomes quicker and their understanding more efficient and satisfying.

These relations are the basis for constructing a mutual internal image. The infant "internalizes" the caregiving mother as a benevolent entity, telling it about its ability to build a sense of trust in the world, as a safe and protected place. The mother, on her part, learns, through her infant and its reactions, to remember it as a benevolent entity that returns her love. These mutual memories become increasingly numerous and gradually expand themselves into more and more needs and wants. In this manner, an internal system of a "memory store" is built in each of the partners, serving them for increasingly larger segments of very short, initial separations required in their lives. Awaking wet, hungry, and making sounds of distress, the infant can relax for a few moments because it has heard its mother react verbally to it. It is not the words she has said that build the temporary calmness (as it does not yet understand their verbal meaning), but the sounds of her presence, the calming tone, and the familiar "music," promising that "very soon... here she comes..." The ability to relax prior to the concrete response is possible thanks to the small memory store that has already been constructed, characterized by the security of an "internal" maternal presence. It is obvious that the ability to be assisted by the internal store is still limited in duration and intensity, but it already provides the moment of secure distance, enabling them to get organized. Hearing her infant calm down for a brief moment, the mother returns to it with her full practical ability to provide proper care and an actual response, and from a restless, upset infant, she once again gets a calm, satisfied, and satisfying infant ("telling" her with its reactions that she is the only one in its life who can completely meet its needs).

This repeated cyclicism in their shared lives is nowadays expanding thanks to the gradual joining of the shared journey by fathers. Although they do not have a basis of primary familiarity, but as intensive, active participants in the communication and care cycle, they too have a chance to gradually build a memory of the good infant inside them, and provide their infant with the experience of the second benevolent figure.

Infant researchers describe these relations as a multi-area process, including several components and sensations: Oral satisfaction (according to Freud, in Muuss, 1982, who intends to emphasize that most of the satisfaction is related to the feeding experience and that the mouth forms a central focus for pleasure as well as frustration); Symbiosis (according to Margret Mahler, 1975, who emphasizes the relations of interdependence and merging of the two); Basic Trust (according to Erikson, 1951, who emphasizes the nature of the experience built in the shared relations); and Secure Attachment (according to Bowlby, 1958; Ainsworth, 1963; Spitz, 1965 and others, who emphasize the experience of a secure relationship built between them).

Parenthood researchers emphasize and describe this period as a period of total parenting (Anthony & Benedek, 1970), emphasizing the parent's need to be in a position of exclusivity regarding the entirety of the infant's needs, and responding to them at every moment and matter. The need for totality originates from the time and complexity required of the parent to "study" his/her child in the safe, protected climate of the absence of competition with someone else who will invade the shared bubble and intervene in the primary relations that are just beginning to develop, and might "steal" their child's attention and love. For these and other reasons, modern social reality that prematurely invades total parenthood and demands, both from the parent and child, to enter into an expanded relationship prior to having established the total parenthood, takes a heavy toll on the parents, of anxiety, weakening and parenthood under conditions of hunger for the experience of the benevolent infant and total parenthood.

A new stream in current research, the Dyadic Approach, puts an emphasis on the shared parent-child relations (Fonagy, 2001, Fonagy, Gergely, Jurist, & Target 2002) and describes this stage as a stage requiring an experience of a fit between the parent and infant (Stern, 1985, 1995; Stern, Bruchweiler-Stern & Freeland 1998). At this stage, the parent is an organizing and regulating entity for the infant (Greenspan, 1992; Greenspan, & Wieder 1993) and enables a relaxed couplehood between them.

Klein, M. (in Segal, 1979; and Winnicott (1988, 1998), emphasize that these continuous relations will be experienced by the infant as **Secure Object Relations,** which will lead to their internalization in the infant's memory and form the infrastructure for mental health and resilience. They will also enable an ever-increasing distance between them, thanks to the ability to rely on the internal memory in situations where the concrete parent or infant are apart from each other (for a limited period of time, of course, and suited to age and needs).

The complexity of these relations between parents and infants leads, upon completion of the first year of life, to a shared experience of familiarity, falling in love and internal trusting of each other, combined with internalization of the positive mutual memory. These enable the infant to distance itself gradually and securely, and the parent - the ability to move away without an exaggerated fear that the child will "fall in love" with someone else, a stranger, and prefer him or her to the parent.

| Attachment Disorders: A Learning & AD(H)D Disabled Infant-Parent

Many children, who during their childhood and growing up are diagnosed as suffering from a learning- and/or attention- and concentration-disability, will be described emotionally and behaviorally, as suffering from difficulties in the attachment relations. Later on, these difficulties influence the development process of social and interpersonal relationships. Attempts to understand these difficulties as only accompanying or secondary to the disability do an injustice to the child and his or her parents. The theoretical-clinical explanation of attachment disorders is based on an understanding of the early characteristics of the disability in the areas of temperament, development of the brain and entire bodily system, and their effect on the course of emotional development from the moment of birth and even before it - during the embryonic stage.

Various disorders characteristic of learning disabled infants might contribute to the difficulty that will form, at a low or high degree, in the infant and parents' relations.

Even prior to their infant's birth, most parents precede its arrival with a psychological experience described as a fantasy about "the ideal child about to be born" (Rafael-Leff, 1993) and are concurrently emotionally attached to the fantasy about the optimal parenthood that every parent wants to provide his or her child. Disorders in early infancy, in each of the areas to be specified next, arouse in the parent - gradually or at once (according to the problem's intensity, time of appearance, duration and consistency of presence) - sadness and anxiety over the loss of the fantasy. This loss forces the parent to transition from one mental state to another, where she or he is required to mourn, but also accept the concrete child, which is far from the fantasy child. The magnitude of the distance is determined both by the nature of the fantasy, which is individual to each parent, as well as by the severity of the infant's specific problem. The larger the distance, the more complex and intensive the work of mourning required from the parent.

What are the phenomena that are destined to disturb and disrupt the process of building attachment between a learning- attention- and concentration-disabled infant and its parents?

A. Temperament Disorders

When the pattern of infant-parent relations is examined, one realizes that the newborn's temperament plays a key role in the parent's ability to get it into a state of calmness and satisfaction anytime one of the basic needs has aroused in the infant and caused the temporary disruption of homeostasis. One can very easily assume how a hungry infant with low regulation ability (a regulation disorder) will behave even after it has been breastfed. Even after the need has been met, this newborn will have difficulty getting itself back into a state of calmness and will continue crying and giving off signals of discomfort for a prolonged period of time. In the absence of the ability to calm and satisfy, the parent associated with it will gradually enter a state of tension and discomfort on his or her own and it will not be long before the feeling of being a "not good enough" parent for the infant will start pervading the parent's mind and emotions.

Regulation Disorder tends to appear in infancy in the form of states such as difficulties in falling asleep, extremely short sleep periods, heightened sensitivity to noise and waking up because of it. Any sensory disorder will only exacerbate the general feeling of discomfort and confront the parent with a tense infant that has difficulty reaching a state of homeostasis.

A low sensory threshold and/or high reaction threshold intensifies the states of discomfort from the infant's point of view and generates long crying reactions accompanied by increased distress signals.

In contrast, infants with another disorder, **Slow Development Pace**, which initially are experienced as "good" by themselves and their parents, will soon cause the parent to experience with fright the gap opening between them and children of the same age, and the experience of failure or worry and anxiety over their fate will appear here as well.

Irregularity of the Biological Clock – a phenomenon creating a prolonged sense of lack of constancy and inability to get organized toward necessary situations of change in life (transitions between waking and sleeping and vice versa, traveling, getting out of the house etc.) in parents and infants.

Withdrawing Infants arouse worry in the parent in the face of the distress exhibited by them when confronted with any change or new stimulus in their lives. As opposed to these, **Approaching Infants** tend to put themselves at risk out of unregulated curiosity, and necessitate strict oversight that is sometimes burdensome for the parent.

Too short or long attention span, heightened distractibility and more – these will already appear in the first weeks as a forming experience of difficulty engaging the infant and an intensified urge to pacify, engage again and again and introduce novelty, or alternatively, to reduce and minimize stimuli.

Such temperament disorders might also intervene and damage the sense of fit between the infant and parent's temperaments. The experience of lack of fit will interfere with the quality of the parent-infant relations (primary Object Relations) and will create a continuous feeling of gaps and difficulty being in a dyadic (parent-child couple) relationship.

B. Motor and Sensory System Disorders

Infants suffering from heightened sensory sensitivity or a high degree of hyposensitivity, make the process of caring for and pacifying them very burdensome. Disorders that also involve sensitivity to light touch (tactile), deep touch (proprioceptive) or in the sense of balance (vestibular), especially increase this difficulty and create a disturbance in the attachment relations. Every clothing or diaper changing, bathing (and later on, hair washing, haircutting, nail cutting, and more) are accompanied by tension and difficulty in relaxation, both in the infant and parent.

Looking for a holding position that is suited to the infant, lack of ability to hug it in a calming manner, looking for clothing and bed linen with cloth textures that are suited to the infant's sensitivity, lack of flexibility in lying or holding positions - all these arouse, in both, sustained experiences of discomfort in the relationship and affect the quality of Object Relations.

Breastfeeding, feeding difficulties, difficult transitioning from being breastfed to food with a texture and taste requiring chewing, difficulty in finding a suitable pacifier or nipple for sucking and more, only increase the mutual pain. Muscle tone will, to a great degree, determine the course of motor development (turning over, crawling, sitting, standing, and walking), and its flaccidity will create a feeling of over-worry among some parents.

C. Specific Health Difficulties

Chronic ear inflammations, proneness to asthma and suffocation anxiety, illness accompanied by high fever with or without a tendency to convulsions, dermatitis and more - these are all "medical" phenomena, appearing largely in infancy among learning and attention-disabled children. However, their existence, per se, impairs the attachment relations and the sense of good infant and good parent. The experience of rearing a child with "medical" difficulties is more difficult than and different in quality from life experiences with a relatively healthy child who grows up without any special disturbances.

D. Memory and Executive Function Difficulties

The association between neurological damages and their effects on the world of the psyche (neuropsychiatry) is becoming increasingly central in the work of researchers and therapists in the mental health field (LeDoux, 1996; Solmas & Turnball2003). The accumulating knowledge about the effect of neurological (normal and pathological) processes on various mental states has led to significant breakthroughs in recent years.

Brown (2000, 2005) emphasizes that what is common to all disorders defined as learning-attention- and concentration-disorders is damage to the executive function located in the frontal lobe center. This central function manages and controls essential tasks in regulating practical and emotional organization: setting priorities, attention focusing and splitting, attention regulation and processing received information, emotion management and withstanding situations such as frustration, operating the working memory, and supervising the regulation of activity.

When the infant is in contact with its parents, the executive function acts as an element responsible for receiving, processing, and storing sensory information. In situations where the infant is required to wait, when an actual parent is not present momentarily, the executive function acts to retrieve sensory information as a temporary soothing source, based on the secure memory provided by the parents.

From the first moment, learning- attention- and concentration-disabled infants interact with their parents while this essential system is not complete and its functioning is impaired (minimally or maximally and in the range in between). This sustained situation, then, is responsible for inefficient receiving, processing, managing, or usage of the parental memory store. Therefore, from the beginning of its life, the infant is left struggling to achieve Basic Trust from some point of lack - while faced by a parent who is completely unaware of the existence of the difficulty, treating the child as if it were an ordinary infant and only sensing the not-good-enough results - but not knowing the reason. Moreover, when the parental feeling is, "I am not succeeding in being a satisfying and reassuring parent for my baby," a difficult experience of parental guilt develops: "It is my fault the baby is not relaxed." This guilt is "supported" by the environment, which also suffers from a lack of knowledge and understanding as to the source of the difficulty.

On the other hand, in this state, a disorder develops in the infant - of difficulty to produce a relaxed and reassuring memory store from the parent's presence - and therefore, in the absence of the parent, dependency needs and anxiety, difficulty in self-regulation, and a sense of loss of any trust in the world, increase - which from the outside is interpreted as an experience of damage to the attachment relations.

D. The Child's Embarkation on Autonomy, and Parenthood Under Conditions of Shame and Doubt

| Basic Objectives in the Second Year of Life

The fixed pattern of relations that forms between parents and children includes three phases, repeating themselves in various ages and in diverse modes: Attachment, Separation, and Individuation (Mahler, 1975). Paradoxically, the human being is constituted as creature in need of a deep emotional relationship, from which it will embark on an experience of separation and independence for constructing a unique and separate identity. The three-phase journey forms an axis repeating itself in various ages and in various developmental periods, and enables every child to have a deep emotional connection with the parents, but without developing lasting dependence that prevents the child from constructing self as an independent, unique entity, attached, yet separate.

While the first year of life is predominantly devoted to building parent-child Basic Trust and enables the building of a close emotional and concrete relationship between the two, the course of the second year of life is devoted to building the ability of separating from each other without losing the connection and without feeling abandoned in the world. For the toddler in its second year of life, separation is mostly based on its ability to preserve the image of the secure and benevolent parent in its memory and psyche, thereby moving toward the axis of independence while drawing from the memories of the parental figure. When the internalized parental presence is lessened, or when the time elapsed from the last meeting of connection between them is prolonged, or when needs appear that are more powerful than the infant's ability to handle them by itself, the infant will soon be returned to the close relations with the parent, who is still within reach, while accompanying the child's journey of independence from close by. In this gradual and complex manner, separation between them is built: one step forward and one step back, disconnection and getting closer, until the physical and psychological distance between them becomes larger but does not sever the thread of the close ties between them - a flexible distance, enabling remoteness, but not disconnection and risk.

The course of separating and getting out of symbiosis and into independence (Autonomy, according to Erikson, 1951) depends on the fulfillment of several conditions, both on the part of the infant and the parent:

First, a clear and increasing rise in its functional independence in various areas is required from the infant. In this respect, it can be viewed as the first initiator of the journey to independence thanks to the maturing of various sensory-motor abilities, enabling it to act by itself to achieve areas of activity, interest, and mainly mobility. One can see the infant, to a certain extent, already starting to experiment with independence in the first year of life: It tries (is able) to move a mobile on its own, or put a pacifier in its mouth and take it out. However, it is the appearance of crawling, continued by walking, that are the significant gains toward the longed-for objective of independence. Until achieving mobility, the infant will practice the beginning of separation through playing initiated peak-a-boo games with its parents, continued by experimentation in moving away through crawling and walking. However, if in the beginning the range of experience is small and limited, it increases in size during the second year of life and becomes complex and diverse, both in the time distances and in qualities. Hence, from the infant's point of view, mobility is a primary and necessary condition for achieving the experience of separation, and it is accompanied and preceded by operating various toys with the hands and mouth.

A second, no less important condition for the existence of experiencing separation concerns the infant's emotional–psychological state. In order to dare move away without feeling lost or abandoned, the infant requires the secure existence of its parents' schema, which is saved and active in its memory, that which gives it the psychic confidence in their psychological existence even when they are momentarily, concretely absent. An infant dares move away when it feels protected and secure in its internal world, otherwise it will get a fright that will prevent it from repeating the experimentation. Even during natural rapprochement, toddlers tend (according to Mahler, 1975) to accompany their journey with "refueling" activity that is concerned with moving away while returning in order to "recharge the battery" of parental presence, and then moving away again. This process sometimes seems like utilizing the cellular phone battery: It is available and active for a limited time at a known distance, but requires recharging every time by connecting it to the "refueling" charger.

Practically and overtly speaking, this moving away-refueling occurs in various ways within the parent-child interaction: The infant runs ahead, but stops at a certain moment, comes back and touches the parent as a refueler, and then turns around again and starts running until the entire battery has been used up, back for refueling touch, and so forth. On other occasions, the journey will look like bursting forward, stopping, refueling with a look to the protecting parent, and then going ahead again. The parent's presence as an available battery charger is hence critical at this stage.

The toddler's ability to rely on the parental schema (the active memory of it) while moving away is also essential for the success of the journey.

This new presence of the parent is essentially different from his or her presence in the first year of life. This is the first time that the parent is required to exhibit parental skills expressing much love by means of limits and protecting. It is no longer only a caring, facilitating and problem-solving parenthood; not only parenthood that shows expressions of affection and love, but also a parenthood that sets safety limits, prevents, and limits out of the same emotional motive of love for the child. For many parents, the gradual transition from giving love to setting limits forms a crisis, anxiety-arousing phase in their parenthood. While many children react to affection and giving with love-reciprocating signals to the parent, when faced with limits and limitations, toddlers tend to react with dissatisfaction and challenging expressions of "first signs of rebelliousness." They are now both faced for the first time with the parental authority test, while as far as the parent is concerned, it must be passed with maximum success. The parental ability to set limits of love involves several conditions as well.

First, Anthony & Benedek (1970), among the pioneers of the psychology of parenthood, claim that **the transition from "total parenthood" to "part-time parenthood"** (as this second phase is termed by them) is first and foremost dependent on the extent of emotional satiation felt by the parent from the symbiotic and total relationship with his or her infant. Therefore, a satisfying total parenthood is a necessary (albeit not sufficient) condition for the parent's emotional ability to withstand the child's expressions of independence and limit him or her according to necessity and safety. Many toddlers' "refusal" attempts when faced by their parents' first disciplining demands are erroneously experienced by the parents as an expression of the child's lack of love for them. While the child's disobedience is "all in all" a test of the power of the coping forces just recently acquired, without being adapted enough to reality testing, the parent might erroneously interpret them as the loss of the child's love. The more the parent remains hungry for total parenthood at the end of the first year (whether because of early leaving to work and putting the child under the custody of a daycare center or nanny, or because of relationship difficulties due to a learning and attention disability, or for many other reasons), the more the ability to mobilize psychic resources for setting limits will weaken. The parent will try to sustain more and more processes of expressions of affection and forgiveness that might make it difficult for the child to embark on independence and may sometimes even frighten the child. Hence, the test of the parent faced with his or her child's expressions of autonomy is dependent on the maturity and emotional satiation felt by the parent from the full batteries charged with the child in the first year of life.

Another necessary condition that is very much related to the first one, concerns the nature of the relations in the first year. The more parents have experienced their infants as benevolent and reassuring infants, and themselves as good-enough parents for the child, the more the secure infant schema will accompany the parent in dealing with the test of parental authority and manifestations of rebellious emotions expressed by the toddler. A parent fueled with the secure infant schema will be able to withstand the frustration created by a toddler who is testing the parent's limits, and set the required limits with confidence and love, without taking the emotional risk of the erroneous interpretation of "the child who says no to the limits I have demanded is actually saying 'no' to my love". The story "Mother, Mother, I Want Another" (according to the children's story by Maria Polushkin Roberts) shows mother mouse's insecurity concerning her baby mouse's love for her, misinterpreting the words " Mother, Mother, I want another " to mean another mother, who might be better.

The more the relations schema has been disrupted due to various difficulties of the two, the more the parent will weaken and continue searching for the child's love instead of setting limits confidently.

Toddlers who are in need of limits—even though they express temporary dissatisfaction with them—when encountered by a weakened parent who is looking for confirmation of their love, experience parental weakness as abandonment or as an unsafe place in their lives. A parent who delays too much with setting limits and replaces these with dangerous facilitation causes their child to feel abandoned and frightened. The natural reaction of young children is to increase their non-compliant behavior in the form of a "rage" attack, which tries to remobilize the parent to a clearer, more protected place. A cycle of "reverse psychology" develops here.

The child exhibiting overt behavior of insubordination is actually wishing for a confident parent who protects by setting limits. Obeying the limit, while making a momentary protest, is testimony of the parent's correct reaction. The parent who avoids setting the limit because of the erroneous interpretation of the overt voice of the child and lack of understanding of the child's inner and "reverse" needs, not only does not do good by the child, but increases the rebellious behavior, and so on and so forth.

The mutual schema of the child perceived by the parent and of the parent perceived by the child as a schema of secure and loving figures, is the inner element that correctly drives the two. Its absence, in the form of lack of Basic Trust, is dangerous to the infant's psychological development when embarking on independence.

In the discussion of embarking on independence, Erikson (1951) describes the danger of developing **feelings of shame and doubt** at the other end of the experience. Both feelings might emerge in every toddler's emotional life on the way to independence and in them as well lies a danger for the proper development of infantile mental health. Shame, claims Erikson, is related to the fact that a toddler with physical skills of mobility and moving away simultaneously also develops its system of connection and coping abilities with objective reality. Freud (in Muuss, 1982) viewed this phase as the moment when the psychic structure termed **Ego (the Self)** starts being constructed in the child. Unlike the Id structure, which is the primary and basic source of pleasure and enjoyment and responsible for the experiences of immediate gratification, the Ego structure is a key factor in the child's ability to develop a delay of the gratification (in gradually increasing pace and quality) and fit it to the conditions of reality. A key, essential reservoir of forces in the child's process of growth and maturing development, The Ego structure enables the child to adapt to the human and social milieu in which he or she lives. A child who, in the second year of life, starts to acquire the forces and ability related to the existence of the Ego, can gradually acquire considerations of conforming/nonconforming to requirements, right/wrong and to aspire to an Ego contented from reinforcements given by the significant adult. Hence, reality testing is a new mental capacity that gradually develops in the toddler and appropriately to its embarkation on independence. Therefore, Erikson claims, if the actions performed by the toddler are met with condemning reactions regarding actions that are "unbefitting reality" (soiling the underwear instead of asking to go to the bathroom), then its actions will arouse an **experience of shame** for not having managed to self-restrain and act as expected. As opposed to this, the **experience of doubt** forms when faced with vagueness of the adult's requirements from the toddler. Vagueness and inconsistency of requirements leaves the child doubtful as to the extent of correctness of his actions and their fit with reality.

The journey to autonomy causes every toddler to encounter these feelings, but the more the experiences of correct independent doing increase, the more the experience of independence will rise and blossom as an important and positive experience in the toddler's life.

On the other hand, the experiences of shame and doubt can not only be attributed to the toddler, as Erikson was inclined to think, but also to the parent who faces his or her child and tests the child's forces of independence. There is hardly a parent who has not experienced the feeling of being overwhelmed by a sense of shame while facing the child's defiant attempts in the middle of the street, during shopping in the mall, or when visiting relatives - whether it was when the child soiled his pants, yelled in the middle of a quiet ceremony, or when the parent himself got into a rage over a candy or toy that the child had taken without permission in a store. These experiences of shame on both sides (parent and child) - when they are momentary and alongside them there are many experiences of success in disciplining - strengthen the sense of permitted independence in the parent and child, but this feeling will always be accompanied by an iota of shame.

The "culture of abundance" has also not passed over the "abundance" of theories of upbringing, nowadays flooding young parents with readily available media (television, the press, the Internet and more). Many parents are left doubtful and hesitant regarding the correctness of this or that method, or regarding the preference of one reaction to another. The many doubts, trial-and-error groping - all these weaken them and communicate to their young children some sense of vagueness, stemming from their parents' doubtfulness. Due to "zeitgeist" many children will try to intensify attempts at independence through rage attacks over inconsistent limit-setting. They will try to communicate to their parents the critical need for clarity and consistency. This parent will once again react with doubtfulness when faced with temporary expressions of failure, and so the process is repeated - again and again.

The toddler's embarkation on independence is concurrent

with the gradual transition of the "parent with him or her" to a stage of part-time parenthood accompanied by momentary feelings of shame and doubt. The more the parent feels confident in their abilities, the lesser the experience of shame and doubt, and she or he will enable the child a confident and healthy journey to independence. Alternatively, the more the parent is overwhelmed by feelings of shame and doubt facing their child's expressions of behavior, the more the child is led to a weak, unstable, and faulty journey to independence.

| A Parent and a Learning & AD(H)D Disabled Child - Disruptions in the Journey to Independence

As mentioned, suitable conditions are necessary - both practically and psychologically - for realizing a good separation experience for the parent and child. When the toddler in question is one with learning and attention disabilities, the conditions for embarking on independence are not complete and whole. His or her parents as well, lack some of the basic conditions required for this. The result is that minor or severe disruptions occur in the process, and in most cases, their first signs cannot be readily perceived or interpreted as relevant to this issue. If we examine each of the main conditions participating in constructing the separation experience, both on the part of parent and toddler, we realize the diversity of possible mishaps.

A. The Capacity for Independent Locomotion

Learning- and attention-disabled children sometimes suffer from developmental difficulties related to their sensory-motor skills. As a result, their capacity for independent locomotion might be delayed, and with it, the wish to act in the direction of actual physical moving away. For some of them, even if they achieve the locomotor landmarks, the quality of their movement is poor or inadequate and may impair the daring to experience locomotion (due to motor clumsiness, balance difficulties, hyperactivity or difficulties with directions).

B. Internalizing the Protective and Secure Parent Schema

An additional key difficulty in learning- and attention-disabled children has to do with difficulties in the development and internalization of the parent's schema as a protecting psychological presence, due to difficulties in the operation of memory and in the executive function's organization system.

A learning- and attention-disabled toddler embarks on the journey of separating from the concrete parent while often experiencing his self as abandoned and frightened. The lack of ability to rely on the inner parental presence (parental schema) because of neurological difficulties, compels the toddler to quickly return and avoid moving away, or to maintain a complex relationship of moving away, anxiety, or over-dependence. This is a child who relies mainly on concrete parental presence, because when the parent is absent, the inner schema is missing.

Memory difficulties are not the only element acting here in the weakening of psychological security/confidence, but also early attachment difficulties (which, as mentioned, stem from the infant's temperament difficulties) that have caused the parent to be experienced by the child as not benevolent and secure enough. Additional disorders such as sensory difficulties, abnormal muscle tone, and more, might influence the formation of a parental schema that is partial, missing, or not benevolent enough. One can imagine a learning- and attention-disabled toddler embarking on the journey of separateness and the required equipment is missing, partially missing, or is of inadequate quality (a weak, abnormal "battery"). As a result, he or she will feel inhibited or anxious - sometimes avoiding moving away and sometimes doing the opposite - taking an exaggerated risk (also due to a regulation problem).

A basic and key parental reaction to the infant's journey of moving away necessitates steps of setting limits, regulation, and oversight in order to provide the toddler with a "protected and secure space" to experience separation. When, during separation, the toddler is stormy or anxious, hyperactive and restless, or slow and hesitant, the parental safety limits are more difficult and complex. The stormy and unregulated toddler requires an intensified and clear boundary/limit, and the hesitant toddler needs an encouraging boundary/limit.

This need for a personalized response, when based on an incomplete inner parental schema regarding the child, is very difficult for the parent to satisfy, mainly because of a lack of knowledge about the source of the difficulty. The parent is "drawn into" a reaction style that aggravates the infant's difficulties. And thus, in addition to the complex inter-relations at the *Basic Trust* stage, new difficulties are added here, of not-secure-enough limit/boundary-setting relations. The parent's reaction is not adapted to the specific needs of the child and the mutual experience is impaired.

This is an additional source of weakening for parents of children with learning disabilities at this time - parents are exhausted and in pain after a difficult year of coping with a difficult-temperament infant. This sustained state of hunger for total and benevolent parenthood and for a secure infant schema, which are so missing for these parents, often causes them to make further mistakes. Parental hunger drives such parents to achieve love at almost any price (albeit generally unconsciously) and they yearn for positive feedback from the child. Setting limits, in general, is a psychologically difficult parental task. A parent with a satisfying child schema, satiated enough from total parenthood, can use these resources as a source of reassurance when faced with the child's reaction and conceptualize the child's resistance as another way of building a protective and secure relationship. However, the hungry parent who has not derived satisfaction from their child tends to erroneously interpret the overt child reaction of refusal as an expression of the child's non-love. The child's non-compliance is a test of the child Ego forces - asking for more and more protective safety limits. However, a hungry parent tends to view non-compliance as a child's reaction to the difficult parental experience vis-a-vis the child. It seems to the parent that their child is reacting with resistance not to the limits, but rather to the lack of satisfying parental love. The parent feels ashamed and guilty over the child's reaction, as reflecting back the unsatisfied parental experience. This parent will quickly back down from the task of limit-setting and instead, will provide love and confirmations of love and will seek to "placate" the child at any cost and not limit him or her. A hungry parent is a parent whose roles have been switched around, and instead of protecting the child, asks the child to "protect" and express positive emotions toward his or her self.

Hence, a learning- and attention-disabled toddler, who is in need of a clear parental schema, gets an inconsistent, confused, and courting parent, instead of a parent who sets safety limits, who sometimes drastically shifts between an all-embracing prohibition due to anxiety when faced by the child's moving away, and permissiveness and lenience because of the terror evoked by the child's reaction. And thus, to the absence of a secure inner parental schema, unstable and unclear parental behavior is now added.

This parental instability makes it very emotionally difficult for the toddler who is now struggling for expressions of independence. The separation journey combines in it elements of expressions of independence involving a constant increase in the expression of the Ego forces now being built. We witness not only physical and psychological attempts at moving away, but also expressions of a desire to act "by myself, alone" ("me do it myself" when faced with the parent's attempt to feed or dress, sleep "insubordination" when being put to bed at night, trying to climb a forbidden ladder or railing behind the parent's back, etc.). These expressions are very important on the toddler's part and require even more reassurance and clear parental protection. An inconsistent parent might "switch-off" or "switch-on" these expressions in a manner that increases anxiety in the toddler, to which the toddler will react with increasing expressions of rebellion, which will weaken/ tire or frighten the parent, and the latter's reaction will be weakened or intensified according to what suits the parent and not according to the child's needs.

A main focal point for the expressions of these difficulties is in the weaning processes, forming a developmental "peak" in the child's and parent's lives, and serving as a sort of overt "identity card" of the "child's quality" and the "parent's quality. " Out of these difficulties, various difficulties will appear in many children with a learning disability, revolving around parting from sucking for the sake of eating solid food, transitioning from a bottle to a cup and acquiring toilet-training habits. These focal points of change in ways of life, beginning to have to meet requirements suited to adult culture, the adjustment this requires, , and the controlling of the body's independence becomes a "battlefield" in the lives of many children with learning- and attention-disability and their parents.

Like the separation processes, weaning tasks, as well, rely on physical maturity, emotional maturity, and secure adult-toddler relations. When some of these conditions are not met or are partially or inadequately met, difficulties appear in these areas (weaning tasks) as well, and add to the shared experience of difficulty.

Alongside the expressions of rebellion, both the parent and toddler are confused by the struggles for independence, which are sometimes even intensified due to additional problems such as regulation difficulties, poor sensory functioning, neurological immaturity, difficulty in remembering teachings, delayed gratification and more - part of a totality of typical-objective difficulties of a learning- and attention-disabled toddler.

When the stage of achieving autonomy on the toddler's part is discussed, Erikson (1951) indicates the danger of the appearance of shame and doubt experiences. Both these senses originate from the nature of the limits and boundaries as they are presented by the parents; however, in most cases, shame stems from rigid boundaries characterized by over-strictness, and doubt stems from the hesitance and permissiveness - from boundary/limits too wide and not unambiguous enough. Both due to their difficulties in maintaining and "learning" the boundaries/limits constantly and efficiently, as well as their parents' unsuited reactions in one direction or the other (strict and/or lenient demands), children with learning- and attention-disability are at increased of going through this stage while the experience of shame and doubt is dominant over the experience of benevolent independence.

However, their parents might suffer from exactly the same difficulty as well, and instead of feeling an autonomous parenthood, they experience parenthood under conditions of "shame" and/or "doubt."

Parenthood under conditions of shame is born from facing the multitude of "mishaps" created for the parents by the toddler, and mainly in public: dirt on the rug, rebellious behavior in the street or store, dirt in the shopping mall, and so on. These are stressful situations in which the toddler reacts to the parent and to himself in a manner that evokes a sense of parental shame. Many parents of children with a learning- and attention-disability describe a journey of embarrassment vis-a-vis the sense of shame, which they have often felt when faced with the improper behavior of their child at the "war of independence" age.

This shame, which also draws from the weakened inner schema, often evokes doubt and hesitation in the parent, especially around the correct and adapted method of upbringing, and sends the parent on a journey of searching and buying contradictory tips and tricks. Thus the "doubtful parenthood" develops. As the parent does not yet know that his or her child is learning- and attention-disabled, the parent is inclined to think that it is merely a problem of upbringing and becomes a consumer of various methods which, in most cases, increase the shame or doubt and sometimes both.

In this way, an escalating cycle of relations is gradually built, loaded with mutual hunger for a calming, benevolent relationship, which makes its mark on the psychological development of both the child and parent.

E. Phallic Child - an Initiating Child and Parenthood With an Experience of Guilt

| Developmental Objectives in the Third Year of Life

The third year in every toddler's life is colored in shades of taking the initiative (Erikson, 1951) - a stage which is a powerful continuation of autonomy. At this stage, many children are driven to utilize their full new, maturing, and developing skills in order to express themselves as unique entities, separate from their parents. Therefore, Mahler < (1975) termed this stage as the "separation and individuation" stage, while Freud (in Muuss, 1982), emphasized the phallic characteristics and their profound connection with the developing and emerging Ego (self) forces. Many parents experience this period as a stormy time in their children's lives and the relations with them - a time where their abilities to set limits and boundaries, to restrain and regulate, are put to the test - alongside the need to allow the child unique expression in various areas of life - but within secure boundaries that do not constitute a danger to the child itself and/or surrounding environment. Pre-school teachers in kindergartens sense the phallic storm as an existence that is unique to kindergarten, manifested both by an increase in various expressive capacities (construction, creation, verbalization) as well as an increase in the intensity of impulses in the relations of the children among themselves.

According to Erikson (1951), the beginning of initiative as a developmental stage is in the child's need to practice and realize the various skills that appear. Thus begins, for instance, the capacity for inter-sensory integration, which is the basis of construction and creation processes. There is a clear increase in the quality of spoken language, both in quantity and diversity of vocabulary, as well as grammatical and expressive ability. In addition, new cognitive development, termed by Piaget & Inhalder (1969) **"Egocentric thinking with animistic [anthropomorphism] and magical characteristics,"** is apparent. In this thinking, the "I" (Ego) of the child is at the center of the world and the explanations given regarding various phenomena in the world have to do solely with him or her (thoughts, wishes, and emotions). The "other" is only evaluated with reference to his or her "I." The child understands the surrounding world (human, inter-personal and the world of knowing about the existence of phenomena) through his or her subjective binoculars. At the Egocentric Thinking stage, social relations develop with one limitation: The relations are desirable as long as they serve the child's will. When this condition is not met, the child will leave or struggle and sometimes try to "forcefully" change the desires of another. In this manner, the child gradually tests his/her own strength and special place in the surrounding society. Phallic children have interest-based relations between them - to the point of getting into a "world war" in struggles against contradictory desires.

Another characteristic of this period is the child's need for dominance over the world through conquering its own ter-ritory. A phallic child tends to build a "place" from which to observe the world while being protected in his or her "home" that has just now been constructed. These needs for conquering are diverse in nature and ways of expression. They are present at the kindergarten, the playground, and obviously, at home. The need for a "home of my own" or a camp or a watchtower, leads many children to creative construction activity, based on an increasingly growing world of imagination. And thus, a hideout made of a table with a long tablecloth at home, the ladder in the yard, or an old heap of boxes can - each in its own way - serve as an infrastructure for creative construction. The fight over resources, division of property, and delineation of boundaries is very prevalent among phallic children. The need for a supervising and regulating adult, allowing a cue on the structure or "just" division of construction materials, is necessary for the child's secure development.

At this stage, the child's imagination draws much from the animistic (anthropomorphism = attributing life to inanimate objects, as well to plants and natural phenomena) and magical worlds of thought (words and thoughts have power of their own, which can actually exist in their own right). This imagination brings about creative initiative, liberating the child, and enabling safe processing of everyday experiences. Imagination simultaneously operates in the opposite direction - a source for an increase in fears and therefore in aggressive behaviors too - for defense purposes. At this stage, children very powerfully identify with strong cultural heroes, especially those possessing super-natural strength, and with heroes of various types of fairytales. These children tend to use these characters, their characteristics, and tools incessantly. In this way, many children search for any object that resembles a sword, a rifle, a bow and arrow, or alternatively an extremely powerful magic wand, as a weapon for getting organized in life. These tools, possessing assault and defensive power properties, serve the child as an additional source of protection and reassurance vis-a-vis the fears on the one hand and the need to conquer on the other.

The increase in sensory-motor skills, and mainly in the qualities of integration among them, forms another basis for expressing the phallic forces. An increasing and advancing capacity to plan and build, to draw and cut with scissors, to express oneself in the material world, provides the child with an additional place for imaginary processing of the world of needs, as well as a tool for conquering and unique presence in the world. The child initiative now bursts through the creative world as well. Combined with imaginary thinking, any material enables varied emotional expression.

These diverse and stormy expressions of initiative, used by the child both to exhibit uniqueness as well as for emotional processing of experiences, are now put to an additional developmental test. The presence of the Ego structure as a primary element in transitioning from the infantile *pleasure principle* to the toddler's *reality principle*, enables the child to move between wishes for impulse gratification with his or her maximum initiative, and the need to acknowledge the boundaries of reality (mainly as represented by the parents or educators) and to become moderated vis-a-vis these boundaries. Thus, a key conflict in upbringing is born in the third year of life - a conflict between the child and adult, drawing from the child's need to express the impulsive initiative, versus the obligation to moderate self and adapt to the limits set by the adult. When this conflict appears, it serves the child in several directions: It teaches about the secure world presented by the adult by means of the boundaries and limits (despite the storminess and need to create - I am "protecting" you from yourself and from your lack of ability to predict the full consequences of your actions), and simultaneously strengthens the experience of separateness and distinctness from the adult (having different needs shows that we are actually separate and different from each other); enables a release of stormy psychical energy through expressing emotions of anger and rage, but also enables an encounter with a confident adult who is not intimidated by child rage and assists in controlling it.

The existence of these conflicts also stems from the fact that the child possessing the initial understanding of the *reality principle* (as an expression of the increase in the Ego's strength), still lacks full insight concerning the possible consequences of his or her actions and behaviors (a stage that is to arrive later, with the development of causal thinking), and also lacks sufficient ability for emotional self-regulation in the face of his or her own impulses (regulation that will mature with the causal thinking). On the other hand, because the child has a concept of the *reality principle*, he or she experiences the limits and boundaries set by the adult as a possible experience of guilt. When the child's initiative encounters the adult's world of boundaries and limits, Erikson says, it is blocked with an experience of guilt, increasing motivation to act within the boundaries and not outside them, in order to feel that the initiative is safe. The boundaries and limits set by the adult not only serve the child as a practical and necessary safety line, considering the absence of the child's predictive ability concerning possible consequences, but also as a reflective mirror regarding the child's actual initiative itself - approving of it as a desirable and positive matter, or preventing it to protect from undesirable consequences of the child's actions. This process expands and diversifies the relational world between children and adults and gradually increases in the child the full understanding concerning the boundaries of reality.

In Erikson's opinion, when safety boundaries are absent or when faced by overly rigid boundaries, expressing rejection and negation of the whole child and not only of specific actions and initiatives, the child might develop a self-experience of guilt and this might cause profound damage to self-worth later on. Therefore, a benevolent adult is one who can encourage initiative under conditions of safety boundaries with reflection that moderates the guilt experience. This delicate balance between enabling and limiting puts the learning- and attention-disabled child to a difficult and painful test.

| A Learning & AD(H)D Disabled Child at the Phallic Stage and Parenthood With a Sense of Guilt

The disruption of processes in the phallic period in the child with learning and attention disabilities makes this an especially stormy and/or painful period for the child and parents. These children start out with a possible range of developmental disorders, some of them creating an increase in the experience of guilt or over-moderation of the initiative needs of children suffering from a sustained difficulty to reach the longed-for balance. Therefore, in this period, there is a considerable increase in the identification and referral of children "suspected" of suffering from the syndrome. During this period, the learning- and attention-disabled child moves between a normative increase in Ego forces and the urge to express them uniquely and territorially, and the difficulty stemming from an unsuitable 'toolbox.'

The world of gaps that is typical of the learning- and attention-disabled child is now especially prominent. The normative ways of expression rely on **sensory-motor integration capacities** or on the world of increasing verbalization, on the ability to **become familiar with and 'learn' the boundaries of reality and their usage as a primary regulatory element.** The impulse, blocked by reality testing, the conflict with the adult - for the learning- and attention-disabled child - these are done under faulty conditions. Poor capacities in the performance area (poor gross/fine motor control, poor integration ability, unclear sidedness and dominance, difficulty in spatial planning, body schema and image difficulties, disorganization, etc.) cause the child frustration, increasing experiences of failure and an impulsive surge of dangerous initiative, due to the lack of ability to express itself in an adaptive manner. The origin of conflicts with the adult's boundaries is in the child's immense urge (due to temperament disorder) in the absence of efficient memory operation and attention disorders (visual, auditory, either of them or both), and the child's difficulty to preserve in working memory, learned conditions of the real world. The child's unregulated need to examine the world with its myriad dangers leads to a difficult experience in the family and/or kindergarten. Disruptions in language development as a key expression and regulation tool, send some children into a regression of behavioral expression instead of pression with speech.

The difficulty to use the adult's verbal and behavioral cues as boundary guides, and the need to repeatedly experience the conflictual contact with the adult, evoke harsh reactions in the adult, ranging from expressions of aggression against the child (undifferentiated blaming—does not blame the child's behavior, but the child's total self and personality), to expressions of helplessness, limit/boundary breaking, and desire to avoid conflicts through exaggerated concessions. These concessions evoke anxiety in the child and lack of confidence in the unstable and weak adult one faces, and act paradoxically on the child: increase anger and aggression as an expression of a covert wish toward the adult to "improve" performance in a secure and consistent direction, of someone who sets stable and safe limits and boundaries.

The world of imagination that also develops in the learning- and attention-disabled child always needs tools to express the urge for individuation. Moderation of the urge in the face of a **slow-to-warm-up temperament,** or the sense of lack of initiative due to this temperament, alongside the small quantity of developmental capacities, sense of clumsiness and lack of adequate Ego forces - all these make this group of children with learning- and attention- disability - passive, avoidant, or anxious children, who observe events from the sidelines, preoccupied with a defense of avoidance or seclusion. In these children, imagination is often expressed **only in one manner** because of developmental gaps. Therefore, a rigid preference for one activity and avoidance of others is sometimes apparent in them. The need to engage in limited routine activities (perseverative = repeating themselves over and over again, sometimes without variety and without fit to reality) provides these children an experience of inner security in the face of dealing with the familiar and safe; but here lies a focal point for additional depravations, which increase the experience of the disability and might cause secondary damage of lack of sufficient exposure to the surrounding world of stimuli. These children are generally experienced by adults as good and even "too good." They do not draw attention and get lost in the pedagogical process of kindergarten and sometimes of the home as well. The meagerness of their initiative is not disturbing enough, because they seemingly "go with the flow" of the disciplinary demands and do not evoke difficulty or conflict.

Both these types (aggressive and quiet) are at increasing risk of experiencing the phallic period - the period of initiative expressions and ability for separateness - while being saturated with a sense of guilt and failure, which is an additional causative factor in the development of an at-risk personality - both emotionally and academically. Early identification of these children and the construction of an intervention plan tailored to their unique difficulty profile, ensure huge potential for moderating the difficulties, moderating the gaps, and creating conditions for more complete and better development.

Realizing the possibility of identifying and diagnosing these children as early as possible is critical in the recovery prognosis for a more benevolent continued development.

While Erikson (1951) identifies the feeling of guilt as an opposite pole to the experience of initiative that bursts forth in the third year of life, one can view the dualism of initiative - guilt as a characterization of phallic child-parent relations in general, and learning- and attention-disabled children's relations with their parents in particular.

Guilt is an experience appearing in the individual when experiencing self and behavior as inappropriate to the rules determined by the culture and society in which he or she lives. Hence the existence of the feeling of guilt necessitates the existence of reality testing, arising from the development of the Ego and judging ability. At the beginning of the initiative stage, young children might experience a feeling of guilt when faced with "parental reflection" of their actions, as unsuited to the rules and boundaries/limits, or when their behavior causes destruction and harm to those around them or inanimate objects. Parents, who witness the initiating behaviors of their children, are therefore required to perform a highly important educational task - setting safety limits and boundaries for them that will protect the outbursts of initiative and channel them toward allowed territories and behaviors. The attempt to break through the boundaries as a way of contact between the child and adult is hence a necessary stage on the way to achieving an experience of full initiative. A stable parent who is confident of his child's love and is capable of protecting the child and his or her initiatives by way of safety boundaries, will not be frightened by the conflicts and will be assisted by them as another way to instill an ability for restraint and regulation.

On the other hand, among the parents who face their children's bursts of initiative, there are those who are inclined to experience the feelings of guilt for certain periods of time in the face of the undesirable consequences of their children's actions, mainly when the breach of boundaries is public - seen by all - or alternatively, concerns focal points valued by the parent. Parental feelings of guilt might be a spurring factor for the parent to remain clear and consistent in limit-setting. Nevertheless, an inevitable dialogue develops between the initiating child and the parent experiencing guilt. At this point in time, the question arises, concerning the conditions that facilitate or weaken the parent's ability to remain stable and clear when facing the child, being consistent in limit-setting or becoming weak and conceding to the child. Inconsistency of the parent's boundaries/limits, concessions and "compromises" are often perceived by the initiating child as parental "weakness." This frightens the child and causes a feeling of being abandoned and unprotected. This feeling many times results in a child's tendency to increase initiative as an additional way of testing boundaries/limits and as a child's request to the parent: "Please, keep on being my strong parent and carry on protecting me against my unregulated initiative." However, this child's interpretation is not always clear to the parent, who might interpret this in the exact opposite direction - as challenging his or her authority or a child's uncompromising stubbornness. As a reaction, the parent acts in one of two contradictory ineffective directions - making the limits and boundaries more strict, with an aggressive and threatening tone, which might frighten the child and cause an unbearable experience of guilt; or absolute leniency, perceived by the child as parental weakness, forcing the child to continue testing the limits with escalating tones.

A key question here is: What are the sources of the weakening of parental authority - causing their inability to generate secure boundaries preventing them from having a stable and reassuring stance - and instead, leading to lenience or aggression?

As we have mentioned before, contemporary parenthood often exists under the shadow of the hunger for the *Total Parenthood* stage - a stage that is very short nowadays. This hunger causes the parent to continue searching for the symbiotic parent-child relationship, which provides an experience of confidence in the child's love for parent. This hunger causes a role reversal between the parent and child: Instead of remaining an element that provides love and security, the parent becomes an entity that searches for the child's love and security, which the child is supposed to provide. This confusion, caused by the extended psychological hunger, weakens the parent's ability to be a proper educational element, and makes it hard to set limits at such a critical stage in the child's development. Anthony and Benedek's (1970) statement, regarding the necessary connection between the stage of total parenthood as a satisfactory stage, and the parental capability to be an element with stable and clear boundaries, is today proven time after time in parent-child relations.

Parents of children with learning- and attention-disabilities bear many scars from their child's infancy period. Temperament disorders, difficulties in providing care for the child, developmental delays and more, have generated in the parent a persistent experience of a small or large sense of failure in one's ability to love and be loved by the child. This parental searching for positive reflection on the child's part, with the sense of guilt, exhaustion and frustration from the difficult handling of their child already from a very young age, now generates the parental weakening: "walking on eggshells," many parents would say, "just so he doesn't have another outburst." Weakening chronic anxiety, recognized by the learning- and attention-disabled child - who lacks regulation - as a lack of parental confidence, causes the child's behavior to escalate.

Another source of the parent's weakening is parental aggression, sometimes appearing as a desperate parental attempt to prevent the child, at any cost, from "producing" undesirable behavior. This anxious parent reacts with covert or overt aggression at any situation - mainly in situations outside the home - with the intention of protecting oneself and the child from the experience of shame and guilt. This constant pressure is picked up by the child as a negative reflection, generating the infrastructure for a negative self-image later on, and mainly the sense of sustained guilt over being a disappointing and bad child to the parents and environment. Sometimes life influenced by this experience causes the child to give up any effort "to be good" and act as one who realizes what is expected from him or her. The effort to produce appropriate initiating behavior demands much energy anyhow, considering the difficulties created by the disability.

An additional source of weakening for parents of children with learning- and attention- disabilities is their child's difficulty to preserve the rules of reality in memory - a difficulty necessitating increased parental presence and involvement anew in every situation. The learning- and attention-disabled child's lack of ability to preserve learning as an efficient factor in moderating initiative and directing it to the permitted places, evokes an interpretation of the child by the parent as "a child who does not learn a lesson." Alternatively, children from the other pole of the disability, the anxious ones with little initiative, evoke at this stage the sense of anxiety in the parents over "what is wrong with my child?" Children from both poles require enhanced parental vigilance. The parental sense of guilt, mixed with fatigue and anxiety, makes the nature of their disciplinary involvement in these situations very problematic, such as being aggressive (lack of parental regulation when faced by lack of the child's regulation), putting continuous pressure on the child (as a parental effort of forcefully "fixing" the disability), making concessions (in the face of pity and identification with the child's distress) or over-protection. None of these enable a normal course of setting safety boundaries and limits, and might increase in the child the range of undesirable behaviors, methods of avoidance, or the reflection (parental mirroring) of being disappointing and not good enough.

Because the child's initiative is a visible occurrence, present in many places outside the home, including kindergartens or neighborhood playgrounds, it becomes yet more difficult and pressurizing. Erroneous environmental and disciplinary interpretation, viewing the child's behavior as "violent and aggressive" or alternatively, "weak and avoiding," without understanding the origins, increases the pressure on the parent who is already subjected to a sustained experience of guilt.

This vicious cycle leaves the parents of learning- and attention-disabled children in an ever-increasing distress of guilt. Together with the shame and doubt, this guilt is in danger of becoming a dominant parental experience in their relations with their child - unless proper help is received, enabling them to have new parental understanding of their child's needs, as well as providing them with a "toolbox" adapted for action with, and when confronted by their children.

F. Language Development Deficiencies: "When You Run out of Words, the Body and Hands Speak."

The emergence of the first signs of language beginning from the second year of life (at the level of one or two words) and the development of language at the quantitative level (number of words) and qualitative level (sentence structure, expression expanse, grammatical structure and more) throughout toddlerhood, comprise a meaningful landmark in the lives of every child and parent. Language, by its very nature, is the means of communication and expression that is unique to the human species, and it develops with the maturation of neurological functions, on the one hand, and upon the emergence of the need to expand the means of contact and communication, on the other. The infant who initially learned to communicate with simple means, like mime and facial gestures, body language (smiling, stretching out the hands) as well as making various sounds (yelling, crying, or murmuring), gradually acquires a complex, very expressive means of communication, which will serve it in several developmental directions simultaneously.

Basic one- or two-word language strengthens the confidence in the relationship between the toddler and parents, and mainly gradually enables defining wishes and wants more accurately, and therefore, gaining better responsiveness from the parent. The experience that connects between comprehensibility and responsiveness contributes to strengthening the relationship between the toddler and parent, which develops and becomes closer. Hence, Greenspan (1992) views the emergence of language as an expression of the existence of a close emotional relationship between the toddler and parents and a driving force for expanding the connection between them.

Developmentally speaking, the increasingly forming verbal contact between the child and parents enables the expansion of the child's experience of autonomy, alongside making the parent's ability to set safety boundaries more sophisticated. The speaking child can afford secure physical distancing from its parents or kindergarten teacher. As long as the child is within speaking and hearing range, he or she has an increased ability to express wants, thoughts, and emotions without special effort. From the child's point of view, the parent can concurrently restrain him or her, set safety boundaries/limits or direct, without physically limiting him/her. The ability to stop a child with words, as well as allow an independent act while being verbally accompanied from a distance, gradually builds an experience of confidence with secure independence and expands the sense of connection between the child and adult.

Separation that is done with words ("Bye bye, I am going, I will be back later...") or a verbal limitation ("You are not to go beyond the fence…"), guidance from a distance while providing secure protection ("Be careful when you make a turn on the steps..."), and so forth - all these create a sense of deep closeness without harming the need for autonomy. On the child's part, the ability to express thoughts and emotions and construct an inner imaginary world with words contributes to expanding the experience of individuation between the child and parents. The ability for verbal expression is another stepping stone on the child's way to achieving a deep connection alongside separateness and independence.

Countless studies on the various aspects of learning- and attention-disabilities indicate some early disruptions in language development with all its components (Amir, 1991; Barkley 1997; Byrnes, 2001; Brown, 2000, 2005; Lavoy, 2006).

Language is multifaceted: It begins with an innate brain structure, which develops into an internal dictionary, thanks to the existence of constant verbal stimulation on the part of the human environment (the intensive presence of a speaking adult, giving continuous verbal expression to every object, touch or expression in the infant's surroundings). It continues with shaping processes with the aid of which the spontaneous murmur gradually becomes a spoken, comprehensible word, relying on the inner word and goes through a process of adapted retrieval, until the word is pronounced in the relevant context. Normal hearing and sensory-motor integration of the mouth cavity are also associated with an increase in the capability of producing spoken language.

The maturing of language structures in the brain enables, from an early age, the development of language centers responsible for building the dictionary, for structuring the grammatical structure of the mother tongue to which the child is exposed, and for creating the match between non-verbal and verbal expressions of connection.

The interactive processes to which the child is exposed are the basis for language learning: verbal stimulation, shaping the spoken verbal expression, intentional matching between objects and their application, between a non-verbal and verbal behavioral expression ("You don't have to throw yourself down"; "Say you are angry, don't bite"; "Tell him he is disturbing you," and more). After several years pass, the association between the components of the inner and spoken language, with the written and read language is learned, so that each stage is a basis in preparation for the next stage until the entire process of language acquisition is completed.

During the years of varied research, we witness signs showing that a high percentage of children who are diagnosed as learning- attention- and concentration-disabled suffer from some degree of damage to linguistic development (Hulme & Snowling, 1997; Levine, 1987). In some of them, the signals appear quite early - delay in the emergence of the first spoken words, delay in verbal fluency and sentence construction, and more. In others, the characteristic signs of the damage are a little later, more complex, and include disruptions in auditory distinction causing disruptions in verbal expression. Alternatively, integration difficulties of the mouth cavity cause clumsy and insufficiently comprehensible expression.

In others, the disruption in auditory attention has an effect on selective and inefficient distinction of spoken reference to the child and the lack of ability to use the spoken word effectively.

The origin of the damage is diverse and sometimes controversial. The estimate is that it is hypo-activity of brain functions and of various brain activity regions, or a disruption in internal brain communication (chemical, electrical, or both) or difficulties in transferring information between various parts of the brain associated with language development, perceptual difficulties (visual, auditory or combination of both), and more. At any rate, the problem's prevalence compels us to treat the result common to all types of linguistic development deficiencies - their influence on emotional and behavioral development.

In the journey to autonomy, the toddler relies on language as an important means for expressing wants, wishes, and emotions. The toddler can add a word to a gesture or mimic in order to express excitement when a familiar parent arrives, or alternatively, can ask for an object or toy without guessing games. The need for food or drink can be expressed, wanting or not wanting various things happening in its life - this is a key component in the experience of independence and control of the world. Later on, the possibility opens up, of reducing the experience of dependence and moving away from the parent while maintaining verbal contact. By the same token, the parent can enable the child to move away, thanks to the ability to protect and direct the child with words.

At the phallic stage, words become a complex means of expression, on which imaginary activity, experience of strength, and beginning of the circle of belonging are based. What is the meaning of a delay in the appearance of language: **The child is in need, for a prolonged time, of an alternative, limited language that is complicated to express and decipher** - the language of behavior, the language of expressions and gestures, and mimicking with facial expressions or the entire body. The limitation imposed by the linguistic delay on the child and parents becomes a frustrating factor for both (the incomprehensible child and the parent who has difficulty comprehending), or a factor that increases dependence while the child needs independence (the parent becomes the translator of the child's "wants" vis-a-vis the environment). Following the need to preserve physical, instead of verbal expression, the child gradually becomes identified with "aggression" or "violence" (grabs a toy and doesn't ask for it, takes something to express a want, reacts physically to contact because he or she cannot use spoken language efficiently). Also, in the social relations that are increasingly opening up, body language remains the language of emotions, wants, and needs. At this point, the results of the contacts are painful, frustrating, and stigmatizing for the child.

In most cases, the delay in language development appears after other early difficulties, whether in the area of temperament or sensory-motor development, therefore the picture become more difficult and complex. In the child with temperament difficulties, such as low frustration threshold, high reaction intensity, too low- or high-sensation threshold, the reactions intensify. By contrast, in the slow-to-warm-up child, the delay in language further increases the difficulty of moving away from the parents, associating with friends, and being active. This child will continue individual perseverative behaviors, and avoid searching for independence and new relationships, as the inability to express itself joins the slowness of reaction.

Motor clumsiness (which gradually makes the child encounter difficulties from the areas of acquiring independence skills, such as dressing, eating suited to disciplinary demands, or from educational developmental areas such as drawing, cutting with scissors, pasting, difficulty participating in certain types of didactic games and more), combined with difficulties in expressing and acquiring heard and spoken language - these will cause the child to feel inferior, frustrated, have rage outbursts, and mainly develop an inner sense of low self-image.

Exposing the child to varied life environments such as home, kindergarten, playground and more, necessitates flexibility, adaptability, and learning of behavioral codes. These all rely on the existence of normal language; and when this is not present, the learning- and attention-disabled child finds himself or herself in need of a different language - a behavioral language. When, in any situation of need, excitement, frustration and more, automation of the verbal language is absent, it will be replaced by impulsivity, low inhibitions, slow reaction, and more. The sense of lack of confidence in myself and my comprehensibility might cause an impulsive and unregulated over-reaction in the child, or avoidance and distancing - both states that increase the dependence on the adult.

The weakness of the working memory system is critical, not only for the actual acquisition of language, but also for the ability to use it at the right time and situation, and it makes it hard for the child to learn during activity. The lack of efficient ability to preserve verbal teachings in the working memory and use them as a teaching process, causes the child a persistent state of "does not learn the lesson," or "loses the sequence after the second teaching" or "out of it." Development becomes full of deficiencies, behavior arouses concern and results in negative reactions from the environment, and thus social distancing starts, or difficulty being "with it" socially.

All these are faced by a parent who has already experienced early difficulties in parenting this child - repeatedly feeling shame and guilt, pain and failure and, and moving between self-pity and pity for the child, to being angry with the child and hostile toward him or her, or towards the environment that does not understand. The parent mainly feels helpless: how to behave and act. The parental pain becomes increasingly visible and creates unease in the parent-child relations. Many moments during the shared day are accompanied by the experience of losing the "good child I expected."

G. The Oedipal Period - a Never-Ending Journey

| Development at Four-to-Six Years of Age

The age of 4-to-6 - the pre-school years - is a period rich in occurrences in several and simultaneous focal areas:

Acquisition of gender identity while identifying with the same-sex parent develops.

Intensive and complex repetition of Rapprochement (getting closer or distancing) processes between child and parent; but now they are happening simultaneously and distinctly, according to the child and parent's gender (at first, renewed closeness to different-sex parent and distancing from same-sex parent, to the degree of relations of envy and aggression between them, and later on - a reversal: getting close to and identifying with same-sex parent, and becoming distant from the different-sexed parent.)

Increase in importance of the peer group as a supporting factor in expressing independence and separateness from the dependence and exclusivity of the family circle.

Socialization into the culture and values of adult society in which the child grows and develops.

In each of these focal areas of development, processes relying on both maturity and learning take place. The child's ability in the totality of areas become more diverse and complex: Inter-relationships form between the various lines of development; an increase in the quality is achieved both in the intellectual-cognitive area as well as the emotional and inter-personal area and motor and sensory areas; the capacity for restraint and regulation, self-control and release becomes more sophisticated; concurrently, verbal expression ability increases, and a rich world of imagination and complex intellectual world are developed.

The multitude and diversity of processes at this age weigh heavily on the learning- attention- and concentration-disabled child and parents and accentuate the difference between them and normal children and parents.

The Oedipal period is characterized by a multiplicity of urges and drives, by building a place in the social world, by complex relations with parents and adults in general, and by a sense of empowerment due to the multiplicity of acquired capacities and skills. It is not in vain that Erikson (1951) termed this period "building the experience of industry alongside the danger of the development of the experience of inferiority." This stage of *industry vs. inferiority* is mainly typical of children at latency age (6-to-12), but its beginning can already be seen in the development of 4-to-6-year-olds.

Piaget (1969; and in Muuss, 1982) emphasizes the emergence of complex intellectual processes, which he terms "concrete operations," originating from the perception of the constant element in the world. At this age, while experiencing, children discover that various characteristics in the world are constant, such as a quantity of material, time, objects. Grasping the *law of conservation* causes the child to comprehend these concepts of constancy. This insight gradually influences the emotional system in the face of realizing concepts like end (its connection to the end-of-life - death), order and regularity, and social position.

At this age, the child is required to have an ability of conservation and internalization of psychic and intellectual processes simultaneously in the various memory systems, to be served by them during the entire complex journey.

The development of gender identity at this age is accompanied by imaginary play processes for processing the drives and building routes of sublimation with socialization. For this purpose, the child is required to perform complex mental activity, both with respect to the simultaneity of processes as well as the separate complexity of each.

Rediscovering his mother, the male child clings to her and yearns for her love, and is required to simultaneously deal with the anxiety evoked in him by his father's presence due to wishes of aggression directed at him. These processes are mostly internal, but they also have visible aspects - behavioral and verbal. The internal processing of the obligation to distance oneself from the mother for the sake of finding a love object among the kindergarten girls, while simultaneously transferring the aggressive and competitive needs from the father figure to the group of boys at the kindergarten demands from the child a mental ability of transfer of processes, differentiated usage of imaginary and real worlds, learning and internalizing the rules of regulation, as well as developing identification with the demands and representations posed by the parents and later on - by all adults.

A learning- attention- and concentration-disabled child lacks some of the mental abilities we have detailed, and their emergence is late and partial.

Freud (in Muuss, 1988) emphasizes that one of the more complex psychological tasks concerns the child's simultaneous ability to feel conflictual distancing from the same-sex parent, while at the same time internalizing and identifying with him/her, including the behaviors and rules represented by them. In this way, the child builds the infrastructure for the development of morals and the Super-Ego. Therefore, this age is an extremely stormy and difficult period for all involved.

When a learning- attention- and concentration-disabled child's mother acts to regulate and moderate the expressions of attraction to and fondness for her, and redirects him from her to the female friends at kindergarten, she is still certain of his ability to make the so-complex transition. However, a learning- attention- and concentration-disabled child has difficulty in these tasks, as well as in some of the academic tasks starting to appear more intensely. The ability to separate from the mother, moderate the attraction to her, and transfer it to the kindergarten girls requires competence of neurological processes, which are partly missing or disrupted in the child with the disabilities.

Identification with the same-sex parent enables at least partial resolution of the aggressive drive, i.e., reaching the mother figure indirectly through the connection with the father; however, in order to reach this, the child is required to be able to operate complex processes of abstraction and generalization, and these are the focal point of the disabled child's difficulty due to damage, of some degree, to processes controlled by the executive function and working memory of the brain.

The father figure, at first representative of the world of manhood only, and later, of the world of adults, their values and ways of life, remains as a concrete figure in the disabled child's mind, without an ability to deduce about others from it. The need to use processes requiring planning and prediction of results and relying on the recollection of experiences stands as an obstacle for the disabled child. His weakness in managing processes of regulation and inhibition and using drives in permitted directions (while avoiding the forbidden ones) increases the environment's attitude toward the child as an "abnormal, difficulty-provoking, violent" child and so on.

Emotional moderation is another capacity enabled in the Oedipal child thanks to the ability to acquire conservation processes cognitively. The comprehension that there is differentiation between the wish to harm the father and the actual ability, the gradually building knowledge that also a physically distant parent (because he has gone to work and the child to kindergarten) is part of the day - a parent that is whole and protected despite the aggressive fantasy - these are what enable the child to confront his father in the morning and calm down during day. This is not the case in the disabled child, who remains stormy for a prolonged time (relaxation difficulties).

Imagination processes, imaginative play, and role-playing - relying on good transitions between imagination and reality, between the truth and "pretend" - enable the child an emotional pause with processing and internalization of the stormy occurrences. However, when the learning-disabled child predominantly relies on what is present and concrete, or is drawn into a fantasy world without being able to differentiate between it and reality, he/she finds it difficult to close the gaps between them, does not trust the memory bank to preserve knowledge and internalization of the parent figure, and remains with fears and anxieties, this child's moderation possibilities are decreased. This anxiety produces emotional intensification and turmoil, sometimes increasing the child's aggressive behavior as a defense mechanism for protecting the anxious psyche and as a means for releasing the tension created within by the anxiety. In this way, an escalating cycle begins, of anxiety-triggering unregulated responses, which in turn increase anxiety, which increases unregulated behavior and so on.

The process of identification with and internalization of the parent figure as a primary representative of the world of values in which the child lives and grows up, simultaneously with the ability to learn gender identity-dependent behaviors from the parent are the mental foundation for the construction of super-ego - that structure which according to Freud, forms the infrastructure for moral behavior and judgment. Being in contact with the parent figure, the learning- and attention-disabled child, does gradually pick up the moral knowing, derived from the development of the Super Ego structure, and in this respect, his development is normal and normative like all children his age. However, lack of the ability to be assisted by the Super Ego structure as a director and anticipator for the preference of behaviors, or lack of ability to use it as an element regulating and moderating reactions, cause the child additional frustration and anxiety. The ability to differentiate between what is allowed and what is forbidden nearly always arrives late: first the behavior and afterward - judgment of consequences. The central and directing element is the urge's storminess and not the moderating force of the internalized world - the will to be like the parent versus the difficulty to realize this will - the child is stricken by these repeatedly. The result is not only expressed in the quality and intensity of non-age and non-norm-appropriate behaviors, but in the growing psychic experience of a sense of failure, a constant inner struggle between the will to be - to achieve.

The internal parental figure is mostly predicated on mental processes associated with the memory system in general and working memory of the executive function in particular. Therefore, internalization of this figure will be partial, non-integrative, non-complete and not full. As a result, the child operates out of a weakened, inefficient inner schema that is not available at the decisive moment. However, normal intelligence, worsening reactions from both the adults and children's environments, as well as the ability of after-the-fact-judgment - these cause the child to make mistakes repeatedly and feel sustained damage to self-worth and self-image. The widening gap between the desire to achieve age- and need-appropriate developmental goals, alongside the inefficient "toolbox," continues to make its mark. Learning- attention- and concentration-disabled children tend to react to these difficulties in two different ways: Some of them become more upset and stormy, their overt behavior is less and less regulated, they rely more and more on behavioral and less on verbal communication, and they are eventually identified as having behavioral and social difficulties. It should be emphasized that these difficulties originate from the disability itself, however, the frequent negative reactions experienced from the environment will cause additional secondary harm - despair, depression, and sustained damage to self-worth. These painful feelings will be "self-treated" by the child with expressions of desperation alongside escalation in the behavioral lack of regulation. Another group of children with disability will "self-treat" themselves by way of withdrawal and avoidance, reduction, and keeping away, with rigidity and obsessive behavior as a defense mechanism for maintaining some degree of control over the world, where the child feels a lack of control.

When additional difficulties in the sensory-motor area or in activity skills and "academic" difficulties are noticed in both groups, they will finally be referred to diagnosis and maybe the intervention the child needs so much will begin - an intervention combining treatment of the academic, as well as the emotional and behavioral problems.

Parents of Oedipal children sometimes view this period as a long and difficult journey of stormy and confusing relations. The child shifts between expressions of overfondness for one parent and experiences of fears due to the aggressive fantasies toward the other. The child's magical thinking continues, giving exaggerated weight to thoughts and words as having "power" to change things in reality. The child tends to act out, "dumping" the emotional burden by projecting it onto the parents, upon the beginning of expressions of rebellion and insubordination as a way of testing the parent's boundaries, strength, and real ability to protect the child from himself.

The emergence of social needs is a key issue in children's lives at this age. It includes giving exaggerated importance to the kindergarten child group, strong attraction to friendships, and desire to be positioned high in the gang. There is a need for forming a group one belongs to as a place for processing the stormy processes and strengthening the experience of separateness from the parents, and as an independent place for imaginary games as preparation for social life. All these contribute their share to the parent-child relations storm (Plotnik, 2003). However, when the child's development is normal and synchronous, the parent has the chance to properly handle these relations by an intelligent combination of boundaries, rules, and places for expressing autonomy and the gang. Every conflict teaches the parent and child about the limits of what is permitted and forbidden. The emergence of intellectual curiosity, coupled with an incessant need for doing and being active (serving the training of intellectual and sensory-motor processes as a way of gaining ventilation and a means of showing industrious presence in the world), builds a wide field of permitted possibilities for expression that even arouse admiration and positive reflection on the part of the parent. The boy who displaces the confrontation with his father to war games with his friends, and invests energy in building weapons from art and scrap material; the girl who directs her energy to housekeeping games or role-playing of kindergarten teacher and children or sits for hours, drawing and cutting with scissors, building and pasting, arouse sounds of wonder at the new abilities.

Parent-child conversations, relying on expressions of interest and exploration of the world, curiosity to know more and more, endless testing of the language through word games, thinking games and so on, create further bonding between parents and children and generate a new experience of achievement alongside the difficulty.

| "The Expulsion from the Garden of Eden" - the Double Journey of Learning & AD(H)D Disabled Children and Their Parents

The increase in sexual attraction to and identification with the different-sex parent as a complex relationship between the Oedipal child and its parents raises the strength of the "gang" (peer group) for the first time. The parent of the opposite sex must create a complex barrier between him or her and the child: emotional connection and love - yes - sexual attraction and its physical expressions - no. Therefore, the parent must provide the child with a new place to realize the urge - the peer group at the kindergarten. And indeed, many children at this age discover the power of the age gang, and use it with great intensity for processing and realizing their drives and needs.

The gang becomes a very important element in children's lives, and it meets several needs simultaneously:

Processing the complex Oedipal conflict with parents.

Support (cast outs group) of a gang of similar children (therefore there is multiplicity of activities of constructing "cast out camps" as preferred activity of these children at this stage).

Learning and practicing social behavior norms according to social and cultural values (learning done under the management and direction of the kindergarten teacher as representative of the cultural-principled world).

Practicing, learning, and experiencing complex relations between the participants, all of the same age.

Release and venting of emotional loads in relationships through fantasy games, oscillation in social position, role-plays and more.

In a learning- and attention-disabled child, there is sometimes an unavoidable gap between the desire and need to belong to the gang and the difficulty to "learn" and acquire the relevant toolbox for being an invited and wanted part of the gang. At this stage, learning and attention-disabled children have the most intense experiences of rejection, loneliness, and inferiority, often supported by other children's parents who misleadingly view them as "bad/aggressive/violent/undesirable children for their children".

Simultaneously, with the suffering the child is destined to deal with, comes the great suffering of the parents. The duty of "expelling" the children from the family to the double territory of the home and the gang is unbearable for every Oedipal pre-schooler's parents. Discovering through intellectual comprehension and emotional awareness, the existence of differences between the sexes, the expressions of child sexual attraction, the new insights derived from intellectual development and initial, clear emergence of conscience (Super Ego structure) - all these are a shock for both child and parents. This developmental moment can be compared to the moment of discovering truth and morality, as revealed to Adam and Eve after having eaten from the fruit of the Tree of Knowledge: "He said, I heard the sound of You in the garden, and I was afraid because I was naked; so I hid myself." (Genesis, Chapter 3, verse 10).

The consequence of the discovery is clear: The obligation of expulsion from the Garden of Eden, lest Man eat from the Tree of Life as well and live forever. In the Oedipal child's family as well, the experience of discovering sexual truth arises and surfaces, while involving the discovery of the finiteness of life, the arising of awareness of death, and setting out into a new, more realistic world - the gang's court and the struggle for a place in it.

Inside the family, however, the task imposed upon the parents is the most difficult of all: They are the ones who are required to expel their child from the total familial Garden of Eden into the harsher and more complex external world. There is an absolute taboo, across all societies and cultures, of sexual relations between parents and their children, and the parent is akin to the angel expelling on behalf of God, guarding the entrance of the Garden of Eden and preventing the child from returning to the enchanted world of childhood. However, the parent is also the one who is required to accompany the child in dealing with this new world - the world outside - the world of the gang.

This difficult process, defined by us here as the "the expulsion from the Garden of Eden" occurs with more intensity and complexity between parents and learning- and attention-disabled children as well, and takes on a double meaning. Characterized by a stormy temperament and regulation difficulties, these children experience the Oedipal drives as well, with great intensity at home and among their peers, and will often evoke feelings of embarrassment, shame and guilt among the surrounding adults and children, due to sublimation and regulation difficulties. In this way, there is danger that an attraction-rejection relationship will develop between the child and parents, where the opposite-sex parent (the object of the drives) has difficulty stopping the child who is expressing attraction with great intensity.

"He keeps feeling me up...," complains a mother of a five-and-half-year-old learning- and attention-disabled boy. "The minute I enter the house she clings to me, pushes against me powerfully, gets inside my body and walks around after me everywhere without letting go..." -a father shares his distress via-a-vis his learning and attention-disabled girl. "He sits in the middle of the living room, as if watching television, and starts masturbating...," parents describe their distress in their attempt to accustom their six-and-a-half-year-old son to avoid these behaviors. "He constantly hugs and kisses me, to the point of actual embarrassment and discomfort. His touch is so powerful that he nearly breaks my bones…," adds another mother.

These and similar distresses evoke in the parents the need to react in the direction of keeping the child away, to the point of rejection vis-a-vis the intense and unregulated attraction exhibited toward them by the child. And the more the parent's rejection increases, the more the child's anxiety increases and he or she continues to express this attraction with ever-growing intensity.

This intensity, searching for release in the kindergarten as well, among the gang, encounters difficulties once again. Non-disabled Oedipal children feel embarrassed and distressed about the disabled child's unregulated attempts at touching, shame about the attempts at kissing and hugging, and react with avoidance or rejection. The clumsy attempt by the disabled child to penetrate the gang's games and belong, when lacking the toolbox, regulation, and suitable verbalization, often causes confrontations and a "violent" reaction, aimed at expressing the rejected child's frustration and unwillingness to give up.

By contrast, children with a slow-to-warm-up temperament often tend to stay on the sidelines, both at home and at kindergarten, and lack the daring and initiative to express their Oedipal wishes. Instead, they withdraw into their corner or are "content" with self-play with dolls and are described as childish, not belonging, and remote.

Both types do not find a secure place in the gang for processing their new drives. As a result, they are over-dependent on their parents to express their full needs; but their parents themselves feel distressed and embarrassed to serve in the role of the gang's substitute, and now more intensely experience their being different from parents of children without the disability (or sometimes different in their parenting of their other, non-disabled children).

This is not the end of the story. The disability's manifestations in some of the formal aspects of functioning at kindergarten lead to a substantial increase in the number of children identified and referred for diagnosis by kindergarten teachers and the educational system. The emergence of gaps and difficulties in the entirety of skills typical of the Oedipal period, the increase in importance of the concept of "school readiness" and the existence of forms and scales for evaluating readiness - all these lead to greater alertness of the kindergarten teachers to the appearance of the functional, global, or specific gap. Thus, despite the early existence of signals at toddlerhood already, a formal and clear referral is made only now, at pre-school age. Thereby, the shattering of the parental hope along the lines of "until it's time for school he or she will get it together/mature/get organized...close the gap" reaches it culmination. This shattering is another facet of the experience of expulsion from the Garden of Eden - the expulsion of hopes. Thus, the parent of the child with the learning- and attention-disability faces a double expulsion task: One is seemingly normative, but difficult and complex due to the child's disabilities; the other, psychological and unique in the face of the formal discovery of the disability and shattering of hope that "everything will be OK."

This double parental journey evokes in the parents distress, which has many varied expressions. Some of them will react with "over-protection" of their child, further hindering the child's efforts to arrive at the world of the gang - mature and ready for coping. Others will send the child quickly and by force and leave one exposed to the difficulties outside without adequate protection, loaded with experiences of guilt and rejection at home and outside. There are parents who will act in a confusing manner of closeness and distancing, as an expression of the emotional turmoil they are in. Others will direct blame and anger at the system, at the kindergarten teacher, or the one who preceded her and had not recognized and acted properly for the sake of their child. Others will delay their reaction and keep hoping that with time things will calm down and work out.

From this moment, many parents enter a new familial situation characterized by processes of familial work of mourning, with all that is implied by this.

2.

Learning & AD(H)D Disabilities

at Latency Age

(Elementary School Age)

A. Difficulties in Identification, Socialization Difficulties

Children at latency age (approx. 6-to-12-year-olds) arrive at elementary school "equipped" with developmental abilities, affecting the way they act, feel, and think. When not sufficiently understood by the adults accompanying the children in this period (parents, teachers, recreational hobby course instructors, youth movement instructors, and others) these characteristics might mistakenly receive undesirable interpretations.

Entering school is an extremely meaningful stage, because in Western society school is considered the highlight in the achievement of educational goals: acquiring knowledge together with developing a set of values and principles that will train the children to be educated adults connected with society's goals. Lasting at least 12 years or more, this educational process will demand from the child an intense emotional effort, investment of intellectual and behavioral energy, until reaching the point of being able to realize him/her self according to cultural norms and values. Additionally, entering the scene now is the component of measuring capacities and achievements and building preferences and wants alongside the necessity of belonging. Hence, this is a complex and stormy period, where different developmental channels are in action simultaneously, which need to be synchronized as much as possible.

The beginning of the latency age is tangent to the Oedipal storm of compulsory pre-school children, and at its peak, it provides an adapted solution for the conflict as permitted and appropriate in modern society: adjusting the ways the impulse is expressed, learning social relations, and building a place in the peer-group gang. The ability to direct psychic energy to intellectual and other activities - that is the key issue of the period and its objectives.

The beginning of the resolution of the Oedipal struggle involves each male and female child's ability to psychically shift from a competitive-conflictual state with the same-sex parent (in the sense of a wish to "remove" him or her from the way in order to more easily reach the opposite-sex parent, the object of love and sexual arousal) to a state of identification with, and internalization of the parent (in the sense of "if you can't beat them, join them," and in this manner you will reach the opposite-sex parent through and by means of him or her). Being like daddy also means enjoying closeness to mommy; and being like mommy is an opportunity to gain the father's love.

Starting with identification and continuing with internalization of the parent, this process poses a multi-faceted meaning, and not only provides a solution and opportunity in the Oedipal context, but also in much wider contexts like the affinity with society and culture.

Latency age is mainly about the increasingly growing, acquired ability of the child to go through a process of socialization, the focus of which is the wish and will to become part of a social group (of peers) that is part of a community, a society - a culture in which the child lives. At this age, children acquire abilities of relating through social activity, and the focus of interest becomes the peer group and belonging to the gang as a good place to be in, outside the stormy Oedipal struggle taking place indoors at home (a sort of "support group" = "outcasts group," experiencing similar experiences and supporting each other in the process of moving away from the family for the sake of constructing a social identity).

The gang enables, to the same extent, an opportunity to serve as a "practice field" - a place in which to act and practice social skills the world of social values and tools; and additionally, a place to realize and practice developments in the intellectual, emotional, sensory-motor areas, and more.

The Oedipal conflict gradually changes its place and intensity and is replaced by a new struggle - a sociometric struggle - a struggle for a position within the gang. However, this new struggle takes place with new rules, tools, and means, suited to age and its characteristics.

The way to the gang of peers - and from them to grown up society - always passes through the process of identification with the same-sex parent, the process of internalizing his or her figure, including all its varied characteristics: sexual-gender identity, social role, world of values and culture. In this way, the parent at the beginning of the Oedipal resolution becomes the first and important socialization agent. Later on, this duty will be transferred to new, extra-familial socialization agents, such as peers, teacher, instructors, coaches, and so on The child will gradually exhaust the process, in which the parent is viewed not only as a close individual with a deep emotional connection to him or her, but also as a representative figure of the adult world, from which the child will generalize about adult society and the entire world.

The learning- and attention-disabled child's journey at latency age is accompanied by coping with many difficulties, and it is no wonder that when parents lack knowledge and awareness concerning these difficulties, the child might fail and feel many experiences of inferiority.

The journey of identification with the same-sex parent necessitates, first and foremost, closeness and availability between child and parent. Assuming that the majority of learning- and attention-disabled children do indeed grow up in homes where this necessary condition is met, the beginning of identification will be made possible; however, as a complex process, identification necessitates neurological competence as well - both of the executive function as well as the various perceptions and memory systems - mainly working memory and verbal memory. As a learning-perceptual process, identification is conditional on the child's competence in using the parental presence as a major stimulus (over the background of other figures), characterizing it with the key outlines, and preserving it so that it can be used as a directing and guiding element for all mental processes. Identification is the ability to know and recognize the figure, characterize it and act in a similar way to its own moves in reality. This mental activity is difficult mainly when the "test of identification" is the child's ability to feel and act as the parent, while the parent is concretely absent. Most children suffering from learning- and attention-disability have difficulty acquiring the memory of the full figure including all its components, and in its absence, using it as a directing and guiding element, based on memory alone. It is not that they have not been sufficiently exposed to the parental presence, but rather that the disability and the disruption caused by it have damaged the learning system and various types of memory systems. For this reason, the child's ability to use the same-sex parent as a full and effective identification figure is impaired, the child tends to "forget" certain parts in of it, and thus the ability to internalize the parent is negatively affected. Because of this, the child also has difficulty preserving the security and calmness that a full identification process enables his or her peers. An increase in identification and internalization ability means feeling a sort of freedom to move away - to be a separate, independent entity. A child with a good course of identification moves away from the concrete parent, but keeps him or her inside, in the sense of "going without, but feeling with…," but in the learning- and attention-disabled child, moving away many times brings about a fright of losing the figure (which is slightly analogous to a sense of death). Therefore, learning- and attention-disabled children experience feelings of a rise in fears at pre-school and elementary school ages. Another condition for completing the process is the child's ability to make real-time use of the internalized figure, i.e., retrieving the figure from the memory banks, including the characteristics relevant to the situation the child is facing in reality, so it can be used to guide action.

Retrieval at a suited time is another complex neurological operation that is missing or inadequately efficient in some learning- and attention-disabled children. As a result, these children operate either from partly or more than partly disrupted memory schema, or from a difficulty retrieving this schema in real-time as a guiding and/or calming element (by contrast, when the parent "returns" and is concretely present in front of the child immediately after having acted improperly, the child will quickly respond:" I know, I should have acted otherwise." The very arrival of the actual parent makes a quick connection between what is represented by the figure but is not accessible from memory and the behavioral requirement).

The absence of the internal parental presence increases experiences of fear and anxiety in these children in various situations.

At its start, the latency age is adjacent to the Oedipal age; it therefore still makes the child meet the world of aggressive urges that were typical of him or her in pre-school. These urges originating from the competition and envy sensed by the child toward the same-sex parent and the wish to remove him or her, are handled at kindergarten through imaginary-symbolic play: role-playing, group wars, and great identification with "strong," "aggressive," and victorious figures (masculine for the boys, feminine for the girls). Upon the child's arrival at the second stage, of coming out of the struggle, he or she turns back to the parental figure as a source of identification, but simultaneously as a calming and aggression-regulating source as well. When, due to the disability, full-blown and fully effective identification is not enabled, not only does the child lack the internal protecting figure, but also, he or she remains exposed to the world of aggressive impulses for a more prolonged time, is threatened by them, and does not succeed in handling them effectively. Thus, the child remains exposed to both worlds - internal and external - and therefore has more intense accessibility to the world of impulses, but lacks the moderating element. The child senses more and more fright and fear when the parental figure is missing on the ground. When describing the stages of human development and construction of the personality structure, Freud (In Muuss, 1988) emphasizes the stage of identification with and internalization of the same-sex parent as having special importance, being the stage that constructs the Super Ego, the structure of conscience and morality, which now starts developing and taking a central place in every child's life. Freud suggests that through the identification, the child internalizes the parent and encounters considerations. Thanks to the new intellectual development (*concrete operations,* according to Piaget), the child now knows what is and what is not ethically proper and exercises conscientious discretion typical of the Super Ego structure. Being responsible for conscience and morality considerations, the Super Ego is first of all acquired in the identification and internalization process that occurs between the child and the parent. Many other theories from various streams of psychology (Freud, A., 1966; Kohut, in Oppenheimer, 2000; Ogden, 2003) emphasize that the child's ability to begin to become aware of the Super Ego's considerations at this stage stems from additional development and maturation processes that support and establish the process. In this way, for instance, according to Piaget (1969), the fact that the child at this age is capable of shifting from egocentric and magical considerations to rationalistic and operative considerations (cause and effect considerations, the ability to start thinking in reverse), enables and supports the ability to consider conscientious considerations as well.

The maturation of the child's ability for self-restraint, regulation, and inhibition-building also contributes to the reduction of impulsive reactions and brings the child closer to the goal of activity based on conscience considerations.

The expansion of intellectual ability to generalization and abstraction processes enables the child to see the difference and similarity between elements, to extract a common denominator from several elements and generalize it, and so forth - separation into elements and combining them. These mental processes are necessary for thinking and behavior with a conscientious nature, suited to adult demands. The process of generalization enables each child to gradually expand the world of identification and internalization from the same-sex parent to both parents, and from them, to all significant adults; and from there - to increase, during the latency age years, the ability to consider increasingly complex considerations regarding what is right and appropriate for human society, as the child comes to know it ,with its characteristics, values and culture. Being the basis for the development of the Super Ego, the parent, in a process of generalization and abstraction, is "mixed and diluted" with the influences of additional significant figures (human-concrete, cultural-symbolic, such as movie heroes, literary heroes, etc., as much as the child encounters them), enabling the child to construct a moral world for him or herself, which in some parts is similar to the parents and in other parts, to other figures with whom the child has come in contact.

This complex process not only necessitates an encounter and familiarity with the figures, but also the neurological competence to operate this complex course of "learning." Here as well, we witness the appearance of difficulties among learning- and attention-disabled children. On the one hand, the prolonged encounter itself with the adult world, simultaneously with the partial maturation of the neurological structures, enables the child to acquire norms and understandings related to conscientious demands. On the other hand, partial identification with, and internalization of the figures, and mainly, the difficulty to use them as inner regulating and guiding elements, cause the learning- and attention-disabled child to act with an increasingly growing gap: A gap between knowing how one should act (nearly always after the fact) versus the difficulty of performing in practice according to the partial inner guidance. Or, alternatively, the wish to belong and act, while faced with the (at least partial) lack of ability to do so, due to slow reaction time, lack of accessibility to the inner directing figure, and more. This state of a sustained gap and the after-the-fact realization that the response to the impulse has overpowered the regulation and inhibition, and the difficulty of acting in relation to it in ways that are suited to the demands of the Super Ego expose many learning- and attention-disabled children to sustained feelings of guilt. Gradually being built due to normal reality testing, this guilt, which becomes operative after the fact, as opposed to the difficulty of acting correctly during the fact, wreaks havoc in the psyche of the latency-aged child with learning- and attention-disability. Because the experience of guilt keeps growing, it becomes an emotionally burdensome focal point. The experience of guilt that searches for release might drive the child to even more aggressive, uncontrolled, acute action, which will eventually lead to the intensification of guilt, and from it - again to "releasing" aggression followed by additional guilt - an increasing snowball is created that is emotionally and functionally burdensome for the child. The child will be driven by the great distress to ask for help with expressions of despair, thereby mobilizing the frightened adult to help and search for a solution. Sometimes, the child will be rejected again and again, until in his or her sadness and depression, he or she will "fold with sorrow and depression" and only this will mobilize the required help, at least in part.

The existence of the conscience, but the lack of ability to realize its demands sometimes creates an additional focal point for the learning- and attention-disabled child with socialization difficulties. The identification and internalization that have constructed the conscience, but not the abilities to use it on time, efficiently and in the suited way, not only leave the child with experiences of guilt and fear, but also with a sense of inferiority, enhanced due to the danger of being rejected by the group of peers, who find it hard to contain the child's socialization difficulties and fear his or her reactions.

B. The "Outcasts" Gang and the Child - The Development of a Social Learning Disability

As described so far, the peer group takes on an increasingly more central place in the lives of all latency-age children. This gang gradually becomes an "off-limits" zone for adults, where rules and procedures constructed by the children for themselves, by themselves, are dominant, but with a close and tangentitial connection to the learning and internalizations brought by them from contact with the world of significant adults.

At this stage, the majority of learning- and attention-disabled children find themselves having great difficulty becoming a significant part of this gang. The reasons for this lie in the nature of the disability and its behavioral and overt manifestations. These manifestations create an experience of rejection by other children surrounding the learning- and attention-disabled child, leaving him or her outside the social "playground."

Children with a stormy temperament characterized by a disability combined with hyperactivity and/or impulsivity might find themselves in the focal point of rejection by peers around them, also due to association prohibitions imposed by parents who view the learning- and attention-disabled child as a "bad," disruptive, harmful, and violent child.

Children with a "slow-to-warm-up" temperament without hyperactivity characteristics will remain on the sidelines - devoid of ability for social initiative - having difficulty keeping up with the social pace, are passive, and therefore - remain outside.

Those with a significant linguistic disability, for example, will have difficulty keeping up with the pace required for verbal expression of their wants, emotions, and wishes. They will prefer behavioral expression, now considered as inappropriate, disruptive, and arousing resistance reactions from their peers.

Others, suffering from organization difficulties, will have difficulty getting organized for making an orderly approach to the peer group and might be perceived as invasive, touching, and inconsiderate. Those who have clumsiness problems will have difficulty keeping up with the physical pace required from them to receive an entry ticket to the gang. Those with a perceptual-visual disabilities might show difficulty comprehending non-verbal codes, and so on and so forth.

Remaining stuck in the egocentric worldview, typical of many learning- and attention-disabled children, creates difficulties in viewing the world and social relations, and makes the learning-disabled child erroneously seem "pushy," "blaming others" and lacking ability to recognize and comprehend the complexity of relations.

Difficulty in restraining impulses, inappropriate verbal expression, lack of initiative, lack of familiarity with (mainly non-formal) social codes, difficulty in spatial organization, lack of regulation vis-a-vis the psychological boundaries of others and more - these are only some of the disability's characteristics that disrupt the learning- and attention-disabled child's social toolbox, while he or she emotionally-developmentally aspires to and needs the social association like the rest of his or her peers.

Yet other children, mainly those characterized as suffering from a non-verbal learning disability (right-hemisphere syndrome), show an additional difficulty affecting their ability to acquire social insights. The difficulty is explained in the *Theory of Mind* first suggested by several researcher groups (Baron-Cohen & Frith, 1985, Baron-Cohen, 1990; Gross-Tsura & Shalev, 1995; Chagay, 2005). According to this conception, these children are afflicted with a type of psychic-mental "blindness," preventing, or making it difficult for them to think about the thinking of others, i.e., to view the other as being able to act out of a different perception of the situation. The understanding that the other has his or her own wants, wishes, desires and intentions is not clear enough and does not direct the child's behavior. This disability, which according to Piaget illuminates the learning-disabled child's disrupted ability to advance from the egocentric stage to the operant stage, is another factor that prevents the child from fitting in and behaving correctly in the social world.

An additional difficulty, sometimes revealed in learning-disabled children, is lack of comprehension of the main idea underlying a dialogue or situation with another person ("*weak central coherence,*" as termed by Uta Frith). As a result, the child is overwhelmed by many pieces of information concerning irrelevant details, and is diverted from the focal point and prevented from being attentive and connected with the central matter that other children are engaged with. The difficulty to group the details into a complete whole (synthesis difficulty) leaves the child without the perception of the complete situation and from here, the way out of the gang is nearly guaranteed.

The damage to the *transmuting internalization* mechanism (see second Chapter: Social Learning Disability) as suggested by Kohut (in Osterweil, 1995; Kohut, 1977,

1979), creating damage to the self-soothing ability and ability to contain and cope with frustration, is another factor causing the failure of the child's social contacts. The sometimes-uncontrollable outbursts due to a small frustration that is surmountable among the non-disabled peers, once again influence his or her socially unusual place and the behavioral gap.

Like all their peers, such children need and aspire to social association as a place to belong, which is the place for constructing positive self-worth. Remaining outside the field and the overt and covert rejections directed toward them, leave them hurt for a long time. The intense wish to feel "like everybody else," becomes shattered vis-a-vis the rules of social reality, which is sometimes cruel.

The development of these gaps - between the wish to belong and the inability to properly realize it - forms a central source of injury in the learning- and attention-disabled child's world.

The latency age is described by Erikson (1951), one of the most important developmental psychologists, as the **age of industry** (production). The rise in capabilities of doing things, in integration between capabilities, the meeting between intellectual understandings and emotional needs, the need to express post-Oedipal aggression through "civilized" means of competition and ambition - these make children at latency age, a group that is active in a variety of areas. This is the field where the children practice their various capabilities, and simultaneously construct their social place; however, Erikson warns of the opposite experience - the **experience of inferiority** that might develop in those children who have reached latency age with their "toolbox" not efficient and sophisticated enough to make them industrious creatures. These children, the veteran psychologist warns, will withdraw to a standpoint of inferiority, which will accompany them for a long period of time and harm the continued vitality required for the continuation of normal development.

Above all, the experience of industry is a psychical occurrence, expanding the child's limits of "Ego" and enabling him or her to relate to oneself as a part of a wider society. In this manner, industry serves as an experience for extensive expression of self and simultaneously contributes to the experience of social belonging. When this ability is impaired or disrupted, the child encounters the sense of inferiority, causing him/her to feel desperate and to give up, or to incessantly struggle. The sense of being unfit for the new situation - mainly when facing peers - while possessing normal reality-testing ability, contributes to the sustained injury to the "Ego" and to the damage to the belief in, and ability of being included in the peer group, and as a result, in the society and culture at large. This inferiority creates in the child a status of other and different, and might intensify efforts to conquer a place in the gang. The enhanced effort will be counterproductive and cause even more rejection and removal; the child might prefer different and other behavior as a way of making the inferiority experience prominent.

The difficulty of belonging, the difficulty of experiencing

oneself as having value, the experience of being different and mainly inferior - these are to become a sustained experience occupying the child's entire emotional world, and may be expressed on many levels:

a. By difficulty in admitting the existence of the disability, and therefore, refusing to receive help - especially vis-a-vis the world of the peers (and as a result, the child will avoid going to the various help centers located inside the school, will refuse to take tests, and to submit papers in a manner different from the rest of the class, but accommodated according to the disability).

b. Other children will exhibit the inferiority as a central element in their lives and verbally express it ("I'm worthless"; "I don't know"; "I'm not smart like the rest of the kids") will prefer to act as the "class clown" and play the fool, and be the troublemaker - the behavior momentarily turns the inferiority into a seeming advantage (everybody laughs at what I do, meaning I am being related to, I have a temporary place in the gang).

c. There are children whose experience of inferiority will overshadow all their relative advantages, and they will exhibit profound sadness, despair, withdrawal, and give up on the struggle. They will avoid social contact and activity and attempts to study and achieve.

d. Others, with help and guidance, will try to forcefully conquer a place through unregulated "aggression," using a variety of other prominent skills (at sports, with courage, physical strength). This struggle will sometimes be accompanied by an attempt to hurt others and cause the other to feel temporary inferiority (through arrogance, cursing, and humiliation of others who are perceived as rejecting and threatening them).

Each child has his or her style, but they all have one common denominator - the profound hunger for an experience of industry, mainly on the social field. The common dream - being part of the peer group. At this age, the peer group - same-aged children - usually meets in several territories simultaneously:

1. The school domain (both through social association built in the classroom and also affected by academic achievement, as well as that which occurs during recess and is related to the exhibition of physical and other skills).

2. The local, non-formal domain: Usually in the neighborhood or residential area that is geographically close. Sometimes an overlap exists between the neighborhood children and the schoolchildren, and sometimes moving to school increases possibilities and opportunities. Most children still connect with each other through the local gang, sharing a common history and territory. The local gang has a great influence on the nature of recreation during free time, vacations, and weekends, and constitutes a "city of refuge" for all children at latency age. The inability to be part of it robs the learning- and attention-disabled child of a central area for experiencing, for the experience of belonging and for a necessary place of refuge outside the parents' house.

3. The meeting at recreational hobby classes, youth clubs, and youth movements.

Nowadays, many children spend a substantial amount of their leisure time in a task-oriented group of belonging - a meeting based on a common area of interest (practical or ideological). Alongside training in a shared topic (sports, arts course, etc.), they construct a widening world of social ties.

Moving between the three territories affords each child a variety of opportunities for social connections. There sometimes is overlapping between the three, and sometimes the overlap is extremely partial and sometimes these are different groups of belonging. The emotional-social-intellectual capacity of latency-aged children for mental operations of generalization and abstraction, analysis and synthesis, gradually enables them to enjoy all the different worlds and from them, to construct their personal social identities containing several different personal and uniquely integrated characteristics within it.

At this stage, great importance, is given to the adult figures, who direct and guide each territory and enable the child-extensive identification under secure conditions. The adult's role, manner of activity, and status vary between the domains, and enable the child an expansion of the experience with the adult world as representative of the society and culture in which they grow up.

The great danger concerning learning- and attention-disabled children at this developmental period is associated with the unfortunate fact that sometimes one or more domains are run without almost any adult presence, or with only partial and after-the-fact presence. While their friends use the internalization of the protecting figures as a psychological presence, enabling them inner guidance in adult-free territories, the learning- and attention-disabled child relies totally on the concrete presence; in its absence, the child stands exposed and inferior opposite his or her friends.

The school recess is one of many examples enabling us an in-depth understanding of the dynamics that develop between one type of children with learning- and attention-disability and their classmates and schoolyard friends. This example is the most important of all, considering the fact that despite the school being a place "protected," as it were, by adults (the teachers), the manner it is currently run shows this is not the case: The adult's presence is **meager** (a few teachers - protectors on duty by rotation, supervising a large yard containing a very large number of children), it is **insignificant** (teacher-protector does not know most of the children, except for a handful who are her or his pupils), the adult presence is **foreign** to the vast majority of children (it is not the figure with whom they have meaningful daily contact), and is usually run using the **"after the fact"**-method (after the fight or confrontation has started, after the stone has been thrown, after the hurt person has started to cry etc.), instead of prior to, or during the act.

For the learning- and attention-disabled child, the transition from the classroom as a task-oriented, structured and guided place, with the clear presence of a teacher, to the yard is complex, and requires much effort due to the focal points of difficulty he or she has. If we follow, thoroughly and

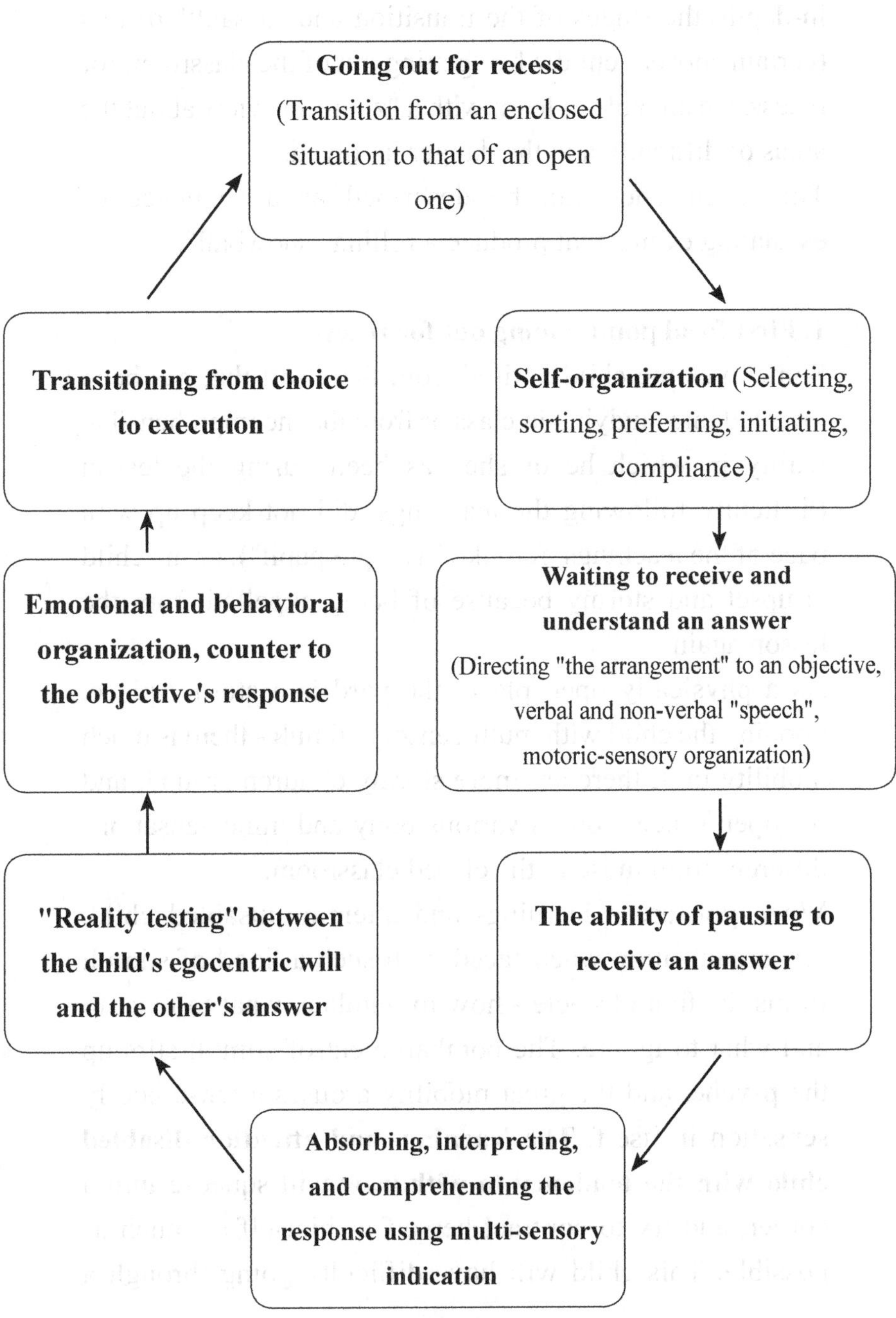
Going out for recess
(Transition from an enclosed situation to that of an open one)

Transitioning from choice to execution

Self-organization (Selecting, sorting, preferring, initiating, compliance)

Emotional and behavioral organization, counter to the objective's response

Waiting to receive and understand an answer
(Directing "the arrangement" to an objective, verbal and non-verbal "speech", motoric-sensory organization)

"Reality testing" between the child's egocentric will and the other's answer

The ability of pausing to receive an answer

Absorbing, interpreting, and comprehending the response using multi-sensory indication in-depth, the stages of the transition and "assault" of this (certain chosen) child when getting out of the classroom for recess, we are able to learn with a "zoom-in" view about the areas of difficulty and the danger involved.

This occurrence can be described as a sequence of escalating events that produce a rolling "snowball".

1. First focal point: Going out for recess

Sometimes the child is tired from the effort that has been invested into studying in class or from the incomprehensible reality in which he or she has been during the lesson (difficulty following the teachings, did not keep up with pace of the teachings, felt like "a stupid pupil"), or the child is upset and stormy because of being expelled from the lesson again.

As a physically open place, the yard is a stormy place, flooding the child with multi-sensory stimuli - there is much mobility in it, there are more stormy children around, and the open space arouses various body and mind sensations different from those in the closed classroom.

When you are a learning- and attention-disabled child, self-organization when faced with such a flood of stimuli forms the first obstacle - how to regulate, what to react to and what to ignore. The bombardment of stimuli stirs up the psyche, and the great mobility arouses a tense bodily sensation in itself. **The learning- and attention-disabled child with the tendency to withdraw** will squeeze into a corner, and try to contract herself or himself as much as possible. This child will have difficulty going through a process of self-regulation from one physical sensation to another. From this moment onward, he or she is completely subject to the mercy of the others - if the child's presence is sensed, then he or she might be invited to an interaction, or they might pass by the child, completely ignoring him or her. Then it will be another entire recess that the child spends alone, doing nothing, as a passive spectator from the side, dreaming of joining in but not knowing how and what to do. **The temperamental learning- and attention-disabled child** will feel he or she must generate some sort of presence to declare behaviorally, "I am here." Being flooded prevents and weakens the ability to verbally approach and get organized, therefore the child will immediately withdraw to a "behavioral organization." On the way, this behavior will have a slightly provocative nature, out of the child's will to be conspicuous over the stormy background, or alternatively, he or she will stick to a leading child, tag along behind, hoping to be noticed by the other. Sometimes accompanied by passive provocation, this type of tagging along might bring about a rejecting and harsh reaction from the non-disabled child. Lacking guidance, understanding, and knowledge, this child translates the learning- and attention-disabled child's behavior as a sort of harassment that deserves to be rejected (passively or actively - ignoring or harshly pushing away), and we again witness a painful situation of being abandoned without being able to join, i.e., inferiority.

Another child, stormy with "impulsive" initiative, will very powerfully try to find a vacant place and declare personal wants. Sometimes the proposition will fit the other's taste, and sometimes the disabled child will be able to offer a type of successful skills that serve him or her during recess (athletic, good at football, etc.). Sometimes this child is equipped with "valuable commodities," such as an attractive iPod, an expensive iPhone, etc., through which he or she will attempt to "buy" others. Sometimes the work of seduction will be done by generously offering candy, "academic" equipment (stickers, markers, and valuable crayons, etc.)

2. Second focal point: Self-organization

Getting out of the classroom for recess means a sharp transition from an adult-directed place to a place of self-choice and organization. This seemingly simple process of choice involves a variety of mental processes that are generally difficult for the learning- and attention-disabled child. These decisions require sorting processes, emphasizing one stimulus over other stimuli in the background, attention, suitable attentional focus without distraction, sticking to one choice and persisting with it (and not "running around" between several stimuli acting on the child simultaneously).

A child with Executive Function disability might have difficulty in choice, might shift between several focal points without succeeding to be in one continuous focal point - or alternatively - "lock" onto one focal point and refuse to show flexibility considering other"s wants (see lack of Theory of Mind pp. 115).

3. Transitioning from choice to execution

The transition often involves a combination of verbal approach processes with behavioral organization. The verbal expression difficulties, a stormy, impulsive temperament, a too-slow reaction pace, difficulty in splitting attention - all these might cause the child to prefer behavioral implementation and to read the social map incorrectly at that moment (weak central coherence, according to Frith). Children who have additional difficulties from the areas of flaccid or increased muscle tone, sensory-motor disorders, motor clumsiness, and more, will find themselves "behaving the will" but in a manner experienced by the other as negative.

4. Waiting to receive and understand an answer

The dialogue that takes place between children in the process of social organization involves verbal and non-verbal negotiation simultaneously. The capacities required for deciphering and understanding the messages and implementing their meaning often become shipwrecked in the face of the learning and attention-disabled child's difficulties to wait until receiving an answer from the other, deciphering and understanding the meaning of the answer, and acting accordingly ("mental blindness" - non-verbal learning disability), and the result will be an experience of a presence that is unfitting, disruptive "not with it," and not fitting the pace of the course of affairs vis-a-vis the rest of the children.

5. "Reality testing" between the child's egocentric will and the other's answer

At this important junction, the child is required to exercise a great deal of restraint and regulation, on the one hand, and at the same time, to have an ability to correctly see and recognize the others' collective will. This encounter between conflicting forces, between my will and the other's will (lack of Theory of Mind), between the need to fight and the necessity to compromise - is very difficult and sometimes leads to misunderstandings and commotions in relations. Abandonment and rejection of the learning-disabled child by the other friends, or a power struggle over enforcing his or her will on others, in either case the child will be left with a painful sense of failure and lack of fit between his or her wants and what is possible.

6. Emotional and behavioral organization

Assessing the situation as being in fit or lack of fit with original wants necessitates the child to prepare accordingly. The child who has managed to find a framework that fits his or her wishes will now enjoy the fruits of the effort (unless other problems develop). The other, feeling betrayed and discontent, is now required to cope with a frustrating experience, which is sometimes beyond the regulation and restraint abilities, or beyond the ability to contain the pain resulting from this. One will react with overt rage, the other will withdraw and avoid and again view the social field as a "hopeless" and futureless place for him or her. They are both hurt - their reaction style is different and gives off different signals to the environment. The overt one will arouse stormy counter-reactions, which might repeatedly get him mixed up in the focus of fights and brawls. The other - his or her injury will not be felt and will cocoon into sadness.

This organization is the last chance to be a part of (belong) - or not - to have a chance to invite and be invited later on, or be repeatedly rejected and lonely.

As a result, the child will return to the classroom - content or frustrated, stormy, withdrawing, or momentarily happy. This emotional instability will also be the emotional basis of the next encounter, and the child will set out with it to the next social occurrence.

Repeating itself many times, this experience will gradually determine the child's social capability and self-image.

The way to assist children with learning- and attention-disability in the social field is open to a variety of possibilities and interventions:

1. Forming groups for social remedial teaching within and outside the school (see Section 6 Chapter 2 pp 209).

2. A change in the setup of the adult presence at the school and training a regular group of teachers as yard and recess teachers (see Chapter 2). Their duty will be to routinely and regularly accompany the children through these processes, while constructing their presence as regular figures, to whom one can become attached, associated with the activities, and therefore, viewed by the children as having status and value.

3. Training these adults as teachers for instilling social

skills, who possess capacities and abilities to "teach" this complex subject matter in real time (during recess) and not theoretical time (during the lesson inside the classroom). Their protecting and directing presence at the time of occurrence, and not prior to or after it, can lead to a significant breakthrough in the school's contribution to the learning-disabled child's educational = therapeutic process in the social domain.

C. Children With Industry Needs - Parents With an Experience of Inferiority

As mentioned, according to Erikson (1951), the latency age is characterized by the construction of an experience of industry, while on the opposite side, the danger of the development of an experience of inferiority lurks all the time. This polar world of experiences enables us to grasp the two major aspects of the functioning of children of this age.

Industry is a sense of great positive self-worth that develops in the child in the face of an increased rise in capacities and abilities from various areas - motor, sensory, linguistic, intellectual, emotional, social and more - and mainly in the face of the ability to act with coordination and synchronization of several capacities. All these enable the child varied self-expression in a widening circle of areas.

The need to produce varied self-expression likens the child to an industrious ant, busy for many hours in the "creation" of a positive presence in the world. The child learns, acquires friends, struggles for his or her place in the children's gang at both school and the neighborhood, enjoys expressions in the areas of movement, sports, plastic art, construction, drama, and social games. The child acquires mastery in a variety of areas - reading and writing, computer skills, and sports games. The child is also multi-faceted in the sense of social belonging: to the family, to childhood friends in the neighborhood territory, to the new children he or she has met in class, and to friends at recreational hobby courses. The child drifts between the worlds, with each one enabling a new position, a toolbox for self-expression and increasing social ties.

To meet the entire range of tasks and wants, the child must be competent and mature for maximal utilization of his or her new capacities. The encounter with a task that is beyond the child's limit of ability might cause him or her to encounter an experience of inferiority. **The experience of inferiority forms a major source of damage to self-image and self-worth.**

As a developmental danger in this segment of life, inferiority has an additional inner source: reality perception. Simultaneously with the development of various capabilities, the child acquires and establishes the *reality principle* as a central directing conception. This ability, the buds of which can be seen at the second year of life, with the beginning of the development of the Ego structure, gradually enables the child to evaluate his or her various actions compared with the demands of reality (as presented by the significant adult) and relative to the abilities displayed by the other children in the vicinity. The more the reality principle becomes a directing element in the child's life, the more he or she is exposed to a sense of self-criticism concerning various achievements and performance.

In this sense, the learning- and attention-disabled child has normal reality testing, but lacks some of the capabilities required for implementing the various tasks and wants. The child is therefore in a standpoint of constant inferiority, and often feels far from the objective set by others or that he or she has set himself or herself. The gap between wanting to succeed and the difficulty in realizing it, due to the disability, makes the child a chronic casualty of the inferiority experience.

This danger sometimes becomes worse due to competitiveness and ambitious urges typical of the latency age. These urges originate from the psychical-aggressive energy that developed during the Oedipal stage and underwent "educational-cultural" refinement under the conditions of society and culture (sublimation and socialization). Through this refinement, the aggressive energy was transformed into drives of ambitiousness and competitiveness. The drives are now directed at two directions: The child **is competing with self** and wants to beat self anew each time, and concurrently, wants to compete with, and beat other children in his or her social reference group. Anyone who is exposed to children at latency age is familiar with the difficulty experienced by these children under conditions of losing or failure, whether in a social game or any other area. The learning- and attention-disabled child has such drives as all his peers, but reality testing on the one hand, and the wish to win and achieve under disability conditions, on the other, might too frequently cause the child to feel defeated and inferior.

The chronic presence of the inferiority experience is unbearable but is also hard to evade. The attempt to construct a different and unique scale of achievements for the child is not willingly received because his or her reality testing is normal as is the ability to judge achievement compared to the others who do not have the disability. This troubling state of mind often causes the child to use vigorous expressions of frustration, taking the form of anger, blame, wanting to destroy the competition or the competitors; or alternatively, to choose avoidance, give up in advance, or escape to places that are deemed by the child to be lower and safer.

The manner in which the sense of inferiority is demonstrated by the learning- and attention-disabled child is closely related to the child's temperament and other better capabilities. In an attempt to disguise and hide the inferiority, the child will prefer coping styles that only increase the experience of inferiority. Some of them will prefer the role of the clown ("it's better to make him laugh than to be laughed at"), others will prefer the role of destroyer and disrupter ("it's better that they think I don't want - and not know that I can't"). There are those who will react with a great deal of aggression (it's better to hurt others, as long as I am not harmed" - a sort of "defensive aggression"). There are those who will react scornfully and with contempt, ("let them l think I am not interested as long as they don't know how eager and unsuccessful I am"). Another choice is to reject any invitation ("rejecting in advance is preferable over the possibility of being rejected afterward").

The demonstration of the inferiority experience in various guises is often perceived (both by the other children and significant adults) as the child's conscious and chosen statement, and therefore is erroneously interpreted as a direct continuation of the overt behavior; the reverse message behind it goes unnoticed. And thus, instead of being wanted and invited, encouraged and supported, the child "gains" an increasing dose of indifference, or anger and rejection. The child's parents witness all these situations and experience an inferiority experience of their own through and with the child. The parental inferiority experience typical of many parents of children with learning- and attention-disability is a continuation of the intensification of feelings of guilt and shame from earlier stages. Parental inferiority is a difficult emotional experience mixed with pain, helplessness, and a sense of lack of ability to change anything in the child's state. Characterized by behaviors that are not suited to the environment and demands of reality, the learning- and attention-disabled child's expressions of initiative make the parents' sense of parental inferiority extreme and cause the parents themselves to be very distressed. The repeated contacting of the parents by the educational system - to come and assist in restraining their rebellious and undisciplined child, to increase the child's motivation, to mend his or her ways - only increases their sense of inferiority. It is not only the child who feels inferior now, but the parents are also deep inside with the child in an intense emotional trap.

Some parents will at this stage try to offer assistance to the child. They will try to resolve the inferiority experience by using their own initiatives and actions - equip the child with attractions that will enable the momentary "buying" of friends; others will intervene in the child's favor when relating to other children and even other adults. Many parents report an uncontrollable feeling of anger that develops in them toward children who do not enable their child to be part of the group. Others will feel this way toward teachers and adults who mirror their child's inferiority. Driven by the pain of inferiority, these parents' active and unsuited involvement is usually not useful and in most cases eventually only increases the experience of inferiority. The range of industry-inferiority, as depicted by Erikson (1951) regarding the latency children, is expanded into an additional channel in the sense of adding difficulty to an existing difficulty - child industriousness with learning and attention disability characteristics, confronted by a parental sense of inferiority as well. The ambition and competitive needs of the child's world affect the parents as well, and therefore, the child's failures are the source of parental inferiority.

In most cases, parents who experience inferiority have difficulty generating the correct setup of help and support that their learning- and attention-disabled child needs so much. They vacillate between wanting to solve problems for the child thereby saving him or her the pain of inferiority, and the inclination to increase the pressure and demands from the child in order to do - achieve like everybody else. Both ways are counterproductive, and will only "contribute" to increasing the sense of inferiority.

Other parents will prefer a style of avoidance, i.e., minimizing the encounter with the extra-familial world (school, friends, expanded family), in order to avoid feeling the experience of inferiority in public. The entire family gradually gets into a spin of a life of loneliness and avoidance as a central defense mechanism. This loneliness leaves parents and child with a sense of pain and failure.

D. The Eternal Triangle: A Learning & AD(H)D Disabled Child - School - Parents

The thought that upon the completion of the Oedipal conflict the charged relationship triangle with the child in the center will come to an end is but a wish. Life's dynamics throws the schoolchild and his or her parents into a new conflictual relationship triangle, no less charged and full of tension than the original triangle. The triangle's characteristics and manifestations are different, and the coalition-opposition relationships are dynamic and variable.

A latency-aged child is obligated by law to attend school. The child's parents can be considered as "expellers" who are compelled against their will to send their child every morning anew from their home to the other play and study house. "Expulsion" by law weakens some parents to a great extent, even if they are not aware of it. They are obligated to act not from an inner-psychological degree of freedom, but out of accepting a law that is external to them. Compulsory education law, which nowadays is in effect in most countries of the modern Western world, draws the parents - although with invisible ink - as people who must be "threatened" to act in the interest of their children. This is a certain weakening of the parents due to the social no-confidence demonstrated toward them by the government.

This is the starting point underlying the unconscious conflict involved in parents-school relations (although the conflict has many additional sources). Concurrently, the great extent of identification of a substantial part of the parents with their children, and mainly with their difficulties, affects the relationship. In situations of contention or difficulty, the parents might be their children's allies against the school. Generally speaking, children themselves go to school out of a will to distance themselves from the family world, to a wider world of identifications and new relations that are opening up for them. At the same time, children have an inner need to acquire a productive ability by means of the world of academic knowledge now being spread out before them. In this sense, they make a sort of an alliance with the school and view it as a source of power against their parents. A common example of this alliance is the situation in which the child asks his or her parents for help in solving a homework problem in arithmetic, writing, or any other subject. The parent mobilizes the full world of knowledge that he or she has, in order to provide the child as much help as possible. The angry child's reaction to the parent: "You're not doing it right, it's not like this, the teacher taught me differently…you don't understand anything." The parent in response: "So what if the teacher thought differently? There are more ways to deal with the problem…" The child persists: "I want only what the teacher has taught, only she knows… you don't know anything." This common conflict, often caused by frequent changes in the ways knowledge and skills are instilled, makes the parent seem like an empty vessel - inferior and of lesser value compared to the teacher's superiority. In this manner, children-teacher-parent relations vacillate repeatedly "between alliances and wars." When the parenthood in question is of learning- and attention-disabled children, the issue is much more emotionally charged. These parents act with the influence of their child's inferiority experience at school and in the company of same-age children. Therefore, the starting point of the relationship is several times more difficult.

| 1

From its very essence and tasks, the school emphasizes the existence of the disabilities vis-a-vis the requirements of being a productive pupil. It is at this period that the disabilities are usually identified, while the demands directed toward the child make the difficulties prominent. The child's world is colored in the shade of the inferiority experience, as is the parent's world. Because each encounter with a school employee might be about their child's difficulties, parents go through difficult and complex emotional states, the majority of which will be directed toward the school - "the institution that produces and is responsible for the experience of inferiority."

The child identified as learning-disabled at pre-school age, and certainly the child identified for the first time at school, both begin as pupils with a sense of inferiority and difference (at some intensity, moderate to severe), while "delegating" to their parents these hard feelings against the educational institution. And the parents themselves, being in the process of work of mourning (see Chapter 5) as part of their journey of coping with the discovery, "I have a child with some type of disability, and I am a parent of a child with a disability," have a complex and emotionally-charged dialogue with the school, ranging from hoping for an absolute resolution of the difficulty, to wanting to "destroy" the school, thereby releasing themselves and their child from difficult feelings.

The parents' style, the disability's degree of severity, and the coping ability demonstrated by the school professionally - these are the conditions determining the nature of the whirlwind of relations that will develop.

| 2

The helplessness, often demonstrated by the school lacking the skills and resources for coping by itself with the child's needs, burdens the parent with tasks that are beyond his or her abilities and greatly tires the parent in dealing with the system. Parents of children with Attention Deficit and Hyperactivity Disorder (ADHD) describe a saga of life characterized by telephone anxiety. In a moment, the telephone will ring (and in the cellular phone age - anywhere, anytime) and the parent will be called to come "rescue" the child from the school and the school from the child. The problem has erupted inside the school, but the solution is demanded from the parents. In this manner, feelings of resentment and no confidence develop in the parents toward the educational system, which is often perceived by them as hostile, weak, helpless, and sometimes even abusive of them and their child.

The life order of the parent - who is already pressurized and exhausted, considering the difficulties created by the disability at home - is disrupted again and again, and the parent lives in constant tension and pressure involved in it, and in the uncertainty of when he or she will be alerted to school again as the child's bodyguard. The need to a repeatedly apologize to coworkers, subordinates, or supervisors - like the difficulty of constructing an independent course of life at times when the child is supposed to be under another's oversight - is burdensome for the parent and takes away his or her peace of mind.

If to this we add the enormous investments in therapeutic actions demanded from the parent by the school (from remedial teaching, through para-medical and medical treatments, to social and emotional treatments) as additional time devoted to the family, then we can see that more pressure is put on the parent. The accumulated psychological experience is that the parent is the main party responsible for treating the disability and the school only serves as a mirror reflecting the child's state: advancement or "being stuck" and even regression. In this reality, the conflict between the parents and the school worsens and sometimes between the parent and child as well, in the face of him or her being the "generator" of the difficulties.

The parents' reaction to the difficulties is on a continuum of reactions built and affected simultaneously by psychological and realistic components - ranging from "cooperative" parents, who comply with every demand of the school, up to parents who avoid any association and contact, through "angry" and hurt parents who direct their rage toward the school. The school does not know how to handle parents' parenthood in general and the parenthood of children with learning- and attention-disability, in particular. The relation between them often becomes a long saga of mutual hurting, conflict, blaming, and insults.

The result is that a child with learning- and attention-disability, who more than anything needs cooperating systems, with similar demands that support each other, is faced with the worst of all - the experience of living in a "divorcing" family under the most difficult conditions. The child vacillates between the wish to placate the parents and meet their expectations from him or her, and the need to comply and go with the flow of the school's demands. But, the lack of cooperation makes the child torn between the two with difficulty in choosing who to believe in and with whom to go. Thus, an additional difficulty is added to the existing difficulties.

| 3

From the school's point of view, it is in an impossible reality: The compulsory education law applies to it as well - compelling it to accept the learning-disabled child and provide for the child's full needs, but sometimes it lacks the resources and knowledge required to do this.

However, the worse contradiction is that most of the help needed by the child requires parental consent by law. This means that the school must act according to two sets of laws that are seemingly contradictory to each other: The child is at the school by law, but consenting to treat him or her requires parental consent. The school is between a rock and hard place - between the commitment to treat the child and the dependence on the parent's consent. Such consent will only be achieved if the school acts correctly - professionally - and succeeds in harnessing the parents to reach mutual understanding and agreed-upon and shared goals. Obviously, the parents' psychological and material resources are also necessary for them to give their consent and cooperate.

In order to harness the parents, the school must train itself and acquire knowledge in the psychology of parenthood in general and parenthood of children with disabilities, in particular. This training is still lacking in the majority of educational systems. As a result, the school often finds itself involved in difficult and even harmful relationships.

| 4

The difficulties experienced by the children within the school, whether in the academic area orin behavioral and social areas (all stemming from the existence of the disability) make their stay at school a difficult experience. Some of them gradually become school refusers, who attend school while encountering many difficulties. They have difficulty getting organized and arriving on time in the morning, have difficulty in performing home assignments associated with the school, and "dump" their difficult feelings by projecting them onto their parents - in both in a clear verbal manner and in the form of aggressive verbalization (they curse the school) as well as in a behavioral-emotional manner (acting out - they run away, cause trouble in order to be suspended and more). The dumping of the negative emotions developed by the children toward the school creates an inner conflict in the parent - to issue the child an "expulsion decree" every morning and send him or her to a difficult and painful "land of punishment," or to yield to the child and risk a conflict with the school (control of absences etc.). The home conflict often becomes an inter-system conflict: The parent dumps and projects onto the school the difficulties dumped and projected onto him or her by the child, and so forth.

The school's lack of understanding and awareness concerning what happens in the relations within the home puts the its overt conflict with the parent and the conflicts with the child at school at the center of the relations.

Thus, the relations triangle shifts up and down while being charged with emotions and behaviors that often tend to escalate themselves.

3.

Learning & AD(H)D Disabled Adolescents and Their Parents

A. The Danger of the Adolescent's Identity Diffusion

The beginning of adolescence is tangential to the end of the latency period (around the ages of 11-to-12 years), but is personal and varies between individuals. It is usually associated with physical and hormonal development and its ending is a dictated "axiom" in social law that has been determined as the age of 18 years in most societies of the Western world. Nevertheless, many adolescents complete this period prior to or after this, according to their individual pace of maturation.

This is a unique age division where the body's needs are contradictory to the adolescent's social and psychological tasks (while in the younger sections, toddlerhood and latency they fit), and therefore contradictory and confusing experiences occur in the psyche of each *one of them*.

Unlike the previous age divisions, more than being

physiological-psychological, the origins of adolescence are social-cultural. The integration of this age division as part of psychological development is associated with social-political revolutions undergone by the modern society from the nineteenth century to this day. While in the past, this age division was considered as the final phase on the way to full adulthood, an additional time period (post-adolescence) of sustained moratorium, associated with the changing of social conditions and increase in importance of academic knowledge and professional training, has nowadays been added to the continuum - from the end of adolescence to the completion of formal training processes, and sometimes even beyond that.

One can see, then, a direct connection between the age tasks developmentally speaking, and conditions that are becoming more and more complex.

The occurrences typical of this period can be described with four parallel axes, typical of every adolescent, but sometimes varying in intensity when the adolescents in question are ones who suffer from learning- attention- and concentration-disabilities. These include: the physical-hormonal axis, the social-interpersonal axis, the emotional-familial axis, and the academic-intellectual axis.

| The Physical-Hormonal Axis

The beginning of adolescence is associated with invisible hormonal changes followed by prominent physical changes in males and females. It is the accelerated action of the sex hormones that is responsible for the adolescent's physical, behavioral, and emotional changes. This age can therefore be defined as an age that first and foremost deals with consolidating the body schema identity and sexuality.

The end of the latency age comes after a long period of constancy in the physical and sexual schemas; therefore, the entry of the sex hormones into the teenager's bloodstream generates sensations, experiences, and discoveries that sometimes cause discomfort, distress, and even fear. This is the loss of body schema constancy to a schema that is constantly changing: each morning the adolescent discovers a new change in his or her body: hair growth, height, acne, breast buds, and more. The accelerated physical growth and change are sometimes also associated with somatic sensations of "growing pains" and discoveries of loss of control over the body, such as nocturnal emission and the appearance of a menstrual period, and more. It is no wonder, then, that many adolescents are so emotionally invested in their bodies and external appearance as a coping and adaptation mechanism to the incessantly changing physicality. More than this - one can understand the emotional instability accompanying these situations as due to the continuation of the incessant changes - sometimes "twice an hour" and sometimes during sleep ("surprises each morning").

As mentioned, physical change is the herald of adolescence, and although its beginning is invisible, to many adolescents it is too conspicuous. The change in body proportions, change of voice, various sexual characteristics - all are at the focus of emotional occupation of every adolescent

- hence their preoccupation with external appearance, clothing, hygiene, and adaptation to a different biological clock.

A learning- and attention-disabled adolescent might experience an intensification or slowing down of the symptoms, whether because of the existence of the disability or because of the associated clinical characteristics.

In many learning- and attention-disabled adolescents one can see relative extremism in physical maturation processes. The physical-hormonal change joins the neurological disability (Spencer, Biederman, & Wilens, 1998; Tyano & Manor, 2001). Some of them are characterized by premature, extreme maturation, expressed by all processes appearing earlier, and this is probably due to neurological irregularity affecting the body's hormonal organization as well. These children, therefore, already at the end of elementary school feel conspicuous and different from their friends in height, secondary sex characteristics, and physical phenomena typical of adolescents - premature hair growth, early appearance of menstrual period, and more. So far, they have felt different because of their disability, but now they feel even more different due to their early maturation.

It should be emphasized: The early onset of maturation does not occur only in learning-attention- and concentration-disabled individuals, but the phenomenon is prevalent in many of them, and coping with it is much more difficult when accompanied by the disability's characteristics.

On the other hand, the phenomenon of "late blooming" is no

less prevalent among learning-attention- and concentration-disabled adolescents. These children experience themselves for a prolonged period as "small," "undeveloped," and childish relative to their friends' average development. In the past, it had been suggested that slow growth rate occurred in some of those who took medication because of side effects (now proven incorrect); slow growth rate is one of the disability's characteristics. These children will close the gap in their growth rate at a later age, at the stage of completing adolescence (17-to-19 years, and sometimes even beyond this). Therefore, the emotional and social characteristics as well, stemming from the changing of the body, will last into late age, and this will last longer. The "late blooming" will be experienced by the learning-disabled as a continuation of the experience of inferiority, difference, and low ability.

| The Social-Interpersonal Axis: Between Identity Consolidation and the Experience of Identity Diffusion

The social subject is a key factor in adolescence. The adolescent's integration into a group of belonging with characteristics of a "counterculture group" is a central goal in every young person's life.

Erikson (1951), the social psychologist who researched and wrote much about this life period, characterizes these youths as being on a continuum whose goal is **consolidation of self-identity**, while the danger of the youth remaining in a state of **identity diffusion** looms. The definition of identity consolidation as a central developmental goal is closely related to the "invention" of adolescence by modern Western society; at this age, society has assigned the youth tasks of acquiring academic and other knowledge, and of a prolonged professional training period. The multiplicity of human knowledge in the modern age has increased the need to equip the youth with tools and ability for coping with this abundance, on the way to his or her adult role.

The consolidation of the adolescent's self-identity is a psychological-individual task, while the social, interpersonal relation has a central role in the process. Often, the consolidation of identity is done within a social, and not only intra-personal context.

The consolidation of self-identity is a central psychological goal, derived from changes in the adolescent's body schema, alongside cognitive and emotional changes typical of this age. These changes open questions before the youth, concerning reorganization of the personality (self) with an adult's orientation.

Adolescence has therefore been determined as a necessary stage on the way to the definition of the adult self.

The identity consolidation process is a prolonged process, interfacing with an adolescent's process of renewed separation from his or her parents. The increase in drives also puts restlessness into the inter-familial relations. The disillusionment that the adolescent goes through regarding the parents' psychological power and size, "sends" him or her to search for additional figures to be influenced by and identify with - outside the family circle. Some of these are admired figures with whom he or she comes into cultural-social contact (such as cultural or sports heroes, and others), some of them are figures playing a role in the adolescent's life (instructors, coaches, teachers), and some are people his own age with whom he or she is in continuous contact because of shared interests and tasks.

The identity consolidation process entails a transition between three continuous, but also simultaneous positions: the chaos derived from the physiological confusion; the narcissistic-depressive position, stemming from the loss involved in disillusionment with the parents' power and depression vis-a-vis the "temporary abandonment experience"; and the rediscovery of the object, expressed by the intense need to love and be loved as an existential part of the "self" (Blos , in Muuss, 1988).

The transition between the stages and journey of discovering new forces of influence inside and around adolescents causes them to sometimes "park" in depressive feelings, also supported by hormonal restlessness. The key question is the duration and intensity of the depression, and the normal forces for getting out of it and discovering new things in life.

Every outing and encounter with a concrete or cultural figure, which has (temporary or prolonged) significance in the adolescent's life, leaves its mark on the consolidation process of the "Ego." The consolidated "Ego" at the end of adolescence will be, then, a unique integration and synthesis created by each adolescent for himself or herself from the array of influences encountered during this period that have been partly or fully internalized. The sum total of all encounters and influences that have left their mark on him or her (psychological internalizations) will form the entirety called the "Consolidated Ego." This "Ego" will contain a clearer definition of the personality characteristics, positions regarding a future profession or occupation, traits and capabilities, as well as weaknesses and failures ("I won't be able to be like …"). This "Ego" will later on direct the young adult to search for his or her personal-familial-social and professional, as well as ideological and moral way.

One can understand from this short description that emotionally and mentally, this is a complex process, necessitating intensive and simultaneous involvement of neurological-brain activities in varied areas of ability. One can hypothesize that in the state of incompetence or gaps between abilities, as they exist in learning- attention- and concentration-disabled adolescents, this occurrence will be difficult and complex, sometimes stormy or depressive, and undoubtedly influenced by the entirety of capabilities as well as difficulties.

Because the entire process is done over the background of the separateness struggles that the adolescent goes through in relation to the parents, i.e., the need to gradually disconnect from the membranes of the intensive tie and replace it with a rebellious, different, psychological tie, the adolescent needs a support group in the form of the peer group - rebelling against their own parents. This group has immense weight in every adolescent's life, not only as a "city of refuge" in the face of the struggle against the parents, but also as a place suitable for realizing the need to practice, examine, and test onself with the myriad identities and internalizations adopted during growing up.

The emotional remoteness that develops in the rebellion process and the anxiety derived from it send many adolescents to examine themselves "in practice" (albeit quite temporarily) as cultural heroes, like various identification figures. In this way, in the presence of the friends, the adolescent tests his or her inner and visible worlds with different figures. The adolescent's external appearance and overt behavior are but a prolonged "journey of costumes," while each costume leaves another layer of the adolescent's impressions and identifications, including all the reactions experienced by the friends from the group of belonging.

The journey of costumes is definitely a temporary journey, but due to the intensity of adolescent perception, it appears at each given moment as if it were absolute and total. Many adults tend to be frightened and get caught up with the concept of temporary absoluteness and with the fear (or enjoyment of the temporary costume selected by the adolescent for himself or herself with fashionable figures or ones that fit his or her additional developmental needs, such as a "freak," "geek," "philosopher", "model," "studious," "actor", "dancer," and more).

The adolescent's room slowly becomes similar to the outfit basement of any respectable national theater; but here there is no order and no dresser, and the "outfits" are thrown in a pile accompanied by the unavoidable statement, "I have nothing to wear," which often means: "I have switched a costume and role, and I am not equipped with the items required for the new role" (the trousers that have been very appropriate for the "laid-back" role, cannot serve me now, when I am at the dawn of a new role - a "geeky student" etc.) It should be noted: This intensive preoccupation with the costume journey serves the adolescent in the achievement of several objectives simultaneously - engaging in the consolidation of the new body schema, in the process of becoming separate from the parent, and the struggle for constructing the sexual identity and placement in the peer group. Each costume and role also has a social-sociometric role: the desire to test my place as accepted/not accepted, my status as a leader, follower, someone who belongs, is rejected, and more. Sometimes the switching of costumes is intended to serve a covert or overt desire to change the group of belonging or sociometric position.

Some adolescents perform this task with overt and high intensity and others, with a low - and minor dosage, each person according to his or her personal temperament.

Here as well, the adolescents with learning- and attention-disability often stand out, going to each of the extremes. They prefer adhering to one "costume" that has shocking power, serving them as a defense mechanism, as well, for camouflaging their personal distress, as if saying: " I prefer that people are occupied with how I look rather than how I feel." Alternatively, they will adopt a provocative outfit enabling with overt "behavioral problems," to shift the focus of interest to the outside - how I look and behave and not my difficulties derived from my disability - a costume that camouflages a sense of inferiority, or alternatively intensifies unique and rewarding external attributes. Obsessive adherence to a certain line of clothing is also a way of avoiding uncomfortable physical contact due to the increase in sensory sensitivity, and more.

The "peer group" is the central training field, on which the adolescent will practice the need to consolidate his or her personal identity with all that is implied by it. Therefore, the adolescent should be equipped with a social toolbox and be connected to a group of rebels - similar people.

Learning- and attention-disabled adolescents find themselves having difficulties due to social disability. They discover that for them, this period is even harder, and the social distress has enormous implications for the quality of psychic life and their ability to adapt to the changes characteristic of the period.

| The Emotional-Familial Axis

The emotional lives of adolescents are closely related to physical change, and at the same time, with the emotional and intellectual changes they are undergoing.

In its historical context, adolescence has not at all been defined as a developmental stage. In societies that preceded the Enlightenment Period, youths aged 12-to-13 were defined as adults (fitting with their sexual-physical maturity) after acquiring a profession and social position (which occurred at latency age, between 6-to-12, with social techniques of an apprentice or helper of an adult professional) and were intended for marriage, establishment of a family, and economic and functional independence.

With the rise of education as a decisive factor in the training of youth, several social changes occurred - associated with familial and psychological changes. Despite being physically competent to have a sex life, the adolescent youth enters a holding pattern (moratorium), legally-socially forbidding him or her to realize such physical potential. What is preferred is the extension of apprenticeship years designated for acquiring knowledge, extending socialization, and prolonging waiting for a later age (18 years in most societies) - when the individual is more competent and possesses the ability enabling adaptation (professional training, higher education, and ability for economic independence as necessary conditions for starting a family). Extending the waiting time forces the adolescent to live under contradictory conditions: On the one hand, he or she is very much influenced by the physical-hormonal process, arousing drives and attachments related to a couple relationship and realization of sexual identity, and on the other hand, a social and educational-psychological taboo forbids this and requires him or her to focus on the academic-social world.

This paradoxical situation arouses in the adolescent restlessness in the relations with his or her peers (mainly with members of the opposite sex as part of life in the rebel group) and in relations with parents.

The rise of drives in the nearly mature body reopens Oedipal relationship triangles and emotions within the family unit, and requires both parents to relate to this intelligently - the obligation to comply with the taboo of the prohibition of intra-familial relations (incest) and the obligation to encourage the adolescent to find release through the social relations outside the family unit. This move supports the ambivalent position of the parents, who are still responsible for their adolescent child's wellbeing, who want continued connection, closeness, and intimacy in the relations (out of a will to remain influential and significant), but are also "expelling," setting limits, and standing on guard vis-a-vis their adolescent's needs and restlessness. These relations provide additional support to the construction of the teenager's experience of separateness from the parents, supported by the "rebellious outcasts" group, and arouse in him or her a complex attitude toward parents, which includes renewed falling in love, devaluation (expressed by a sort of criticism, contempt, or distancing, while the adolescent has difficulty diminishing the parent due to his her power), and preference for closeness and intimacy with peers - to the parents' joy as well as discontent

In adolescence, the restlessness resulting from the drives is responded to in sublimative ways (fitted to the spirit and values of the society in which the adolescent lives and grows up into), such as masturbation, increased interest in the sexual world with its various types, intellectual interest (which fits in with intellectual development), power struggles and rebellion, various types of wild behavior, engaging in physical activities (sports, dance etc.), connecting with groups for recreational activities ("hanging out"), and many other ways..

Adolescent rebellion is therefore a developmental

psychological goal, which is intended to serve the adolescent's wellbeing and simultaneously, that of his or her relations with the parents. At the same time, this rebellion serves the psychological remoteness required for separateness-needs on the way to consolidating the new identity.

However, it is important to examine the ways that the adolescents' parents and other significant adults, like teachers and instructors, cope with the manifestations of unrest and rebellion in the face of the age tasks related to studies and education. It is very important to keep a watchful eye on the group of "rebels," lest they become empowered in dangerous directions - through legally and socially prohibited behaviors, such as drug and alcohol abuse, delinquency, forced sexual relations and more. The fact that adolescents "distance themselves" from their parents often endangers them because they are abandoned-rebels. The difficulty in finding the parental balance - between enabling distancing but avoiding severance and lack of oversight - causes tensions and many dangers to many adolescents in Western society today.

A group that is undoubtedly at high risk during growing up is the group of adolescents with learning- and attention-disabilities. The danger stems from their disability's characteristics and from its presence at significant developmental junctions.

A key problem that the learning- and attention-disabled

adolescent is faced with is the problem of regulation, which exists anyway as a difficulty in most adolescents, but in this case is intensified - mainly when the disability in question is of the hyperactivity, impulsivity (ADHD), or oppositional defiant disorder (ODD) types. In these adolescents, the work of regulation is far more difficult. The learning disorder also causes difficulties in planning and organization and therefore, mistaken judgment, (temporary and momentary) loss of reality testing, and risk taking ("thrill"-seeking) while repeating mistakes. The factor that controls their behaviors and choices is the immediate impulse and not reality testing. Alternatively, they have a tendency to simultaneously withdraw and avoid contact with parents and friends.

The partial competence of the executive function–a disruption typical of most adolescents, who suffer from the syndrome, might cause difficulties in discretion that necessitates factor integration, thinking while splitting attention, and simultaneous awareness of various components in a situation. Difficulties with the Inner Language might cause preference for behavior that replaces emotional or intentional expressions, due to the difficulty in verbal expression, and this way, they find themselves in the eye of the storm again and again, "behaving" their emotions and desires, and being judged as violent, aggressive, bullying and so on (see Chapter 2 - social learning disability).

Secondary school and academic tasks serve as a sort of dominant life field that also determines social range. For many among the learning- and attention-disabled adolescents, it is a place of inferiority, failure, and vulnerability and of a wish to "destroy" and damage the place that causes pain - or alternatively - a place to avoid. The difficulties in the social area and difficulty finding an appropriate group of belonging often cause learning- and attention-disabled adolescents to "pick" a group of similar ("rejected") people. Together their power endangers them even more. The possibilities of escaping into worlds providing immensely intense thrills - emotional connection under the influence of sedatives or pain-alleviating agents, such as alcohol and drugs; "wild" anti-social behaviors as a way of expressing the feeling of non-belonging; intensifying the rejection from a standpoint that seemingly shows control of the situation - these are available and tempting options - as they provide moments of grace of moderating the pain accompanying the disability.

You will sometimes see them preferring extroverted behavior of going wild or wearing blatant and provocative clothing, as if telling themselves and their environment that they "prefer" to be considered as socially deviant and not neurologically disabled. Often, under the cover of provocations, eyes of deep sadness, despair, and sorrow are seen, camouflaged by heavy makeup (mainly in the girls), a hat or disheveled hair hiding their faces (many boys), or loud clothing that seems like it prevents any suspicion of pain. **Going wild is a defense mechanism against the pain.** Another group with a slow-to-warm up shade of attention deficit disorder (ADD) and temperament, will often prefer the extreme withdrawal and avoidance that includes not going out of the house, avoiding social contacts, hooking up to the computer as a substitute-virtual world. This behavior is no less worrisome for the environment. The rebellion against the parent will be expressed by an extreme move of severing contact and ties, of withdrawal into the room while maintaining constant physical and psychological distance, as if protecting themselves so that their distress will not be exposed.

Yet others will move in opposed axes of avoidance and dependence, helplessness, and risk-taking simultaneously, and in this way greatly confuse their adult environment regarding their true needs.

| The Intellectual-Academic Axis

A central place in the lives of all adolescents in the modern Western world is designated for the broadening of education (both compulsory and voluntary), which becomes extended in years.

The definition of adolescence as an artificial-developmental stage in modern society is closely associated with the rise in the need for years of waiting (moratorium) for extending education. Intellectual and academic development has a key influence on the consolidation of all adolescents' psychological identity.

According to Piaget (1969, in Muuss, 1982), at this stage the ability for abstract thinking (abstract operations, and mainly the hypothetical-deductive sub-stage) reaches its peak. The adolescent no longer needs conceptual linkage between a concrete object and a thought, but can develop thinking that has value in its own right, disconnect thoughts and ideas from the familiar, and use hypothetical illustration. In addition, an enormous growth occurs in the ability to generalize - deduce one thought and knowledge pattern from another, link idea types, make assumptions and critically test them, and deduce from them about other assumptions. This accelerated development creates in many adolescents a thirst for extensive knowledge from various content areas - not necessarily those studied in school. The adolescent is willing to embark on an endless journey of debates over ideas and basic assumptions encountered by him or her, and develop a pattern of an argumentative philosopher, who often annoys teachers, parents, and other adolescents. The new mastery of the world of higher-order thinking, accompanied by good verbalization ability, often serves both the adolescents and their social milieu. The endless need to rebel, coupled with the intense need to test ideological positions, make adolescents in many societies an ideological revolution group - the pioneering task force of demonstrations, rebellion, and new ideas.

Adolescents are eager to undertake such tasks because they are simultaneously served by them in all the axes: intellectual-ideological, social-collective (revolution always takes place in socially or ideologically unified groups), emotional-familial (rebellion against adults), instinctual-impulsive - ventilation of the intensity of the drives (to demonstrate means going out to do something exciting, liberating, and impulse-driven, all at once).

The need to confront a teacher in class or a social-political position formulated by parents and a social milieu creates an extensive basis for consolidating the separate identity while developing intellectual capabilities. One can gather from this that if the learning- and attention-disabled adolescent and his or her intellectual toolbox do not in fit with the required capabilities, or if the school's demands externalize and accentuate the disability, or if an ideological group is joined only on a partial basis due to the verbal or cognitive difficulty, then psychic life is compromised.

The learning- and attention-disabled adolescent has a difficult experience of inferiority, followed by blaming others. At this point, blaming (the disability and/or the parents as generators of the disability) often forms a key obstacle to providing the adolescent with the needed help. The sense of rage directed toward the school and teachers as responsible for, and intensifying, the experience of inferiority, causes the adolescent to act with "aggressive," blatant, and "destroying" behavior, toward them or alternatively, to avoid contact with school and teachers, and engage in frequent absences from the pain-causing area ("skipping school" and being absent until a state of covert and overt dropping out is reached).

The intensified sense of failure sends a few of these adolescents to join revolutionary groups, which are content with action devoid of complex thinking - or to avoid these groups totally, lest the limitations be exposed again. In a few adolescents, inferiority takes on the character of great rage - in others - sadness up to depression that jeopardizes their wellbeing.

For these adolescents, the emphasis put nowadays on measurement and evaluation of intellectual abilities through grades and tests, certificates, and groupings externalizes the disability and therefore prevents the mobilization of motivation for coping with the obstacle. They therefore might comprise a risk group for dropping out of school, mainly when it is accompanied by extroverted behavior rebelling against the school as a place that perpetuates their disability (overt dropping out), or when they extend the time of avoidance within the school (covert dropping out).

B. Parents in a Struggle Between Dependence and Independence

Parents of adolescents in modern society are often faced with extremely difficult parenting tests. The complexity of modern life and the belated moratorium of their children "ensure" in advance an enormous obstacle on their way to good parenting for adolescents; and when the growing up process takes place in the shadow of a learning disability, the parental task is much, much more difficult.

Several unique tasks stand before parents of learning- and attention-disabled adolescents, in addition to those of parents of their contemporaries:

First, this is parenting that involves a continuous experience of worry and anxiety about the adolescent's fate and future. The disability's presence as a factor that jeopardizes success in school makes school and studying a field of constant struggle. Some parents give up in advance in order to avoid a confrontational encounter, which is no less painful for them than it is for their children. The experience of inferiority accompanying the studying makes their parenting extremely painful. Under the rationalization of independence, responsibility, and separateness, some parents tend to avoid contact with the world of difficulties. They give preference to paying for tutoring lessons over assistance with organizing the studying or creating binding situations and directive involvement in the son's or daughter's difficulties. If parents also lack parental knowledge and skills needed to assist the adolescent, then their situation is many times more difficult.

In a home where child-rearing takes place without any extraordinary difficulties, an experience of trust forms, not only of the teenager in his or her parents but concurrently of the parents in the teenager and his or her strengths and abilities as well. Parenting a learning- and attention-disabled teenager is characterized by constant damage to the basic trust of the parents in the teenager, with the difficult sense that he or she "cannot be trusted." The need to supervise and oversee is no less an emotional obstacle than a practical difficulty. The sense of lack of trust replaces the wonder and enthusiasm that accompanies many parents in raising their children. The lack of wonder and enthusiasm on their part acts as a painful mechanism for the teenager who "returns" the pain to the parents in various forms.

The gap between the learning- and attention-disabled adolescent's dependence needs and the task of separation and independence creates sustained misunderstandings and confusion in relations. Therefore, a disrupted relationship forms, of holding and letting go, bringing others too close, and over-rejection. This parental mechanism is painful and tiresome for both parties.

The anxiety of receiving reports of improper acts done by the teenager at school, in the street, in the neighborhood, or in a recreational hobby course leaves many parents tense and in a constant sense of helplessness. This is how a learning- and attention-disabled adolescent, who is in need of a psychologically strong and protective parent, gets a weakened, frightened, anxious, and worried parent. Such a parent frightens the adolescent and creates a sense of abandonment and loneliness that causes the adolescent to make the difficulties seem more extreme in order to try mobilize the parent again - and so forth.

The difficulty in predicting the teenager's reactions, the lack of confidence or trust in his or her choices, the need to be "constantly on-call" - these are the factors that cause parents to shift from patterns of permissiveness and responsiveness. i.e., immediate meeting of needs in order to preserve moments of bogus good "ties" to make up for the suffering out of identification - to patterns of severe punishment, denial of rights, anger and rejection - , i.e. an attempt to forcefully "correct" the disability or a sense of rage over the overt failure. Already suffering from difficulties in organization and predication of his or her behavior and its consequences, the teenager now gets an environment more massively devoid of backing - making organization even harder.

Regulation difficulties, disruption of the biological clock, and leftovers of sensory and motor difficulty cause many learning- and attention-disabled adolescents to have difficulties in their daily life cycle. Awakening and sleep processes, organizing a daily schedule, transitions from home to school, stopping an activity to fulfill an obligation, disengaging from the computer or television in order to perform study tasks or home chores, showering, arranging the clothing closet, buying clothes, maintaining hygiene, and more - all these become focal points of struggle and difficulty, weakening the parent, and following the parent. The adolescent, who is weakened anyway, but shows this with resistance or avoidance intensities, is erroneously evaluated by the parent as having power.

The social choices of the adolescent, who might sometimes stick to "fringe" society in the face of interpersonal difficulties and inability to resist the temptations of the street, arouse anxiety in many parents who find it hard to let their adolescent be independent.

Parents know that their child's disability is invisible and that the overt phenomena are erroneously judged by the near and far environments as behaviors of a "disturbed" violent child; and that they themselves are also erroneously judged as people who do not know how to provide proper upbringing, as failing. All this, together with experiences of guilt and shame, make every outing from the protected concealing house a subject of indecision and avoidance.

The restlessness typical of the learning- and attention-disabled adolescent appears very intensely at home as well.

The reduction of options in the extra-familial world and the experience of inferiority and frustration often cause the adolescent to discharge his or her pains and release wrath inside the home. And in this way, the children's parents, siblings, and other close family members sometimes live in the shadow of "tension and terror" in fear of the adolescent's and/or parents' next outburst. Nothing is expectable or certain because of the inability to predict properly the learning- and attention-disabled adolescent's will or reaction.

Parental pain is often not well contained by pedagogical and therapeutic service providers. The parent is blamed and criticized by them as well, causing the parent to feel threatened. Parents react by sometimes blaming and being aggressive or being avoidant and giving in. In the absence of an understanding professional language, these parent's behaviors are erroneously judged by the environment as impaired parenting, and not as a sustained reaction to parenting a learning- and attention-disabled child. This mixing up between cause and effect in the complex relationship with a learning- and attention-disabled adolescent often disrupts the intra- and extra-familial worlds; and if we take the hereditary aspect into account, then when a learning- and attention-disabled parent lives under the same roof as an adolescent suffering from the syndrome, the emotional complexity is even greater, and sometimes obstructive.

Partially and selectively being responded to by the adolescent, the dependence that the parent attempts to develop in his or her adolescent child is often intended to keep the teenager under conditions of over-oversight in order to reduce the development of problems in the disabled adolescent's behavioral, social, and emotional processes of choice. However, dependence is a tiring experience and contradictory to the adolescent's needs on the way to separation. That is why he or she reacts to it paradoxically: being needy and rejecting; rebelling and moving away; returning and becoming dependent. The inconsistency reflects some of the disability's characteristics itself - returns to the parent the experience of lack of trust and helplessness and causes the parent himself or herself to shift inconsistently between the two extremes. This is how a difficult and painful cycle of relations forms and becomes intensified.

It is important for parents who are frightened by the intensity of the pain and lack of clarity accompanying it to know that it is precisely the high emotional involvement they exhibit toward their learning- and attention-disabled child that causes the child to try to distance himself, try other ways, get confused, and not know what is right. Were it not for the parent's high emotional involvement with the child, such highly complex parental feelings would not have developed.

C. The Dilemmas of Adolescents Parents: to be a Friend or to be an Authority?

An additional axis of lack of clarity in parent-adolescent relations, in particular, with learning- and attention-disabled adolescents, concerns the parental standpoint, shifting between the wish for closeness and friendship with the teenager and the need to maintain a certain remoteness by way of an authoritative approach.

The wish for closeness and intimacy between a parent and child is right and legitimate; however, this wish often becomes a will to be the adolescent teenager's intimate friend. Many parents nowadays bear memories of being remote from their parents and tend to "compensate" in an erroneous attempt to be their child's friend. This wish of friendship between the adolescent boy or girl and the parent is one of the representative signs of the current generation and the modern era.

For many parents of adolescents, the early childhood years have lacked sufficient emotional satisfaction in symbiotic relations. The early transfer of the child to an extra-familial framework, the quick going back to work to further develop the career and the need to be a "modern" parent have left many parents "hungry" for satisfying quality time with their child. This early abandonment is experienced by the parents as guilt, for which they are required to "expiate" without at all checking what their child's need and experience is: Is it a uni-directional hunger, or does the child feel a lack as well? Whether the 'hunger' is uni- or bi-directional, the ways of making up for the lack pose a key obstacle in parent-adolescent relations.

The will to expiate by means of permissive approaches causes the adolescent to feel flooded, but not satisfied by his or her parent. Desperately seeking a positive reflection in the child, the parent "buys" it by means of permissions that jeopardize both the adolescent as well as the parenting. The social support of approaches enabling permissiveness and pleasure satisfaction only exacerbate this disrupted relations cycle. The lack of differentiation between honor relations and boundary blurring, between love and permissiveness, between enabling or limiting experience, and avoiding the regulation of the child, exacerbates the world of relations more and more. And thus, the parent who seeks identification with, and approval from the child, instead of serving as an identification model, leaves the child devoid of a significant parental figure.

An additional parental difficulty stems from the modern conception that prefers skepticism, pondering, experiencing, and permissiveness to totality and unambiguousness. This is an outcome of the World Wars trauma, which has associated between totality and belligerence, between leadership and tyranny. The Western world has chosen the liberal educational approach as the correct way, even though this way is sometimes dangerous. An overly permissive parent is often a weak parent, who has difficulty in protecting the child, setting safety boundaries and limits and providing liberty within the limits of the allowed and possible (Blank and Fuchs- Shabtai , 2004). The cultural revolution of the 1960s that gave preference to the world of youth has been economically supporting a global market of the youth preservation industry and quickly pervaded education and the family unit as well. Parents of adolescents often identify with and reinforce their children's young appearance and culture, instead of setting an adult identification model. The complete adoption of the youth language, appearance, culture and areas of interest by adult parents compels youth to make an effort to constantly produce cultural and fashion radicalizations that will serve them in their rebellion. Parents who "steal" the signs of age from them over and over again, necessitate the continuation of adolescent radicalization.

The parent's drawing near to, and imitation of the adolescent child, in the sense of "looking like, feeling like, being like…," while having an adult body and mind not suited to youthful appearance, creates difficulty in maintaining psychological distance - necessary for the adolescent.

The longing for friendship with the child instead of being an authority figure is further reinforced in this era of electronic equipment. The mastery and agility exhibited by the youth in operating the modern devices, such as computers, music playing/recording devices, smart phones, and more, create a dependence of the parent on the child, instead of the other way around. The wise old man of the village - the spiritual guide of the tribe from the past - is no longer relevant because he does not have mastery of the culture's secrets; the human tribe is now run by the hi-tech youth. This is the case in the external world as well as in the family unit (Strenger, 2005). I have often heard an adolescent "punish" his or her parents by not giving assistance in using software or operating a new appliance at home - unless they allow him or her to receive, go, be, and do just as he or she wishes. Being a good authoritative parent - means coping with momentary or sustained reactions of the adolescent, who reacts with discontent to the limits set for him or her. Being authoritative - means daring to withstand the adolescent's anger and rebellion while having constant confidence in the correctness of the limitation and that it serves the child's good - that which is hidden from him or her at this moment. A protective parent is a parent who allows the rebellion to take place in a safe territory; a limiting parent enables the formation of conflictual relations in the service of psychological separateness that the adolescent needs so much. A parent who shifts between allowing and limiting guides his or her adolescent child along the sequence of accommodated processes; however, for this, the parent must have confidence in, and trust the child and the relations with the child. The parent must know the adolescent child's developmental needs and must stand steadfastly vis-a-vis the child's frustration. Under the cover of a modern-permissive ideology, the weakened parental-psychological resilience makes it impossible for the parent to hold his/her ground..

When parents shift from a parent-friend to parent-protector, they need to feel inner confidence in themselves and/or their child - to feel able to regulate and accommodate themselves not to the child's changing mood - but to his or her present and future needs.

It is easy to imagine how many difficulties are involved when the parents in question are parents of learning- and attention-disabled adolescents. In this case, we often witness a parenthood that moves within an experience of sustained parental hunger, intensified by the painful years of the experiences of failure and (overt and covert) difficulty. The disappointment with the teenager and his or her difficulties, and sustained burnout from dealing with the disability weaken parents to the point of inability to differentiate between the teenager and the disability. These parents might be afflicted with over-permissiveness as a defense mechanism against the pain of rejection that arises in them - as a way of avoiding bringing the difficulties to the surface by means of an "'ideology" for hiding rejection and abandonment experiences.

D. Learning & AD(H)D Disabled Adolescents at Secondary (High) School and Onward

The rise in the power of academic education coupled with the centrality of school as an institution that trains and teaches have intensified the preoccupation with the phenomenon of learning- attention- and concentration-disability.

The need for accommodation of curricula, teaching, and test-taking methods has been causing great commotion in the last decade, both in the school world and in society as a whole. The increase in the number of adolescents who are compelled to stay at school for more than 10 years in order to build their future has expanded the identification and diagnosis of those finding it hard to meet the demands of school tasks despite their normal intellectual capabilities.

Together with this, the public debate over the extent of the disability and its essence versus issues of motivation, laziness, lenience, and more, has intensified. In this way, many adolescents suffering from learning- attention- and concentration-disability and their parents often find themselves in the eye of the public-social storm: Is it a scam-or a real problem? Are the increase in the prevalence of diagnosis and the recognition of needs derived from the identification of the syndrome correct, or are they the result of a scam bought by money? In addition to the difficulties of the disability itself and coping with it, its existence and truth must now be proven as well, or a public apology must even be given for the existence of a neurological event in the body of a student who seemingly appears normal and normative.

One can assume that on the fringes of the increase in the number of those diagnosed is a negligible group that uses the diagnosis and its derivatives for the sake of personal interests, which are not sufficiently based on the disability's aspects; however, the vast majority, of diagnosed adolescents, which keeps increasing, reflect the real picture.

When shaping an educational policy and economic investment in education, one must take into account that the more the acquisition of education requires increased learning and training time, the more the study loads increase. These increased loads will lead to the collapse of more and more adolescents, who in the past have survived the framework or have met its demands adequately despite their mild disability, but in light of the increased duration and extent of study, their disability is exposed and becomes burdensome. Adolescents need support to enable them to succeed in spite of their disability; these conditions enable them to realize personal and intellectual potential despite their minor or major disability.

The statistical change we are witnessing, and which is about to increase in the future, stems from the fact that building the future of the graduate is predicated on more years of education and larger extent of study. and in this way, more and more youth with less severe disabilities will enter the circle of diagnosed students in need of accommodation.

Every secondary (high) school is today preoccupied with the definition of the disability's characteristics and ways to assist. The more grades and meeting the demands of tests and academic tasks become the portal to adult success, the more the number of those in need of assistance at school increases (Hallowell & Ratey, 2004; Tuckman, 2007; Barkley, Murphy & Fischer, 2008).

From their very essence, the demands of school act in opposition or contradiction to the needs of adolescents with learning- attention- and concentration-disability. Try to imagine the heroes like Tom Sawyer or Huckleberry Finn as prominent representatives of talented youth suffering from the disability.

Many adolescents with learning- and attention-disabilities possess high abilities precisely in areas that differ from those required at school - specific capabilities in the areas of performance, art, manual competence, excellent visual perception, and more. Were it not for the demand for general and verbal education, evaluated by matriculation test grades mainly based on the verbal domain, by SAT scores that depend on performance speed measured by time, and more, these students could have integrated into capability-suited tracks and experienced some reparation of failure; however, the dominant preference nowadays for grades, mainly reflecting theoretical study capabilities acquired in an institution called school, necessitates an in-depth discussion of their ways of coping, psychological experience, and ways of assistance.

The encounter with a student suffering from a learning disability and/or attention deficit disorder necessitates **multidisciplinary preparation** on several levels simultaneously by the school institution and the entire educational system (a systemic multi-disciplinary approach):

1. Ability to identify, diagnose and focus the difficulties - both as a unique syndrome distinct from other difficulties similar to it in the overt aspect (such as mental retardation, emotional disorders, being underprivileged, communicational disabilities, and more), as well as a unique profile of the individual, in order to identify both the need for constructing bypasses for the difficulties, as well as the need to strengthen and rely on especially good strong abilities. The earlier the identification and diagnosis, and the more the intervention starts early and in extensive aspects, the less the secondary damage (experience of failure, inferiority, gap increase, expansion of functional and emotional difficulties), and the higher the chances for adjustment and success.

2. Ability to (dynamically) construct accommodated teaching programs, to develop unique learning methods for providing help both on the individual and general levels. A program based on remedial teaching (an approach that constructs alternative teaching methods, suited to both the disability and ability profiles) provided both individually as well as on the classroom and grade level, can be beneficial to a wide variety of students. The remedial teaching can also serve students with other temporary difficulties.

The prevalent approach to excellence in school nowadays must be dramatically changed: from a setting measured mainly by the achievements of the high-ability students to a setting measured by the achievements of the maximal number of graduates according to their potential, and without dropouts.

Remedial teaching constructs learning strategies suited to the students' various profiles, and leads them with unique approaches to the ability to study in the mainstream. Instead of limiting the training in remedial teaching to teachers from special education only, an alternative approach could integrate remedial teaching in the training of every teacher (in the professional continuing education programs and in the learning staff room) - whoever he or she may be. The more remedial learning strategies and teaching methods can be integrated by a larger number of teachers into the teaching process of the specific discipline taught by them, the better the overall course of teaching at school will become and the study climate will be better suited to a wide variety of students.

Systemic-educational experience has taught that the good integration of a student with a learning- attention- and concentration-disability in a regular class is an indication of the student's wonderful abilities and of the teacher's capabilities and good personality. All the students benefit, not only from the ethical aspect, but also from the net professional aspect. A teacher who succeeds in integrating a struggling student is in most cases a good teacher for all the students. This teacher knows how to deconstruct the learning processes into sub-areas, to construct a clear and directive set of directions, to create structured learning conditions and clear guidance, and mainly to utilize creativity first and foremost in the student's ways of expression and output. For example: usage of the following methods by all teachers will lead to the empowerment of all the students:

- Mediation and advance introduction of the lesson's content and study assignments
- Integration of memorization elements into principle comprehension processes
- Acquisition of strategies for knowledge focusing and various means for differentiation between the main point and details that are of secondary importance
- Deconstruction of study directions into short sub-directions in a short sequence that is updated all the time
- Working while the process is dynamically supervised, intentional intervention while work is in progress (monitoring), training for sequential execution

of assignments, work process and environment organization, and more

- Replacing written-verbal output with performance output (illustration, sand table, drawing or flow chart, presentation)
- Use of facilitating means of input and output (recording, using a word processor, shortened text with big fonts, frontal teaching and oral test alongside written teaching, written output, and more).

Beyond the specific training with which remedial teaching teachers are equipped, support centers for teachers can be created at the school (parallel to those for the students), where a remedial teacher will assist the subject teacher in building accommodated lesson plans.

3. Intervention in social and interpersonal processes inside and outside the classroom.

Learning- attention- and concentration-disabled students are often characterized by social disabilities as well, stemming from the same source. The manifestation of this in the social domain leads to worsening of the vulnerability and to difficult personal-emotional feelings.

Nowadays many schools suffer from various types of violence (starting with young children), from the penetration of street dangers such as drugs into the school to the development of "negative" social norms - gangs with delinquent norms, contempt for and injury to others, vandalism, and more. There is an increased need for the construction of intervention plans that not only relate to the academic aspect - a need that has become a contemporary must.

The learning- attention- and concentration-disabled students' inadequate integration into the regular academic stream often creates an experience of estrangement, rejection, and abandonment in them, and causes them to be active or passive ("joining") accomplices to the infiltration of the above-mentioned negative phenomena in the schoolyard. The regulation problems, social difficulties, negative emotions, the anger as a defense mechanism from the shame and more - all these affect their involvement in those phenomena.

Constructing an intervention program that is based on improvement and learning of social and functional skills will not only improve the disabled teenager's quality of life and ensure his or her thriving, but will also influence the climate and norms in the entire school. The reward will be twofold. For this purpose, specific preparation is required, that includes acquisition of **social remedial-teaching** approaches, and constructing a different, accommodated presence of adults who intervene throughout the entire school. This program has three components: first, it necessitates the construction of boundaries; second, the clarification of norms and rules; and third, allocation of professional intervention and an ability-building work force. The combination of the three might bring about the longed-for change, both at the individual as well as the system levels.

Updated findings regarding the deviations lying in wait for adolescents who do not socially integrate in the "peer group, " but in substitute "'groups of the different ones, " such as delinquency, drugs, and alcohol abuse (Tyano and Manor, 2001; Einat T. and Einat A., 2006; Barkley, Murphy & Fischer, 2008) indicate the real danger. In the absence of integration programs, the percentage of overt and covert dropping out of school increases and expands the danger zone to the street, the neighborhood, and community centers.

4. Construction of individual therapeutic support sources that address the emotional aspects of the students and their parents.

Learning- attention- and concentration-disabilities can be dealt with by a variety of therapeutic-interventional means, according to the individual's needs and personal profile. In general, an intervention plan is required that is based on a variety of professions and the coordination between them.

During their lives, many teenagers need professional intervention, which includes medical services (neurological and psychiatric diagnosis and treatment), mental health services (psychotherapy, social work, expressive therapies, therapy and support with animals, therapeutic gardening, horseback riding, swimming, and more), services from the physical treatment field (physiotherapy, occupational therapy, horseback riding, therapeutic exercise, swimming, and more), and from the field of remedial teaching.

A treated teenager might find himself or herself moving between the various therapeutic service providers (nowadays mostly outside the school), while the coordination between them and the school and family is minimal at best. Sometimes these treatments are even contradictory to each other. Constructing multi-disciplinary treatment centers inside, and in the vicinity of the school will enable the minimization of difficulties. Integrating treatment hours within the study schedule might alleviate the difficulties of many parents and adolescents, both from the practical as well as social-emotional aspects - release of tension during the study day. Nevertheless, a few adolescents might have reservations about receiving this help openly within the school, (such as being been seen by their friends and teachers.) For the sake of these teenagers, regional, outside-school centers can be established, equipped with proper means of communication with the school.

Centralizing the treatment resources inside and around the schools will also reduce the distress of the schools, which are nowadays coping without sources of support, will reduce the need for burdensome communication with an endless number of intervening treatment bodies and with too many approaches, and will enable a similar therapeutic language for all students in need of it. Internalizing therapeutic approaches will eventually empower the school. The integration of accommodated teaching methods, testing methods accommodated to a specific disability, and systemic and individual treatment channels - all these will create a safety net that will benefit the students, their parents, and the schools, and will lead to the pooling of forces and softening of the encounters between them. Nevertheless, it should be noted that the process undergone by each adolescent and his or her parents, from acknowledging the disability to accepting it, has variable pace and stages; teenagers sometimes cannot enjoy the full resources at their disposal before being psychologically mature. And because many of the disability's characteristics are opposed to the school environment, they make adjustment and functioning difficult.

Constructing a good treatment network is not a guarantee for the disappearance of the difficulties, which are intrinsic to the disability, but a promise of creating a tapestry that understands the difficulties, is capable of deciphering their origins, and containing and limiting them professionally and in a beneficial manner. The intention is not to develop programs that completely prevent the difficulties, but rather programs that construct a substrate on which every teenager can grow in all areas, according to his or her potential and in the personal pace suited to the teenager and the family.

E. Social Learning Disability at Adolescence

"Social Learning Disability" is a conceptualization of the development of social adjustment and integration difficulties of teenagers diagnosed with disabilities. The social aspect is an additional facet in which the disability is manifested, similar to its other aspects (behavioral, academic, emotional, and more) - hence, the great importance of understanding the aspects of social disability and later on, developing relevant intervention programs. Social disability appears for the first time at the age of three to four, a time when most children show the first signs of social interest and start acquiring the ability to be part of the peer group. At pre-school and elementary school ages - the period where socialization becomes a central focal point - we can clearly diagnose the pain and distress aroused by the disability among the children suffering from it (see Chapter 2).

An additional cycle of social anguish will occur at adolescence, when the rebel gang becomes a source of attraction and a central territory for social encounter.

At all stages, social disability can be described as an additional manifestation of the general disability's aspects. Therefore, intervention programs should be constructed along the lines of "social remedial teaching" in order to provide a response for the difficulties of the children and adolescents.

Social skills already appear at toddlerhood, as an inner and natural expression of the maturing of a variety of capabilities and needs. Starting out in the egocentric position, the young child needs friends so they will serve his or her current needs, while from the child's standpoint, he or she is in the center of the world.

This uni-directional and self-interest-oriented attitude is typical of all 3-to-4-year-old children and that is why it has been given the title of "the egocentric period" - a group of children playing side-by-side and requiring interactions with each other for only a few moments of meeting needs and activity. The moment there is a lack of interest or lack of fit, they disengage from each other and move on to the next child, as so forth. In most cases, situations of conflict of interest will lead to overt physical confrontation (biting, hair pulling, spitting etc.) or to moving away and avoidance (the child retreats to another place, to a different object or to a child who is willing to accept his or her requests).

Entering pre-school life at the Oedipal period expands social contact with aspects of being considerate and acknowledging the other. The gang games now serve as a source of emotional ventilation from the Oedipal death and castration fears, a way to lessen conflicts with the parents. These are also initial attempts to operate according to law of conservation and concrete operations, enabling the gang to acknowledge the existence of permanent rules and procedures, with the beginning of moral discretion and the development of a wider altruistic standpoint. In order to reach this standpoint, the child needs neurological competence in all development lines. This competence is missing (to a greater or lesser extent) among learning- attention- and concentration-disabled children and its absence sabotages normal social development.

Another characteristic of social learning is the place of occurrence and the "learning methods." In most cases, social skills are acquired in non-formal learning processes (modeling, imitation) at times that are not exclusively devoted to this, in an indirect framework, and in the presence of many people, both children and adults. The scope of social learning is not only the product of the multi-disciplinary approach, but first and foremost a result of a multi-stimuli reality that obviously cannot be deconstructed into the various learning components. Most children are assisted by processes of attachment with adults and generalize them to gang relations, and they develop learning while experiencing diverse situations in daily life. Their friends who suffer from the disability are left behind - hungry for social connection but experiencing great difficulty in realizing it.

The disability with its various aspects damages or disrupts fundamental processes that construct the ability to have normal socialization relations:

1. Damage to some of the perception channels.

Damage to some perception channels might disrupt the ability to recognize and control non-spoken interpersonal centers - for example - deciphering-based visual or auditory information, intonation, the music of speech, phonological awareness, visual cues that form gestures, mimics, or various body postures. Each of these components has an important contribution in understanding others and the situation, and for the construction of the continued social process. Sometimes the disruption in the perception of a certain component comes in addition to a non-verbal learning disability and damages the ability to understand the theory of mind.

2. A delay in the development of language and /or communication capabilities, and later on - difficulties in developing the Inner Language.

The delay in the appearance of spoken language and later on - difficulties in deciphering language and its components, like the difficulties in pronunciation or auditory perception, make verbal communication a delayed and disrupted channel of expression in these children. It is possible that additional problems in language development or in communication processes will create additional obstacles. The required transition from behavioral expression to verbal expression is not only associated with the development of language and communication components, but with the maturation of additional neurological processes such as regulation, frustration threshold, transfer, and more. As a result, children with learning and attention disabilities tend to "get stuck" for a prolonged time in behavioral rather than verbal expression, in speech that includes "hand language" and body language, and less spoken language. By contrast, social life becomes increasingly established on verbal communication with all its complexity. The difficulty to participate and become a part of this communication sometimes makes the learning- and attention-disabled children rejected and unwanted.

The difficulty at a later stage, of developing an Inner Language, which will be a channel for planning and control over behaviors and social connection, adds another difficulty to the existing one.

3. Damage to sensory-motor control and general sensory functioning.

Social connection also draws from the ability to plan physical-personal presence within a group space. Motor planning, maintaining a proper psychological distance, the ability to act and move according to age norms - these serve as milestones in the development of group play (both motor and didactic).

The ability to keep a reasonable distance from others; to wait in line without delaying the cue, or without seeming pushy and pressing urging; showing physical capabilities that are compatible with group activity are some of the social capabilities required by children. The sense of threat due to sensory hyper-sensitivity, or touching others too much and too powerfully due to hyposensitivity and/or lack of sensory regulation, contribute their share to the difficulty as well.

4. Executive function difficulty: time place, transition management, flexibility

The damage to the executive function with its myriad functions and components arouses an experience of chaos among children, and therefore, some of them are afflicted either with social anxiety - expressed by avoidance, withdrawal, and seclusion - or enthusiasm, exuberance, bursting out and dominating others. While the individual with a "slow-to-warm-up" temperament-, who suffers from (hypo) regulation difficulties, will turn to the withdrawal side, the one with the "difficult" temperament will frequently be described as pushy, hurting, inconsiderate and so on.

5. Damage to memory, concentration and attention abilities

The damage contributes to the development of focusing difficulties, orientation difficulties and ability to stay "with it," without falling into associative processes disconnected from the matter under discussion by society.

Schema internalization, abstraction processes without concrete presence, trust relations, abstract rules, and more - all these rely on competence and flexibility of memory processes and being able to work under conditions of split attention. In their absence, the child is managed on the basis of concrete thought, without the ability to be flexible and without "learning a lesson."

6. A delay in transition between cognitive stages.

Many adolescents with learning- and attention-disabilities remain in the egocentric social standpoint due to the non-advancement of conservation and splitting processes, deficient attention, and deficient generalization and transfer processes. The delay leaves them without adequate capabilities for acknowledging the permanence of rules in the world of relations, as well as in the world of play. The need to learn anew the rules of the situation, or of the game, or of the suitable behavior for the place, every time, creates an adjustment and accommodation difficulty, and various feelings of deviance and inferiority form instead. Sometimes, rejection or avoidance on the part of other children in the gang also form, as the child is viewed as burdensome, annoying, and "not to the point, a "misfit."

The major part of these difficulties continues with more intensity during adolescence as well. The renewed entry into the world of drives, physical-hormonal changes, increase in drives, the need for separation and consolidation of the identity under the presence of the disability - all these cause especially difficult social adjustment conditions.

The increase in academic and emotional loads, the

continuous need for social belonging also as an expression of self-worth, the incessant sociometric positioning struggles, and the will to construct a personal world outside the family unit - these make the learning- and attention-disabled adolescent a person who bears many difficulties and frustrations. The uncompromising struggle to build a group of belonging or to belong to an existing group as an existential need - versus the abandonment and absolute giving up on the others - are two polar reactions typical of learning- attention- and concentration-disabled adolescents. The rise in sexual drives feeds these feelings more intensely, hence the increase in the level of regulation, restraint, and adjustment difficulties.

The social network, both within the school world (inside and outside the classroom) as well as in the extra-familial and outside-school (the gang) worlds, is the training and socialization framework for the adult world. Learning-disabled adolescents who have no place in the net due to their disability, will drag this void with them into the future, and it will intensify and overshadow all further adjustment processes. Intervention at elementary school age and senior high school by way of social remedial teaching is therefore necessary and crucial for the teenagers' rehabilitation processes and mental health.

The sustained existence of these distresses often drives some adolescents who suffer from learning- attention- and concentration-disability to the "choice" of belonging to fringe groups and being attracted to hazardous and prohibited behaviors.

A teenager who has had no success in connecting with a class/neighborhood/recreational course group might find his or her "friends" who are similar in their distress, on a street corner. The creation of a group of belonging of people who are similar in their disabilities might constitute fertile ground for the development of a gang that is dangerous to itself and its surroundings. Preference for "delinquent," provocative, and prohibited behaviors forms compensation for the rejection, gives release to the experience of inferiority, builds meaning for the injured "Ego" - even at the cost of abnormal socialization.

The attraction to drugs and alcohol as substitutes for medical treatment (at a heavy price of addiction and additional damage to physical and brain vitality) temporarily alleviates the pain, momentarily moves depression away, and provides a social objective of secretive belonging and a temporary sense of euphoria (intensified methods of achieving excitement). However, at the same time, they escalate existing difficulties.

Male and female teenagers who need medical treatment due to their disability - but do not receive it because of familial or personal objection, because of the popularization of medical treatment objectors - harm themselves twice: Not only do they have difficulty surviving the academic and social system, but they are also harming their psychological ability to construct an "Ego" consolidated according to the age task.

The consolidation of the "Ego" versus the experience of diffusion, as a developmental task, requires complex processes that are difficult to realize in teenagers with neurological disabilities. The importance of medical treatment for some of them as a necessary condition for both academic-emotional and interpersonal normalcy is impaired and leaves the adolescent in a state of identity diffusion. It is a painful experience when you do not know why you keep failing.

The difficulty to achieve consolidation under the sustained conditions of the disability might lead these adolescents to a sustained difficulty in shaping psychological identity in an endless journey of costumes and with a "false-self" experience - identity switching, attempts to imitate figures and behaviors, and a difficulty in consolidating and connecting with an identity of your own, with which you identify and are identified by. A sustained state of living with a "false-self" involves constant pain and discomfort, tension and restlessness, which also contribute to the danger of depression and despair (Barkley, Murphy & Fischer, 2008).

CHAPTER TWO

"Social-Remedial (Corrective) Teaching"

Guiding Principles for Intervention With Social Problems in the Educational System and the Treatment Settings

1

Social Learning Disability-
Developmental Background

As described in the previous chapter, social disability is another aspect of learning disability and attention deficit disorder. The origins of social disability are a combination of structural aspects (neurological - innate and learned) and secondary aspects to the primary disorders. The appearance of social disability matches the child's age and development: its primary aspects appear in some children at a young age (playschool and pre-school) during the period when pre-school children start social and group life. In some, its overt manifestations appear with high intensity only upon entry into elementary school, i.e., with the expansion of the children's occupation with a more varied social life (in the classroom and during recess at school, in recreational hobby courses, in the youth movement or in the neighborhood after study hours), and continue during all the adolescent years as well.

Social disability includes varied difficulties from many sources, but has common aspects: a sense of excommunication and/or rejection by peers, being labeled as disruptive/violent/harassing or alternatively - an avoidant/withdrawing child, who is not actively rejected, but avoids social life and interpersonal connection and maintains them on a reduced, minimal level. What they all share in common - ongoing damage to self-worth and self-image.

Among the children who need help in the social domain, groups of those possessing syndromes from a common neurological-academic background, can be listed:

1. Children suffering from Asperger Syndrome
2. Children suffering from verbal and other learning disabilities
3. Children suffering from non-verbal learning disabilities
4. Children suffering from attention deficit disorder combined with hyperactivity, impulsivity and defiant behavior (ADHD, ADID, ODD).
5. Children suffering from attention deficit disorder (ADD) with a slow-to-warm-up temperament.

Alongside these groups is another broad group of children with a spectrum of syndromes related to various types of communication disorders - cognitive, physical, sensory limitations, and more.

The emphasis on the groups is that we are dealing with children whose social difficulties are a product of the specific disability. In spite of their normal intellectual ability and their intense developmental will to belong socially, they experience failure in that area as well - a failure that casts a great shadow over psychological quality of life and their self-image. The disability prevents spontaneous learning, does not enable the "learning of a lesson," and leaves them again and again hurt and "outsiders."

It is true that in some of the cases we identify children whose social capabilities are precisely the positive-key aspect in their development, in spite of the existence of some specific disability. These are children whose language capabilities, physical abilities, and personality-leadership power enable them to turn the social field into the area of strength in their lives and to a focal point of escape and immersion vis-a-vis the academic and other failures; however, they too are prone to "trouble." They might find themselves leading at a high cost of over-investment, facing a multiplicity of conflicts, and obsessiveness with all that concerns their control needs. At certain periods and ages, they might - alongside the success - experience anxiety and failure within. These difficulties might even sometimes route them to "negative" use of the leader's power - a harasser, a "clown," a lesson "buster" - leading to dangerous and forbidden behaviors, such as pranks, on the verge of forbidden acts, risk-taking, and wild behavior. The transition from a positive to negative leader is sometimes fast and incomprehensible to the child and milieu, and conceals aspects of the child hidden from himself, such as anxieties and the complex, threatened self-image. Sometimes, the fear of losing the only positive center stage leads these children to making decisions that are dangerous to them and their surroundings. In this way, strength sometimes becomes a breaking and risk point, and so on and so forth.

2.

Social Learning Disability With a Developmental Approach ("Self Theory")

Theories about the development of the self as a central element in a person's life and mental health appeared in the second half of the previous century. This field of knowledge has importance for the understanding of human beings - their development processes, as well as their difficulties and distresses. "Self Theory" by Heinz Kohut (1979) is a cornerstone and a breakthrough in the field. The "self" and positive self-worth as a developmental factor vital to a person's adjustment and thriving, have become part of the basic concepts for understanding the human psyche.

According to Kohut (1979), the sense of self-worth is the driving factor in a person's development, and the need to feel as one who has self-worth drives a person repeatedly until this sense is gained.

The sense of self-worth forms and develops through the environment, which already relates to the child from infancy. It is a process where the ability of the adult in the child's environment to form mutual relations builds the basis for the child's internalization of itself as a positive entity.

When the parent serves as a regulating and soothing agent

for the young child (the emotional regulation stage according to Greenspan (1993) at a stage where the latter is not yet capable of doing so (regulate and sooth) by itself, the child gradually develops a sense of **transmuting internalization** (Kohut, 1977). In this process, the child gradually develops its own ability to serve functions of soothing, regulation, and restoration of self-worth - functions that have been previously fulfilled for the child by the parent. Children with learning- attention- and concentration-disabilities often go through a negative process of transmuting internalization or difficulties in developing it, both due to the difficulty in soothing interaction with the parents out of their own difficulties (see chapter on early childhood) as well as the difficulties in executive function and working memory, which make the internalization of the process difficult.

Children's sense of self-worth is constructed via interaction with an adult who serves in the role termed by Kohut (1977) as "self-object." It is a close person who also serves in the role of the child's self, and assists it in calming down when upset and restores the "self" for the child when it is hurt or injured. When the child does not get a self-object as needed, a conceptualization of the world as a bad, hostile, unpleasant place develops and forms in the child. By contrast, when the experience is reassuring and containing, a positive worldview develops (similarly to the *Basic Trust*, as Erikson (1951) described it.)

During the entire course of development, the child needs an available "self-object," who will mirror containment, recognition and acceptance, make "sounds of wonder and enthusiasm" simultaneously with an ability to help and soothe. This is how the sense of self-worth forms and consolidates in children. The development and consolidation of the self, then, is greatly dependent on the quality of interaction between the child and the "self-object" and on the nature of the child's self-reflections as a result of these repeated encounters.

Conversations with parents and later on with pre-school and school teachers of children with learning- attention- and concentration-disabilities show how few are the moments of positive reflections compared to the multiplicity of "negative" reflections and lack of enthusiasm with the child's poor achievements - not to mention reflections having the nature of prohibition, anger, criticism, and more. The structure of a person's "self" provides three main abilities (Osterweil, 1995)

- The ability and need to be in contact with others and persist with this
- The ability and need to attain emotional regulation
- The ability to regulate and attain a sense of self-worth.
- These abilities are formed constantly and developmentally - first through the ways of relating existing between the child and the adult serving as self-object and later on - as part of the child's self-structure. When a person's "self" is constructed, it contains fixed activity patterns that repeat themselves. The structure of an individual's self according to Kohut (1979) is, then, a psychic (mental) structure that contains two poles inside it, with a mediating zone in the middle:

1. One extreme contains the ambitions, forming the part that aspires to experiences of accomplishment and success. These experiences develop through the appreciation and acknowledgment (wonder) received from the close environment. From the wonder and enthusiasm over being of value and unique, the child receives approvals of being what he or she is - positive and special (the individuation stage according to Mahler, 1975). The reflection and wonder that parents provide their child in response to an action or doing that has come from the child's own initiative, and not only out of a will to placate them, are the evidence for the child, of existing as a person who has value. This unique, repeated reflection given to the child by an adult who has value of a "self-object," provides the child with positive acknowledgment of his or her actions - they are his or hers, and are wanted. This is an essentially different experience from the reinforcements given to a child following an action the child has done (behavior shaping) out of a will to reinforce or extinguish it (reward and punishment). In this case, the motivation is external to the self. The reflection according to Kohut, returns a positive-unique value to the child for having chosen to act as he or she has acted.

It should be remembered that while positive reflection builds positive self-worth, negative reflection achieves the complete opposite. A child who is fortunate to receive positive reflections from the close environment and adults serving as a "self-object" derives additional developments from them, which gradually become a part of his or her "self."

How is the ability for the regulation of self-esteem formed? Just as the child requires positive reflections, he or she is also gradually exposed, to a certain extent, to failure. When the extent is balanced (quantity- and intensity-wise), the child develops the ability to take these failures without feeling destroyed and falling apart, without being completely dependent on the value reflected from the environment, by the "self-object" - but rather, adhering and staying close to one's self-worth, and an ability to stand one's own ground (assertiveness), which is neither exaggerated (grandiose) nor defensive (arrogant and condescending). Assertiveness, then, is the ability of the "self" to stand its ground - even when there is sometimes disagreement with the environment - and to remain feeling vital and valuable. This is the child's ability to regulate self-esteem.

When the child grows up in an environment that only reflects negation or criticism, and a criticizing and limiting "self-object" is internalized, a constant deprivation will develop, which the child will try to fill through receiving amazed approval from the environment. Instead of developing a self-ability, the child will develop into a person who is constantly occupied with listening outward - for the environment's reactions, for approval, for comparisons with others. There are children who, in this continued situation, will construct a defensive setup of arrogance and condescension over others. Despite outwardly projecting over-confidence, the origins of this confidence are actually the product of continued vulnerability and unregulated self-worth. Any small (real or imaginary) failure will cause such a large experience of failure that the child will react to it with criticism, vulnerability, anger, defensive aggression, rage, or disregard and contempt.

Another development is the ability to produce vitality, purposefulness, and persistence. Wonder and enthusiasm by a "self-object" (such as a parent) over the very production of initiatives and activities originating from the child, build an experience of vitality. By contrast, the absence of such wonder and enthusiasm causes the child to be dependent on formative evaluation that placates the parent's will. Such external appreciation, which does not pass through the transmuting internalization, deprives the child of the possibility of gaining vitality as part of the "self."

The emptiness that will or might befall the child, drives action only in the context of deceiving others, therefore it depletes psychic energy. The child has difficulty acting from within (intrinsically), and instead, acts out of reactivity to the environment. The child has difficulty persisting in activities intended to achieve his or her own goals (purposefulness), and will instead be occupied with placating others (lack of persistence). A child who has experienced a "self-object" who had faith in the former and his/her abilities will believe in their own "self," and that is why such a child is capable of persisting and acting toward the accomplishment of self-set goals. This child has inner vitality that fuels efforts, and overcomes frustration in order to actualize the "self." On the other child, a "false" fake "self" might be formed here, which is entirely charged up by the environment's reactions and devoid of contact with the inner truth. The development of ambitions is tangential to the autonomic and phallic periods of life and continues into the Oedipal stage as well. Children who are in these stages of development are engaged in a variety of actions and interactions with their environment and construct their set of ambitions according to their strengths and abilities.

2. A second extreme in the "self" structure is the one that concerns the development of values and ideals. The sense of value is that sense of appreciation experienced by the child in the continued contact with a close and regarded figure (first the parent, and educators and others later on). For the child, the very fact of being associated with a valued figure **provides him/her with a sense of his or her own value.** In a process of transmuting internalization, the child operates and constructs an idealization (over-evaluation and accentuation of only the positive sides and in an enhanced manner) of this figure. This value and idealization are two components of the child's "self" pole, and they gradually enable, through transmuting internalization processes, the construction of processes of **self-regulation, self-control, and commitment.**

Self-regulation is formed in the merging process that the child experiences with the caregiving parent. Out of the merging, the ability to self-soothe is formed (similar processes are described by Mahler, 1975, when discussing the concept of symbiosis; Greenspan, 1992, when discussing the stage of the parent as a regulating figure that builds the regulation of the child "self"; and Ainsworth, 1963, with the concept of attachment.) Feeling threatened by drives, anxieties or lack of balance, the child experiences the parent's calming being when hugging (merging) with the valued and admired parent. Later on in the child's life, the internalization of the soothing parent will become an experience, an ability for self-regulation.

One can assume, then, to what a great extent such an experience is sometimes missing for children with learning- attention- and concentration-disabilities. From the outset, it is difficult to provide them with an experience of calm due to innate difficulties. However, even when this is reached, the limited ability for transmuting internalization (due to memory and conservation difficulties) leaves them without the inner personal ability.

Self-control is the ability that forms in the child to maintain the self-soothing even in situations of especially intense arousal. The toddler experiences a deep connection with an admired and ideal parental figure, which provides an experience of control through supporting and limiting - controlling drives and channeling them to permitted processes (sublimative according to the values of the environment in which the child lives). This parent not only enables the child to conserve processes of self-soothing, but also an experience of self-control vis-a-vis powerful, intense sensations arising from within. These abilities enable the child to gradually detach from complete dependence on the parents as focal points of help and regulation and grow an inner ability arising from the "self, i.e., becoming self-reliant." Children who have not experienced these processes in full, due to their own disability or deficient parental functioning, are subject to long periods of unregulated frustrating experiences, leading to uncontrollable outbursts of rage, addictions to instant pleasures, and dangerous acts - despite their ability to afterward return to normal reality testing.

Commitment is the developing ability in the child to consistently feel that the things done and accomplished by him or her have value and meaning, the ability to share one's own things with others, because others believe in and are involved with him or her. Commitment is formed through the process of transmuting internalization experienced by the child in the relations with the parents, who demand persistent behaviors in goal achievement, even when difficulties appear. Hence, commitment too, is formed on the basis of normal parent-child relations, while normal neurological mechanisms are operated, enabling the existence and conservation of the transmuting internalization process.

The Twinship pole is a late addition in Kohut's (1977) work, where he describes the need to be close to a similar other, who will alleviate the loneliness and provide a sense of belonging. Twinship is a psychological experience formed while examining the similarities and differences between close people and magnifying the similarity for the sake of connection between them. From this place, Kohut identifies the child's early will to feel similar and close to the same-sex parent. Later on, during the separation and individuation stage, the desire to have this experience of Twinship with someone other than the parent-someone similar, of the same age, and with the company of similar people is revealed. Similar people means the group of belonging (peer group) that is so central in the lives of latency-aged children and youth.

Nofar-Yishai and Chen (2006) describe the sense of self-worth as a key motivator in human development. When the primary interaction between the child and its environment does not meet the needs of the "self" for structural-neurological reasons, innate or otherwise, the child might develop a sense of low self-worth accompanied by experiences of frustration, loneliness, inferiority, and rage. These feelings harm the child and are manifested by the child's adjustment and/or behavior difficulties, that fit in with the learning-attention- and concentration-difficulties. Learning- attention- and concentration-disabled children grow up in a familial and later educational reality, where they do not receive the reflection they need. Instead, there will in most cases be a statement that they are not succeeding in acting in an appropriate and accommodated manner, that they are disappointing, and very far from what is required of them. This negative reflection continues during their encounters with adults in educational systems as well, and later on, with their peers.

The difficulty does not only involve the reflection processes and inefficient transmuting internalization processes, but also inefficient merging processes. The child who bursts out in constant rage when faced with frustration or failure, responded to by a mature figure (parent/teacher) who does not represent the ideal adult needed, but instead, a weakened and frightened adult. An escalating cycle of lack of fit between the child's needs and the environment is created, which makes its own contribution to the continued damage to the self-construction processes, and both parties - the child and the environment - experience emotional and/or behavioral radicalization.

When a normal child experiences frustration at an intensity and frequency within its processing capability, the ability to supply the forces of regulation and coping for itself and by itself develops; however, when the frustration is at increased levels of intensity and frequency, much beyond the child's processing ability, and when the basic needs for constructing the "self" are not met, a continuous injury to the self-worth is created, coupled with severe reactions and behaviors:

- Narcissistic rage and anger outbursts
- A sense of helplessness
- Difficulty being criticized
- Difficulty accepting boundaries and limits
- Avoidance
- Persistence difficulties
- Rebelliousness and defiance
- Withdrawal, depression, and despair

When intensified by the other characteristics of the disability, these behaviors form a vicious cycle, both in the child's relations with the parents and family, as well as with teachers and peers.

Among the characteristics of the disability that participate in and interrupt normal learning and development of the children - in spite of normal developmental motivation - several factors can be listed, present at varying intensities and compositions in each child, but always present (partially or fully) in all these children, and which participate in the injury to the child's "self" and in his or her difficulty in acquiringe proper social behaviors:

1. Stormy temperament (children characterized by a "difficult" temperament belonging to this risk group from early childhood). These are children (see Chapter 1) who show difficulties in regulating their biological clocks and regulation difficulties in general and low intensities of stimuli perception, compared to an especially high reaction threshold. They tend to pounce on stimuli and lose interest quickly, suffer from attention difficulties, and any possible combination of sensory flooding (hyper-sensitivity) or hypo-sensitivity. They are characterized from infancy by difficult and prolonged adjustment processes to any environment and stimuli.

2. Slow-to-warm-up temperament. Different from the first group, these are children who in most cases have a low-perception threshold, and the intensity of their reaction is also slow and low. They are characterized by a tendency to avoid situations that are overwhelming with respect to stimuli and sensory information, and have difficulty keeping up with the pace of occurrences in their social environment.

3. Abnormal sensory-motor development and sensory-motor integration. These children have difficulty operating in the social environment, have movement organization problems, inefficient spatial orientation, a sensation that they are being touched whenever something moves in their vicinity - or alternatively - they have a tendency to touch others with unregulated force. They have difficulty fitting in with some of the physical activity that is typical of the beginning of social relations and show difficulty maintaining proper psychological "distance" from others (unknowingly too far or invasive). Their organization is slow or clumsy, their surroundings are sometimes untidy, and therefore, their integration is difficult or arouses difficulty in the other person.

Sensory hyper-sensitivity might also cause these children to recoil from densely packed areas of human contact, or to experience other people as attacking them, and to react with avoidance, escape, or aggression when the sensory touch is unpleasant or overwhelming for them.

4. Impaired lingual development. In this group all children whose (spoken) language is delayed, whether due to specific disabilities or sensory-motor difficulties in the speech area (mouth and its internal organs), can be included. This group additionally includes children with a spectrum of difficulties in the areas of auditory perception, sound discrimination, retrieval of talk, sentence organization, verbal regulation, and more. In most cases, these children suffer from difficulties in organizing and managing the

Inner Language as well, and that is why they tend to approach their friends in a behavioral manner and less and less in an accommodated verbal manner.

5. Perceptual difficulties (visual and auditory). Awareness of auditory and/or visual cues, or both together, is a key focal point in understanding social communication and behavior. A difficulty in discerning between tones, sections, music of an approach and more, can lead the child to great confusion regarding the meaning of what is being said to him or her during social interaction. Difficulties in deciphering visual cues of gestures, mimics, and body language also contribute their share to the formation of social difficulty due to the inability to recognize, understand, and act according to accepted social codes.
Children with auditory sensitivity, for instance, cannot stay in an environment that is noisy and overwhelming; they tend to evade or avoid or react with defensive aggression to the difficulty of coping with the load that overwhelms them.

6. Spatial-orientation difficulties, motor planning, and directionality. These children often find themselves bumping into others or into objects, stepping over others, or experiencing others as stepping over them. They become lost in the space where the social activity takes place. Their movement is in most cases clumsy and it is hard to be around them in a defined space.

7. Non-verbal learning disability. These children have

a wide spectrum of difficulties that cause them to misunderstand non-verbal communication. The difficulty in understanding the motives of others and acknowledging others as separate entities possessing their own wants, and difficulty in understanding the key idea in interpersonal communication are serious obstacles when dealing with interpersonal relations.

8. Difficulties in concentration, focusing, and regulation. These difficulties are burdensome for the child in the correct direction and channeling of the social path: choosing one focal point over a background of a multiplicity of stimuli; staying engaged with one activity for an adequate period of time; withstanding frustration due to waiting, arguing or conflict; showing flexibility vis-a-vis the other's will. The child is easily distracted due to being overwhelmed by internal stimuli and temptations.

9. Difficulties related to the emotional experience of inferiority and low self-image. This emotional experience is the product of emotional, academic, and behavioral failures, causing the child to seek compensation in the social world and leading them to act with a an overly high level of sensitivity and vulnerability.

10. Difficulties in executive function and working memory. These types of difficulties make the majority of those who have them, act from a feeling of emotional overwhelm in the social field, but without a planning

and delaying ability. Such individuals have no ability to learn a lesson from previous mistakes and mainly, have no ability to make efficient transfer from normal understanding to performance that fits. Instead, a widening gap opens between understanding (mostly after the fact) and performance, which is controlled by other sources such as impulse, vulnerability, motivation to belong, and more. This gap causes the development of guilt feelings, and later on, covert depression that may intensify into overt depression. Many times, the struggle with difficult feelings shifts on a continuum between hyperactivity (ventilation of the difficult feeling), aggressiveness (mainly defensive, to remove the distress and its sources), and withdrawal and avoidance.

These difficulties appear in varying compositions in all children suffering from learning-attention- and concentration-disabilities and make them "warriors" who are all the time at the front, on a daily struggle, hour by hour. The gap between the normal need and the inability to realize it makes most of them vulnerable, scarred, and reacting to the pain in a manner that only moves them away from the chances of integration.

3.

An Escalating Cycle of Relations With Adults

A learning- attention- and concentration-disabled child who shows his or her difficulties in front of parents and/or educators often arouses in them restlessness of their own. A male or female educator who struggles over their place in the classroom, sometimes finds themselves drawn into the storm or withdrawal demonstrated by the learning- and attention-disabled child. In such a situation, the attempt to set limits and restrain the child, or make functioning demands of the child, is done, not out of a containing, restrained, controlling, and balanced standpoint, but rather from a standpoint of threat, helplessness, and anger of the adult who feels he or she has failed in dealing with the child. An optimal situation is when the teacher sets himself or herself as an ideal figure, which enables transmuting internalization of regulation, restraint or doing processes. However, when the adult is far from the ideal figure, because of the feeling of helplessness aroused by the child in the situation, or due to an inability to understand the origins of the disability (and instead of this there is an "educational-therapeutic" interpretation of an undisciplined child, lacking habits, rude and more), the adult also loses control and increases the child's helplessness and lack of control.

This escalating relations-cycle poses a complex challenge for the education system. Setting up a specific intervention plan by this or the other professional, who acts with detachment from the total functional and social world of the child, is not sufficient. Instead of this, systemic teamwork is required, in which all adults participate, each from their own position, and serve as ideal figures, "social remedial teaching teachers" as a central or associated topic in their educational practice.

The division of work in the team necessitates the development of knowledge, insights, and uniform language regarding the source of the child's difficulties and intervention methods. The prolonged dependence of learning- and attention-disabled children on the model set by various adults - those who intervene in, assist with, or exacerbate their difficulties - becomes critical at the school. The intervention plan and methods of helping children who suffer from social disability are varied and are on a wide continuum of individual and group treatments integrating body and mind or only dealing with one of these. Each approach has its advantages and disadvantages, and each of the treatments can achieve different aspects of advancement. The majority of treatment modalities lack a critical aspect - teaching social skills in a direct and intentional manner, which deconstructs the sequence of interactive, multi-area occurrences typical of social contact, gradually building a toolbox for dealing with this complex playing field.

Social-remedial (corrective) teaching with a systemic approach is an educational-therapeutic approach that deems it necessary to act in the social context as the focal point of intervention, simultaneously or separately, parallel to or in combination with the therapeutic needs shown by each child.

This approach combines aspects from various fields: from the field of academic remedial teaching, through the field of group therapy (psychological or expressive therapy) to specific and unique principles of intervention in social life. The systemic intervention is done simultaneously in each child's natural environment (pre-school, classroom, during recess) and in a therapeutic environment oriented for this purpose. The treatment service providers are the educators present in each child's life, alongside specific therapists who have or will train themselves for this purpose.

Pre-school teachers, schoolteachers, and recreational hobby class and youth movement instructors can all be leading elements in this approach, if and when they train themselves for this, alongside therapists from the mental health field who are equipped with their diverse toolbox. The joining of forces with a systemic perspective is critical in order to assist the child to transfer the experiences from the protected field (therapy room) to real life (the pre-school and classroom, the yard, and the hobby course). Continued and daily meeting of the children with significant socialization agents who speak the same "therapeutic language" enables empowerment of the program and greatly increases the chances of change and their assimilation over time, across various situations. Mobilizing parents to learn this language (through the approach of "parenthood with remedial teaching"- see next chapter) enables the cooperation of all the agents (adults) surrounding the child or teenager.

Social-remedial (corrective) teaching is predicated on the basic principles (see detailed description later on) with their flexibility and accommodation to the nature of the situation - to the child's various types of difficulties and to the adult involved (personality and specific role with regard to the child). Social remedial teaching, then, includes simultaneous intervention in a variety of life situations and social situations, while adhering to the awareness of the adult's role as a socialization agent: The adult serves as an ideal figure for constructing positive self-worth in a variety of situations.

Learning socialization is a difficult task from many respects: It takes place every day, all day long, in various contexts - at home with parents and siblings, in the neighborhood (on the playground, casual encounters), in nightspots (mainly during adolescence), in the pre-school or school classroom, in the yard during recess, in youth movements, or in some hobby course.

4.

Social Remedial (Corrective)
Teaching– Basic Principles

Every social situation, whether spontaneous or planned, necessitates the adult present in it to act according to five basic principles. These principles create an environmental-educational reality that is accommodated to the child's disability and improve qualities of social interaction.

By means of these principles, the various adults in the child's environment can construct a significant circle of relating for building positive self-worth - in the context of the functional and behavioral life and in the relations with family members, peers, or other significant adults. These five principles simultaneously serve in the process of constructing social remedial teaching, as well as basic principles for parenthood with remedial teaching (see next chapter).

The working assumption is that when the child speaks "disabilityese", he or she fails in implementing legitimate needs, drives, or wants that are expressive of the child's "self." To be able to express them in a normative manner, the child must receive continued, present, and available assistance. Effective intervention of the adult who intends to change the child's ways of acting and reacting, is based on the following principles:

A. Protective Presence

Learning- attention- and concentration-disabled children often find themselves having difficulty restraining, regulating, or planning their actions with respect to a desired goal. With neurological competence, the process of adjusting an overt behavior is enabled by the normal operation of structural components . These components include the Executive Function serving as a guide; an "Inner Language" - enabling construction of scenarios, and modifying them as necessary; regulation of drives and converting them to verbal expression tools, as a way of coping with difficulties along the way; motor planning and organization suited to the wish in the child's focus of interest; capabilities of persistence and adherence to a goal, without distraction or quick switching of focal point of interest; good distinction between the main and secondary points in a situation; deciphering verbal and non-verbal codes as expressing the other's reaction, and more.

When neurological competence does not exist (or is not efficient enough, according to the depth of the damage), an external responsible body is required that will "work" in the child's service on the way to social behavior. This body is the significant adult present during the entire duration of the situation and whose presence enables the provision of a response for a variety of missing functions. That being the case, "protective presence" is the first element in the program. The adult has an obligation of being continuously present while the child is involved in various activities. This presence provides the child protection with broad and varied aspects:

- The very presence provides an experience of protection and calming.

- The presence enables the adult "real-time" intervention or prior to this (see next section) and "on-the-go" correction of impulsive or other mistakes the child might make.

- The adult's presence can preserve the child's persistence and focus and bring the child back to the focal point whenever attention "slips away."

- A protective presence can ensure "verbal intervention," which the child lacks due to the verbal disability, and has preference for behavioral expression (a reaction that will cause disturbance and harm.)

- Protective presence exposes the child with the disability to a benevolent "self-object," who is present with an intensity that enables a type of "transmuting internalization." This process is made possible thanks to the adult's correct (regulated) reaction accommodated to the child's needs, as well as to the possibility given to the child to substitute memory, internalization, or information "retrieval" difficulties (in real time) with a concrete person who temporarily fulfills these functions.

Protective presence does not mean an adult who "sticks" to the child and prevents him or her from doing anything for himself or herself, but rather, an adult who is present and watches from a certain distance, comes back and gets closer as necessary, moves away when possible, but is always on protection alert to intervene again, before the next storm erupts or the next failure arises.

The external person is actually a substitute for the inefficient neurological functions, a good contact-figure, serving as a temporary substitute until the child succeeds in conserving it as an internal memory and using it as a memory-evoking cue, enabling accommodated reaction/behavior.

The ability of being, but not intervening unnecessarily is the complicated part of the assistance. The adult must have practice and training, on the one hand, and restraint and an ability to withstand emotional frustration, on the other. It often happens that the "protected" child feels pressurized, threatened or "not free" to act with the spontaneity that is typical of the disability, and dumps the anger on the "protecting" adult. The child will sometimes reject the adult as a test balloon for the issue of rejection ("Go away!" the child will tell the parent, while paradoxically requesting: "Don't go away, and show me you are not frightened by me and are not walking away because I told you, but rather staying and proving to me persistence, tolerance for frustration, and emotional caring." (See the final Chapter, "A Dictionary of Colloquial Disabilityese"). The adult's coping ability not only necessitates practice and withstanding of the emotional difficulty, but also psychological availability and disengagement from everything else for this specific purpose during substantial parts of the child's activity time. Often the claim arises that this disengagement and availability are an unrealistic resource in the life-load of parents, pre-school, or school teachers.

Tracking of the shared life with a learning- attention- and concentration-disabled child shows that the more the adult is missing, not present or unavailable (for justified reasons of load, being divided among many other needs, and more), the more the child will find his or her own techniques of "dragging" the adult to him or her. But being dragged takes up nearly the same time the adult would have devoted had he or she been in protective presence. This time it is under less beneficial conditions - as a reaction and not initiated by the adult, out of anger over the interrupted time and the inappropriate behavior - instead of with intentional emotional regulation that correctly contains the child (transmuting internalization with a negative, instead of positive and regulated reflection). The presence time into which the adult is dragged following the child's storm is no less than the initiated and protective presence time, but its quality and benefits are much less, and teach the child much less about the desirable pattern of interaction.

Time measurements that have been done in many families and/or by pre-school, and schoolteachers who have taken this initiative, show:

a. Protective presence time is no greater than the time required for after-the-fact remedial presence.

b. The quality of initiative is immensely better than that of the reaction.

c. The child's positive learning ability becomes much higher.

Therefore, with time and repetition, the child begins using the adult's cues and the need for the same extent of initial intensiveness declines.

B. Advance preparation

Learning- attention- and concentration-disabled children are always exposed to after-the-fact remedial interventions. These interventions occur after the error/damage/harm has been done and necessitate the child to learn about the undesirable behavior when already in a stormy emotional state, exposed over and over to the sense of failure and feelings of guilt.

"Backward learning" - from the effect to the cause - is much more difficult than "Forward learning," which deals with building a scenario from the cause to a possible effect - both cognitively and emotionally. "Forward learning" requires less attention resources, enables more efficient focusing, and "saves" the time wasted on the error and the outcomes of it.

Advance preparation, then, is a key principle in social remedial teaching. Advance preparation is the adult's ability to prevent the formation of the problem beforehand, to assist the child to choose, decide, and intend before-the-fact. In this manner, advance preparation builds the ability to delay before reacting, the ability to choose "smartly" before initiating something, and to predict success or failure before experiencing something in practice. When the child practices this approach an endless amount of times, he or she slowly makes it his or her own work strategy and adopts it as a social working tool. It is true that, due to the disabilities, much advance preparation is required in a variety of situations - places and people - for all the details to be constructed into a generalizing principle, from the child's perspective.

In addition, advance preparation serves as a preparatory means toward transition or change situations. As mentioned earlier, transition, change situations, or parting from one kind of activity and switching to another are accompanied by many difficulties in these children - like the difficulty to get organized for a new situation and an emotional difficulty (withstanding frustration). An unplanned transition intensifies the child's sense of lack of control and helplessness and the experience of emotional deprivation, and therefore, also the tendency to rebelliousness and insubordination. A transitional situation that has been prepared for in advance by guidance and short notice, gives the child a timeout for parting from a present situation and for getting organized, and thus, there is a rise in the sense of self-control and in the ability to a manage the transition autonomously. In this sense, advance preparation not only constructs for the child the plan that is missing so much, but also allows preparation time that is required because of the lack of flexibility.

C. Mediation and Verbalization

Mediation is a series of conscious actions possessing specific characteristics, presented by the adult to the child while the latter is dealing with the stimuli environment in which he or she is. According to Pnina Klein (1986, 2000), mediated learning is designed to prepare the child for new learning and to make the child more flexible for absorbing new information. What is meant by this is a series of planned actions performed to achieve a change in the child's clarity of perception, processing, and expression. It gradually builds in the child an awareness of the existence of various factors; encourages focusing on the most important of them; encourages observation and attention; and encourages intentional scanning and selection of stimuli that are the crux of the matter to which the mediating adult aspires to bring the child.

Through mediated learning, young children without disabilities achieve cognitive enrichment and development of abstract thinking spontaneously and in a way that increases the effectiveness of their encounter with any stimuli environment. By contrast, learning- attention- and concentration-disabled children need mediation over a long period of life and in different and varied situations: from daily functioning, transitions between different states, to higher thinking functions; and from choices of social focal points of interest to choices concerning academic occupation. Adopting the mediated approach as an effective tool in the interaction involved in social remedial teaching enables the learning- attention- and concentration-disabled child to enjoy a double assistance by the significant adult, in every situation. First, the adult focuses the child on the important stimulus, assists in choosing it, in focusing on it, in avoiding increased and disruptive distraction; and, secondly, assists in constructing the accommodated reaction and its correct ways of expression. In addition, regular intervention by way of mediation constructs in the child a gradual ability to self-mediate. It provides the child in a conscious, repetitive manner, an approach of mediation in various life and learning situations, and therefore, becomes a technique of social remedial teaching.

The more mediation is present and repeats itself in various life situations, the more the child gains - twice: accommodated behavior now and another layer in learning self-mediation in new situations in the future.

Verbalization is an extension of mediation through spoken language. Even when learning- attention- and concentration-disabled children are assisted in choosing and focusing, they still have difficulty organizing the relevant language follow-ing a feeling, a wish, an impulse, or an emotion they sense while focusing on the situation or on the specific stimulus. The higher their emotional arousal, the weaker their ability to focus for themselves the accommodated verbal reaction, and to describe their feelings with regard to the occurrence. As a result, a regression occurs in their functioning and they tend to express themselves in a "behavioral" manner. The absence of Inner Language (according to Barkely) as an essential component of planning that precedes the overt language, leaves them internally exposed to impulsive/emo-tional intensity and the only way to express it is with the early means of "behavioral language." In the functional and social interaction, behavioral reactions are experienced as a "behavior problem," both because they are inappropriate to the child's age and situation, and because there is an expec-tation that the child will advance to communicating with a "mature" language and because they are sometimes experi-enced as "violent," invasive, impolite, and more.

The status created by "behavioral speech" for the learning-attention- and concentration- disabled child, is of one who is disruptive, impolite, non-communicative - or worse still - aggressive and violent, invasive, and disrespectful of the other's boundaries. The more the intensity of behavioral speech is greater and more frequent, the more the child is labeled accordingly. The "language of behavior" is the "language of the disability," and the way of coping with it and enabling the child to achieve a change goes through **verbalization.** The adult who stands before the child and through the child's behavior recognizes the message the child wanted to convey, is now required to verbalize for the child what is happening, as a statement that expresses intention - not the intention of the overt behavior according to an interpretation that lacks understanding of the disability, but rather the child's original intention, as expressed by the behavior: "I understand that you were mad when Danny passed you, but you are not allowed to express this anger by shoving. You can tell him you are mad..."; You are allowed to be jumpy, you are not allowed to curse because of it. You can say you are jumpy or go to your room and let off steam by yelling..."

Obviously, elements such as hyperactivity and impulsivity, organizing and planning difficulties, lack of regulation, expressive difficulties, unclear speech, lingual disability, low-frustration threshold, high-reaction intensity, and more, intensify the difficulty and increase behavioral speech, but they oblige the adult to be restrained, set boundaries and limits, contain and verbalize all at once.

D. Monitoring

"A device used for observing, checking, or keeping a continuous record of something" - that is how monitoring is defined by the *Oxford Dictionary*. The device (monitor) needed by at-risk people is like the monitoring circuit installed for singers on stage, who can't hear the accompanying band and might be cut off from the synchronous context that is so necessary, so children with learning- attention- and concentration-disability need monitoring as well. And an instruction given to them at a certain point in time, even if it has passed through the barrier of attentional distraction (and not opposition to hearing and listening), even if it has been registered in the thicket of stimuli by which they are overwhelmed at any given moment (and not refusal to listen) - it is not sustained for long, because it cannot compete with the distracters. It is not sustained for long because of problems of persistence, focus, and lack of flexibility to disengage from one activity (sometimes favored, like sleeping or watching television or playing a computer game). It is also unavailable to the child due to difficulties in operating his or her Working Memory (and that is why the request is immediately "forgotten"). The presence of an adult, acting as a monitor, keeps the "demand" in the child's area of focal stimulation, externally conserving the instruction in a place where efficient inner conservation ability is missing.

Moreover, due to a low-frustration threshold, organization and transition difficulties, learning- attention- and concentration-disabled children tend to "put off" a task to another time they call "later." Problems with time perception as another characteristic of the disability extend the postponing to a prolonged period of time without limits and limitation. The children "awaken" to discover that the train has left without them again, when it is too late; that they have again not acted as required, have been late or delayed or have not carried out instruction. Derived from the disability, these failure experiences turn their lives into a continuous journey of failure → guilt → inferiority → depression. They are exposed to the continuous complaint of "lack of motivation," "lack of discipline," or "deaf on purpose," while their inner truth is that they are missing out, suffering from a lack of alertness, lack of focus, distractedness, low frustration threshold, and more.

The adults who claim that this problem becomes very much moderated with age, are right. The child even surprises with an ability to execute instructions when an arousing, motivational discovery is made with regard to a desirable task that has very desirable meaning. And indeed, **even in the harsh neurological reality of the disability, personal motivation is a disability-bypassing factor** - but not for long, and not as a factor that enables generalization to other situations. Moreover, the child's preparation for an event that bears great importance for him or her (going to a hobby course, to an outing, etc.) even if it is accurate in time - might encounter the problem of lack of flexibility when it is postponed or delayed or worse still - when it is suddenly canceled - which will drive him or her to react with a harsh behavior of frustration and lack of flexibility to accept and come to terms with what "there is not" now.

Even if the instruction has been registered and the child is preparing to carry it out, or has self-picked the desired reaction, the problem of continuity and persistence in the correct execution still exists. We sometimes spontaneously see an ability for correct choice and diversion from the current activity, but when this is required over time, due to the penetration of new stimuli or distracters in the child's activity field, the problem arises in its full severity.

That is why the existence of the adult, present as a monitor, provides the child with a safety zone; it is an external element that puts the child back on the right track whenever needed. The adult sends the child "clues" in real time regarding deviation and its correction. The absence of monitoring repeatedly exposes the child to the frustration involved in discovering a result after the fact, instead of thinking and planning prior to, and during the fact.

Through monitoring, as a supervising presence over time, the child acquires success in real time, alongside a strategy that is learned from the outside inward - from the adult to the child's inner world through transmuting internalization. A supervising adult with a significant connection with the child creates a double defense - both here and now and by learning self-monitoring for the future.

E. Feedback and Correction

The circle of relating that develops between the child and adult is dynamic and variable. A child who is fortunate enough to have the presence of an adult serve in the role of a positive "self-object," enabling transmuting internalization processes with regard to the child's functioning and construction of positive self-esteem, gains moments of satisfaction - wonder and enthusiasm - alongside correction and control moves. With time, the child needs the concrete presence less and less and can begin relying on the internalizations that have formed internally, in a multi-area manner and in different ways.

This diverse internalization makes it easier for the child when it is time to retrieve the inner presence via one of the strong channels, and be assisted by it as an element that independently directs the child's moves. In order for the process to gain power and momentum, the learning child needs continued reinforcement and guidance. This is enabled by the feedback cycle that forms between the child and the adult.

To a great extent, this stage can be viewed as a reconstruction of an earlier move that forms between a toddler and an adult in the period of constructing Separation and Individuation. Margret Mahler (1975) depicts an intermediate state between Symbiosis and Separation, which emphasizes the child's need to move away from, and get closer to the adult though the "fuelling" of the presence (Rapprochement). The young child, who has just recently established motor abilities that carry it some distance away from the parent, is momentarily frightened by the discovery of being alone in the world. The inner parent schema has not yet been established well enough to serve as a reassuring source, and out of the fright of lack of this schema, the child runs back to the parent, clings physically (holds onto the edges of the clothing or on to the body) or psychologically (with a glance, eye contact, or a word); "refuels" with the parent's concrete and calming presence; gains an exalted moment of the parent's "wonder and enthusiasm" (refueling /reflection: "You run so nicely…", "Well done for stopping on time…" and more); internalizes the parent and the wonder and enthusiasm - and is now fueled and can continue onward.

The learning-attention-and-concentration-disabled child sometimes finds itself moving away and becomes frightened - not finding a way to return to the parent - reacts with panic, or is forced to stop because of a forbidding or unenthusiastic parental demand, ("Stop running so fast, it's dangerous…!"; "How many times have I told you that if you carry on running like this, I will not go on an excursion with you…"), without ability of transmuting internalization. Therefore, the child will lack the parental presence and will be left with negative self-worth.

The rectification of the situation is possible not only with the aid of the four principles mentioned earlier, but also with the cycle of remedial feedback. By the significant adult's initiative, the child who has dared to start acting on its own gains approving and enthusiastic feedback, and from here, is helped by the adult to continue maintaining the ability-or alternatively, to replace the initiated act with a different behavior/reaction that is more suited to the varying situation. In this manner, the child simultaneously gains a variety of self-experiences, ability to make reactions more flexible according to the circumstances, gains the continued protection of the adult but from a more autonomous standpoint, and the construction of positive and autonomous self-worth based on protected experiencing. Gradually, the circles of autonomous distance will enlarge, the child's self-reactions will become more numerous, and they will be conserved by the adult's corrective feedback.

Summary of intervention principles:
1. Understanding the child and his or her motives
2. Awareness of the adult of the child's feelings
3. Providing the child with accurate interpretation
4. Five stages of **Social-Functional Remedial Teaching**

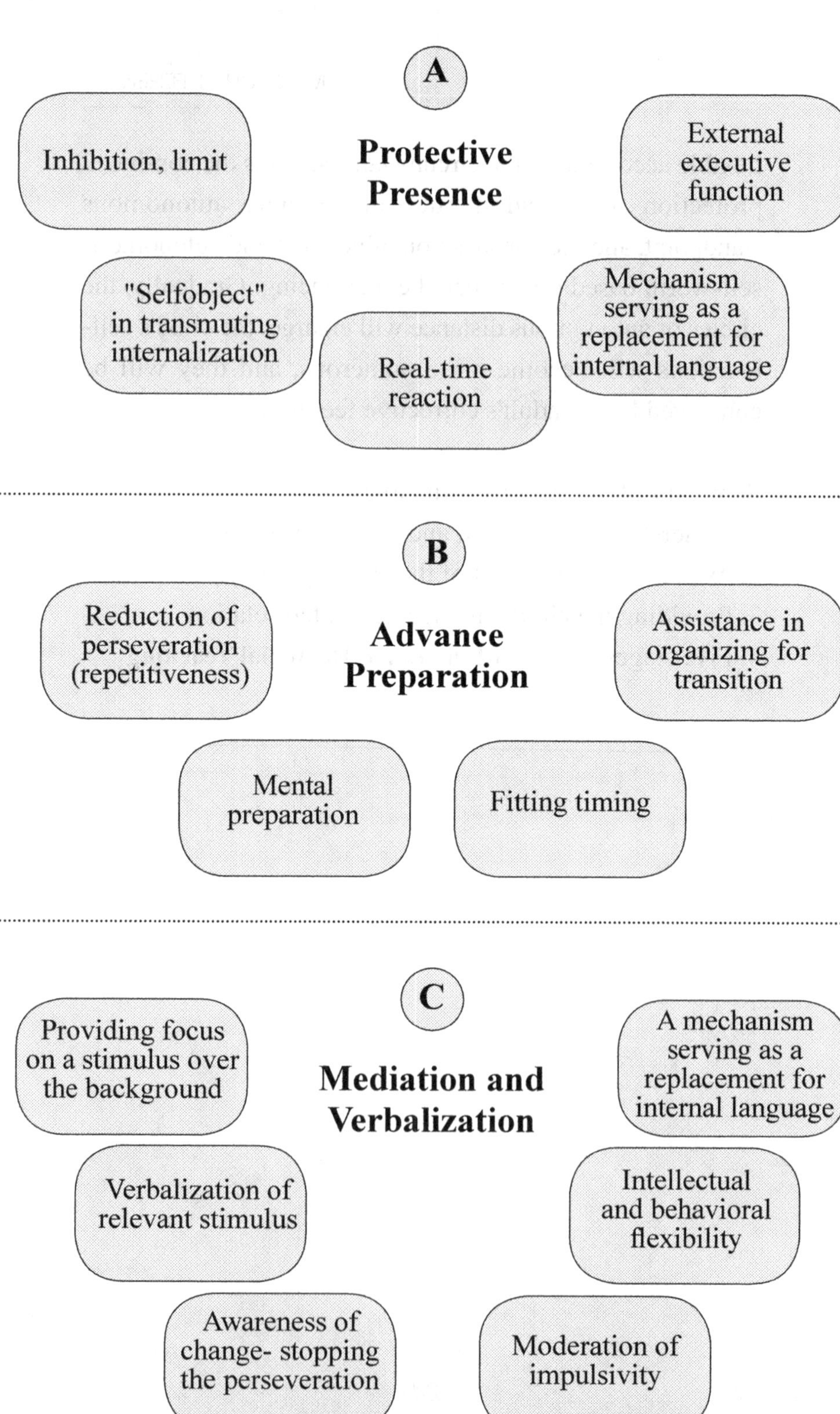
A
Protective Presence
Inhibition, limit
External executive function
"Selfobject" in transmuting internalization
Real-time reaction
Mechanism serving as a replacement for internal language
B
Advance Preparation
Reduction of perseveration (repetitiveness)
Assistance in organizing for transition
Mental preparation
Fitting timing
C
Mediation and Verbalization
Providing focus on a stimulus over the background
A mechanism serving as a replacement for internal language
Verbalization of relevant stimulus
Intellectual and behavioral flexibility
Awareness of change- stopping the perseveration
Moderation of impulsivity

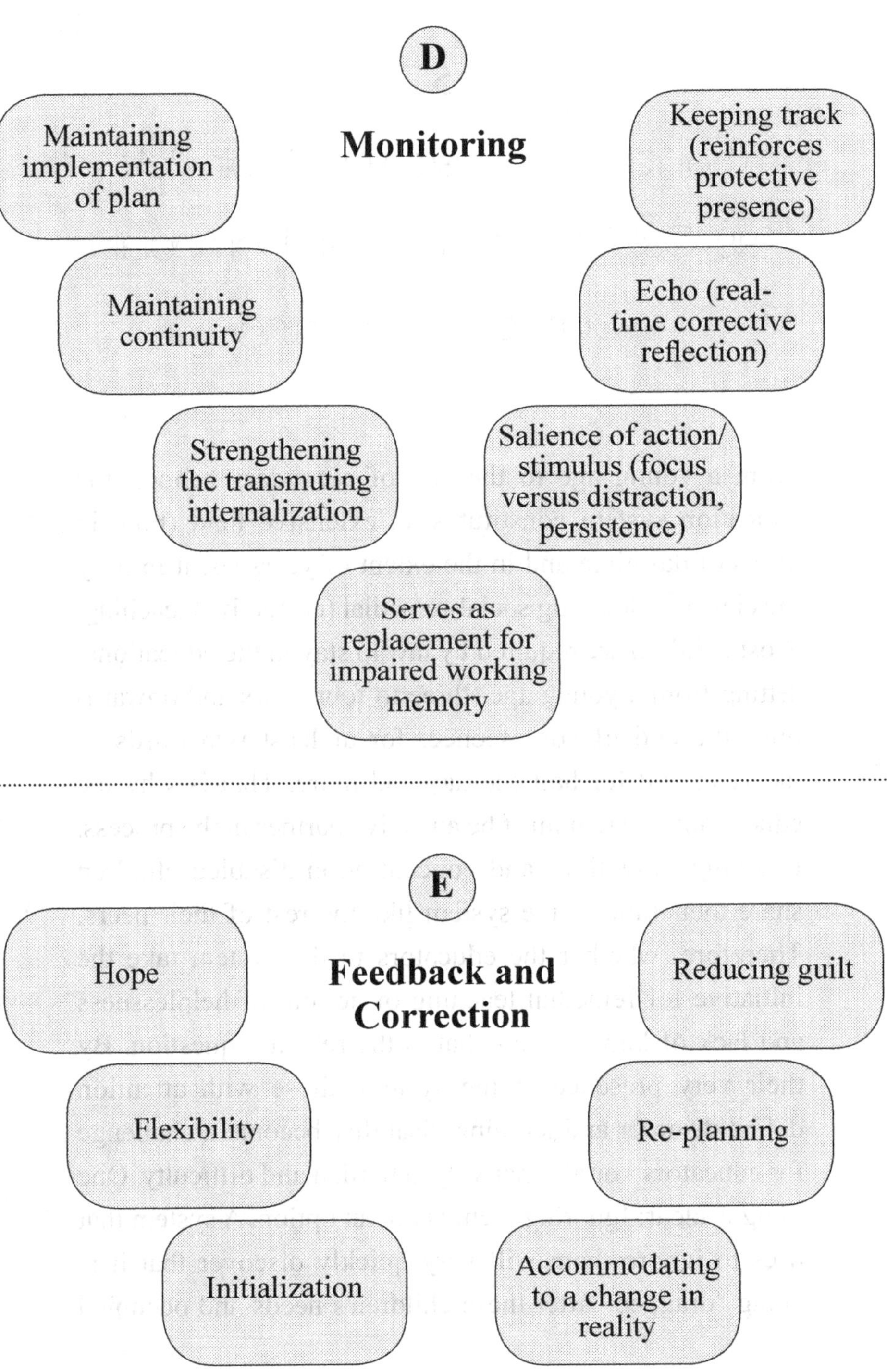

D
Monitoring
Maintaining implementation of plan
Maintaining continuity
Strengthening the transmuting internalization
Serves as replacement for impaired working memory
Keeping track (reinforces protective presence)
Echo (real-time corrective reflection)
Salience of action/stimulus (focus versus distraction, persistence)
E
Feedback and Correction
Hope
Flexibility
Initialization
Reducing guilt
Re-planning
Accommodating to a change in reality

5.

The Yard Teachers and Their Role as 'Self-object' in Social–Remedial (Corrective) Teaching

From a young age to the end of secondary school, the education system constitutes an extensive field (both in terms of day-time and in the extent of years spent in it by the child) for learning social-remedial (corrective) teaching. Most children are required by law to stay in the educational setting from a young age (three to four years and onward) until the end of adolescence, for at least two thirds of the year, and for half the day and more. That is why the educational system must be an active partner in the process. Learning- attention- and concentration-disabled children share their time in the system like the rest of their peers. Therefore, whether the educators in the system take the initiative for remedial teaching or act out of helplessness and lack of knowledge - that is the relevant question. By their very presence in the system, those with attention deficit disorder and learning disability become a challenge for educators - or alternatively, a burden and difficulty. One thing is clear: Ignoring them is not an option. A system that tries to ignore them will very quickly discover that it is being "dragged" after these children's needs and occupied with defensive reactions instead of constructive initiative. To respond to the children's needs in an initiated and goal-directed manner, a professional work force must be allocated and trained. The most effective social remedial teaching time during the school day is recess (as well as the transition times and the various corners inside the pre-school structure and yard). The problem is that in most cases this time remains abandoned without any oversight of educators, or alternatively, it is partially and inadequately supervised by people who are "strangers" to most of the children and cannot serve as an effective "self-object." While the formal lesson time is entrusted in the hands of a fixed person, who forms a significant relationship over a year and more, yard time is mostly covered only by casual teachers ("teacher duty"), who are not known and do not maintain significant relations with the majority of the children (except those few, who on the day of duty, know them as their class teacher or a regular teacher of some subject.)

Remedial (corrective) teaching by a casual adult who cannot serve as a significant "self-object" due to his or her basic characteristics, and in most cases even lacks the specific knowledge and skills required for social remedial teaching, does not achieve its goal. Sometimes the outcome of the encounter between this adult and a learning- attention- and concentration-disabled child is extremely destructive. The very responsibility imposed on the adult, of "solving" problems that arise in the interaction between the children, without familiarity and without any knowledge and skill, exposes the adult to the child's reaction spoken in "disabilityese (behavioral) language" and evokes difficult emotional reactions in the adult: helplessness, lack of control, aggression and anger over the child's behavior and sometimes even an experience of shame and insult ("How dare he speak to me that way…"; "What's with the curses he directs toward me?"; "He's got some nerve!" etc.) And thus, just when the child desperately needs an adult "self-object" who knows and understands, who is capable of providing social remedial teaching (and maybe even intervene according to the principle of advance preparation and reduce the duration of the problem)—the child experiences a stormy adult, who reacts in an escalating, instead of a calming and corrective manner.

Worse still, the teachers' duty comes at the expense of their own recess and rest, which they very much require. Therefore, their entry into duty is mixed with an emotional standpoint of unavailability and pressure. Such teachers not only lack the required knowledge and skills, but also lack the required psychological state.

The **"Yard Teachers"** can come from varied disciplines: education, therapy, physical education, non-formal education and more, as long as their presence during recess times will be the main area in their professional lives, for which they train themselves. In addition, they will be trained as "social-remedial (corrective) teaching" teachers, and will be skilled in providing this ability to the children who need it. The schoolyard is their main classroom and their presence there is fixed. The children arriving at the yard under various circumstances (recess, leaving the lesson, being expelled from the classroom) will always meet them. The constant and regular encounter of the children with these teachers enables them to be in a position of a significant "self-object." As such, they will enable the children to have transmuting internalization processes and the development of safe social strategies.

The Yard Teachers act on three levels simultaneously and thus can enable extensive coverage of the social needs in the education system.

A. **Fixed presence during recess** - in a predetermined territory (the concourse, the court/field, behind a certain structure, etc., each teacher and his/her own fixed territory.)

B. **Initiated presence during recess times** - for building activation areas on different days, to enable structured activity areas that give a response for sublimation and develop social skills (e.g., a boxing corner, box games, ball games, gardening, animal corner, and more.)
The fixed presence during recess enables Yard Teachers to be familiar with, and know in advance, who are the learning- attention- and concentration-disabled children who need them. With the aid of the teacher, these children will get social remedial teaching actions, while these are driven according to the five principles specified earlier. The child will be able to be get help from the teacher at the "before stage" to get organized in a manner suited to his

or her wants; and the child will receive accompaniment of mediation and verbalization, monitoring, and continuous feedback. The eruption of a problem - if and when it happens - will immediately get a real-time response - as opposed to a "postmortem analysis" done by an on-duty teacher who is not involved enough, alerted by the children after an event has occurred. The ability to assist a learning- attention- and concentration-disabled child after the fact is low, and in most cases requires referral to another, familiar figure (the personal educator), who has not been involved at all so far. In this way, an escalating cycle of "second-hand" after-the-fact intervention occurs, at a substantial distance from the time of occurrence, without an ability of correction in real time. As a fixed "self-object" in the child's life, the Yard Teacher is present in real time, builds a strategy "before" and corrects as necessary "during." In this way, social remedial teaching becomes a significant language in the **lives of all the children.** The presence of the Yard Teacher contributes to all the children at the school, to the social climate, and to the development of the social and moral language at the school.

The variety of pursuits and initiatives that can be brought by the Yard Teachers, enables different children to utilize recess time, sometimes even at the expense of certain lessons; and enables them to develop in various areas according to their abilities - areas of interest and strong capabilities (and not only be in areas of weakness and difficulty.)

A Yard Teacher who brings along physical activity, acting skills, connection with nature (plants or animals), artistic skills (plastic art, drama, etc.), extends the child's areas of pursuit within the framework of social life, and enables them to connect, each to an area of personal choice.

C. The Yard Teachers' Presence is Maintained During the Formal Lesson-time as Well - surely, the Yard Teachers' classroom remains the yard, but it absorbs learning- attention- and concentration-disabled children, who frequently find themselves getting out of the lesson (or being thrown out) while being hurt, in emotional turmoil, and have difficulty in regulating themselves (they have lost attention and concentration and gone out for some fresh air, have "interrupted" and been thrown out by the teacher as punishment or to get some air; or have lost control and have had an outburst and therefore have been sent away from the classroom to "cool off," and more.)

In a school without a Yard Teacher, such a child finds himself or herself in one of the difficult moments of the day. Best-case scenario, the child is left alone; worst case is that the child is rejected, lonely, and lacking self-regulation forces. Worse still, the child experiences an intensification of aggression due to the sense of insult experienced in the classroom. At this moment, more than ever, the child is in need of a skilled, regulating adult ("self-object") who knows how to act. The Yard Teacher now serves primarily as a "lightning and thunder absorber" and simultaneously processes (by means of his or her skills) the occurrence with the child and teaches the required and adapted behavior; the Yard Teacher constructs safety limits with the child under conditions of containment and guidance of the child's emotions and reactions. The child is no longer alone and not only receives help in real time, but also gets the construction of a coping strategy for future crisis events.

D. **The Yard Teachers as Talent Identifiers and Aptitude Routers** - many learning- attention- and concentration-disabled children possess high capabilities in their performance intelligence - as opposed to difficulties in the verbal part. The school lessons accentuate their difference and exceptionality, and do little to highlight their higher skills. Entrusted with social remedial teaching, the Yard Teachers can accelerate class, grade-wide, school-wide occurrences that intensify these capabilities - and not only the difficulties: competitions, championships, varied activities, responsibility for technical equipment, gardening, playing music, and decorating the school. In this way, they can turn the tables and give some of the children supremacy. A child who has had an opportunity to win a championship, put up a display, decorate the school, perform in a ceremony, etc., will experience - sometimes for the first time - public wonder and enthusiasm regarding his talents and capabilities, and for the first time will experience positive rather than negative self-worth. That wonder and enthusiasm, which is so missing since infancy, can serve as a first breaking out of the cycle of inferiority and guilt. Focused on creating such opportunities for breaking out, Yard Teachers sometimes act according to different priorities than those of the class teacher, and thus they gradually also become a significant

socialization agent in the educational integration of learn-
ing- attention- and concentration- disabled children.

257

6.

Group Social-remedial (Corrective) Teaching for Instilling Social Skills

The emotional, behavioral, and social distress of children and adolescents suffering from learning- attention- and concentration disability is well known today to all those involved in the matter (parents, educators, therapists). The ways of coping with these difficulties are based on varied theoretical and therapeutic conceptions, which interpret the disability's essence and sources in a different manner.

According to the conception presented in this book, the non-adaptive behavior of these children is only the overt facet/manifestation of the disability's wide, non-visible world, with its entire range of difficulties it arouses in a person from birth to maturity. Therefore, the search for assistance routes for the children is based on this comprehensive perspective.

In the recent decades, we have been witnessing the proliferation of conventional and unconventional therapeutic approaches, given by various service providers who come into contact with children suffering from learning- attention- and concentration-disabilities.

Among the various therapeutic approaches (of which only some have been researched in depth) are those originating from the medical professions (drug treatment); from the paramedical professions (body-mind treatments based on knowledge of physiotherapy, occupational therapy, and therapeutic exercise); from the fields of developing physical ability (self-defense, martial arts such as judo, karate and more); from Eastern doctrines; and from intensive teaching approaches, such as individual and group coaching for children and parents. Alongside these, approaches from the field of traditional psychotherapy (play therapy, verbal psychotherapy—individual and/or group); from the expressive therapy professions (art, music, drama therapy ,and more); and from cognitive-behavioral therapy are prevalent.

Various studies have tried to evaluate the effectiveness of the varied intervention programs, but the impression one gets is that the social side has not received special attention. The change in this area - if it occurs - is associated with preliminary therapeutic definitions, such as regulation ability, improving self-image, raising awareness of the disability's existence and implications, reinforcing desired behaviors and extinguishing disruptive behaviors, treating the experience of inferiority and feelings of failure, and more.

Only recently has an approach focused on providing social skills to children and adolescents with learning- attention- and concentration disability started to develop, and with it, the necessity of developing research tools for evaluating this approach, emerges (Biderman, 2007).

The need for developing a unique approach for developing social skills first emerged in unique educational and therapeutic settings, which viewed the specific social difficulty as a central and immanent facet of the disability, treatable mainly in a manner that is direct and focused on this goal. Moreover, the understanding of the disability as a neurological, multi-area occurrence along the child's total development, and during the time the child's relations with the parents and the human environment are constructed, has enabled the social facet to be conceptualized as a present, immanent part of the disability, and therefore necessitating focused intervention.

Other therapeutic techniques are based on the approach that views the therapeutic process in the protected room as a place for the child's growth and change, from which transfer to "real life" will be made. However, understanding the disability in its neurological contexts shows that transfer alone cannot be a change-generating factor among learning- attention- and concentration-disabled children, because **it necessitates a neurological competence which they lack.** These children need mediation and assistance bodies in real time during the transfer of the experience of change from the protected room to "real life." An assisting body is necessary in order to be capable of containing the change in life in real time.

A **social-remedial (corrective) teaching group** is built, then, on principles taken from several fundamental disciplines, enabling it to operate with tools that are essential for children with learning- attention- and concentration-disabilities.

A. The Therapeutic Approach

A social-remedial (corrective) teaching group is built on a combination of group play- therapy with principles of an activity group, and expressive therapy (plastic art, drama, dance and music) approaches. The content-related world of play or expressive activity, as well as additional social activities, is precisely the main toolbox of children at latency age and adolescence. The social world of children and adolescents is, for the most part, based on these activities, that are acquired from the mid-toddlerhood years, and become central from the age of six and above. The basic idea in this approach: using these tools is the opportunity to "train" and develop social language among learning- attention-and concentration-disabled children, as it is naturally present in the lives of their peers who do not have the disability. Through it, they will be able to maintain the longed-for contact and connection with them.

The language of play, like the language of expression and activity, is the expression tool customary in the social group that plays a major role in the psychological development of children and adolescents (see chapter on latency age and adolescence). The acquaintance with this language and the wish to use it exist in most disabled children, but what is missing is realization in practice. The ability to maintain the interaction rules is missing, therefore the children experience rejection and avoidance.

The introduction of tools from therapeutic languages such as art and drama, role-playing or cognitive clarifications, can be done by the therapists in addition to, and during the active process, to empower and vary the therapeutic process. A child who experiences an increasing ability to play box games (to choose, plan, invite partners to the game, to successfully withstand an experience of defeat or victory, restrain oneself from "cheating" in order to win at any cost, to avoid destroying because, "I haven't been invited," to initiate and dare to play with someone, to express one's own will, and so on and so forth) or engage in creative activity or social games, will gradually be able to transfer these abilities, acquired in the "safe room," to the playground in school or in the neighborhood, thanks to the similarity of the situations, processes, and required manner of functioning. Encountering emotional experiences in the schoolyard that are similar to the ones in the group, will be easier (or less difficult) to regulate and stop, thanks to the similar intensive experience in the therapy group. The joining of forces between a therapeutic group, a parent skilled in language (see next chapter) and a "Yard Teacher" at school (see previously) gives the child the ability to transfer the change from one situation to the other.

B. The Therapists' Functions

In most cases, a social-remedial (corrective) teaching group is led by **two therapists.**

The practical need for two also corresponds with the theoretical-therapeutic conception. What is the practical need? Learning- attention- and concentration-disabled children arrive at the group while being different from each other in terms of the disability's extent, difficulty levels, and temperament ranges: stormy - avoidant. The common denominators do not prevent the existence of individual differences, and they all share an experience of great vulnerability and high sensitivity level. The need to respond simultaneously to the variety of needs for social occurrence to take place puts a tremendous load on the therapist and a great degree of attention splitting. The obligation to serve as a significant "self-object" who can simultaneously contain and set limits, arouse daring, and regulate over-intensity, sometimes creates a difficult experience of duality in the therapist. The existence of two therapists is intended to provide a solution for the complexity of the situation and enable a variety of attitudes simultaneously.

The presence of two therapists not only enables children to experience accommodated and varied responsiveness, but also to be exposed to a dialogue (interaction) between two adults, which is an extremely important social situation for learning by modeling (and sometimes arouses among the children projection reactions that are related to their perception of their place in relation to their parents and siblings in the family).

The therapists' functions are:

- **Oversight and limit setting.** For the group to be conducted with an experience of a safe place for all participants, an intervention with an advance "contract" regarding the code of conduct - what is allowed and safe within the activity room, is required. A common problem in a therapy group is the reconstruction done by the children - of their natural place in the outside world. The aggressor comes with aggression, the victim with the experience of misery, the provocateur, with his/her repertoire, and the avoidant one, with the natural cringing. The reconstruction of roles without safety limits and oversight in real time might fixate the participants and prevent opportunities to experience new and varied interactions. The ability to act **at the time of the occurrence** provides the therapist with a variety of means for creating a physically and humanly safe environment. Additionally, the existence of limits, boundaries, and constant protection enable the children to acquire cues in real time, to adjust themselves to experience success and avoid the reconstruction of forbidden acts, which again arouse the experiences of reprimanding and guilt (the prevalent escalation cycle in their lives). Alternatively, they avoid withdrawing, avoidance, and cringing, which intensify the sense of self-imposed excommunication. **The ability to change direction, while feeling protected by the therapist, liberates the children to dare to change their roles, behavior and interaction.**

- **Containment and empathy**. While in the outside world, the majority of learning-attention- and concentration-disabled children experience a sense of being criticized, guilty, or ignored due to erroneous interpretation of their functioning motives. The group and group leaders facilitate change through empathy and containment processes - an experience of acceptance is created. I want to be who and how I am despite the difficulties I bring along with me. Experiencing unconditional acceptance in the group becomes a new, very powerful psychological occurrence for most children. The need to initially test and escalate forbidden reactions and behaviors to receive unconditional acceptance again, becomes a critical experience in the change process experienced by participants.

Containment and empathy are also achieved through the therapist's ability to correctly interpret the child's motives and verbalize them in the language of remedial teaching, in a manner that will accurately connect between **motivating emotion, overt behavior, and intention.** When the child feels the absence of judgment on one hand, the clarification of sources and motives of behavior on the other, and the ability to express oneself in an understood, different, and more socially and interpersonally acceptable manner, the door to inner change processes is opened. The therapist's containing and empathic presence illuminates a necessary aspect of their function as a significant "self-object" for the child, enabling the construction of transmuting internalization processes under conditions of wonder and enthusiasm, positive reflection/of who the child is - and not only of what he or she has done - good or bad.

- **Real-time reaction.** As discussed several times in this book, one of the difficulties in most of the intervention programs for learning- attention- and concentration-disabled children stems from the absence of a significant adult in real time. Therefore, an extensive part of social learning is done under "after-the-fact" conditions. The therapeutic group setting enables the therapists to address the difficulty as it happens, thus enabling the child to search for real-time change processes. An empathic limit set for the enraged child - bringing him back to the group only when another interaction approach is attempted by him, or accompanying group leader who encourages a withdrawing child to express even the smallest personal will or initiative - these provide the children with a safe environment for immediate changing during the occurrence. This is a critical condition for the existence of social remedial teaching, and it empowers the child's ability to experience transmuting internalization processes, restoration of the self-image, and receiving an enthusiastic reflection during, and not after performance.

Treating behavior in real time, without the need to retrieve past insights from memory, builds alertness to receiving cues from the other person in front of me, and enables the strengthening of awareness of the other - for children lacking this awareness (see Chapter 1: "Difficulties in Understanding the Other's 'Theory of Mind'") and for those having difficulty in reading non-verbal cues or in regulating themselves vis-a-vis the other person.

- **Implementing the five fundamentals of social-remedial (corrective) teaching.** The function of the social remedial teaching group leaders and therapists is all the time interwoven with the five fundamentals discussed previously. The ability to act with constant presence, prepare in advance, mediate and verbalize, provide monitoring experiences, and give feedback and correction all the time, makes this language the language of the treated children. Gradually these acquired strategies will operate out of the children's own self-control - and not only out of dependence on (the therapist's) external control. The construction of a group language network and prolonged experiencing of it (and if possible supported by additional significant adults outside the room, such as parents and educators) empower each participant's ability (according to personal pace) to acquire language and dare to use it in more and more situations.

C. The Therapeutic Setting and Process

1. Constructing the safe environment

The uniqueness of the social remedial teaching group is that each of its participants brings him or herself to the session as they are in daily life. The idea is to enable the children and adolescents to present themselves authentically - and not force them, from the first moment, to accommodate themselves to the session's requirements. In this way, the beginning of a safe process of acceptance and basic trust is formed, with real experiencing of constructing the desired change. In addition, creating the safety in the room with conditions as similar as possible to the natural environment (but more protected than it) later on assists the generalization process required from the child as he or she begins to generalize from the room to the natural environment.

Maintaining conditions - such as a fixed day and time, a fixed structure (building), equipped with playing and activity conditions, but also with a protective physical setting, a fixed space, fixed group leaders, and a fixed social composition - very much reduce the need to go through an experience of adjustment to the situation every time. It helps form a sense of continuity over the fixed background, and from it, leading to change as a main varying factor.

2. Manner of activity

To create a therapeutic environment that is as close as possible to the natural environment, the group operates according to the principle of **free and unstructured activity.** At the beginning of each session, a "collection" process takes place, where each child constructs their own initiative and will, both from the aspect of activity type and human composition. Negotiation (safe and protected by the therapists) takes place between the participants regarding their personal wants and initiatives, activity compositions (everybody together, alone, in a couple, with one of the therapists or without them), and the wanted materials. In this manner, the child experiences the restarting, management, and construction of the interaction each time anew, while maintaining conditions accommodated to both his or her needs and the therapy rules.

3. The open situation

The open situation is a close simulation of every social initiative the child is in need of in the outside world, whether it is reached as an initiator or a respondent. Moreover, the contentions, opposing wants and conflicts are possible as well, and are dealt with in real time, like all the other therapeutic processes. Rage outbursts, low frustration threshold, concession and avoidance, domination and power struggles - are all legitimate language as they occur in real life. The difference is in the presence accompanying the child during the difficulties, as well as during successes. It reinforces what is proper and tries to remove what is improper.

4. The group's structure and size

To create therapeutic environmental conditions that are as similar as possible to the children's natural environment, but enable an accommodated therapeutic intervention, the construction of a small group of children with a close developmental range is required. Therefore, an optimal group is one with 10 participants at maximum (suited to the size of the therapeutic space), composed of children close in age. This simulates a real peer group with development-dependent content and interest areas, as occurs in reality. The close-aged group importance is also in the possibility of providing the children with age-suited language and activity materials - exactly at the stage when verbal language has not yet been established and the language of play is easier and more accessible.

A group of this nature gradually enables the widening of interaction and breaking of loneliness outside the therapy room as well, and creates an opportunity for richer social lives for the children.

5. Duration of therapy-on-going groups

Committing to a therapy group without any predetermined duration might sabotage both the children and parents' motivation and daring to participate in it. Knowing that the disability is an innate, life-long phenomenon is difficult enough; therefore, the participants must be given hope that with correct intervention processes, abilities that bypass/overcome the disabilities can be developed. The duration of the group is limited in time (15-to-20 sessions), and thereby, the threat of total commitment is removed, alongside the space of time necessary for experiencing and achieving some change. Nevertheless, for some of the children, this time frame is but an initial taste, preliminary establishment and befriending of the processes required to generate change. Therefore the groups are defined as continuous workshops. The basic therapy cycle is 15-to-20 sessions long, containing the entire required therapeutic sequence (basic trust contract, familiarity with the language and participants, active participation and experiencing, feedback, summary and farewell). After it, the group reopens to extend itself for new participants - to a continuation contract for the "veterans" in need of it and separating from those concluding the program. This diverse range, protected by the experience of constancy for certain duration of time, enables modeling and flexibility similar to outside life and also accommodates the children's different levels of difficulty.

6. Parents' involvement

When children are referred to any kind of therapy whatsoever, the parents usually remain as a population **accompanying from outside.** The experience of the parent who waits outside is difficult and arouses complex emotional turmoil. There are few articles and books dealing with this issue and its characteristics (Bergman and Cohen, 1994).

In learning- attention- and concentration-disabled children, the problem of the parent accompanying from the outside is twice as difficult. The parent who is "inferior" compared to the therapists and group that are closed in a room, is foreclosed, as it were, from the process of change occurring "inside"; this is not an easy experience for the parent. On one hand, this experience does not benefit or contribute to the entire change process, and on the other hand, it is possible to provide the language of parental remedial teaching at the same time when the child is in the group. Concurrent work with the parents might substantially support and empower the child's change process.

Nevertheless, for some of the parents, the decision to mobilize themselves for an obligating therapeutic-guidance framework is not at all simple. Sometimes parents prefer to invest in the child, but find it difficult to invest in themselves. Therefore, the contact and connection between the children's group therapists and the children's parents might be complex and varying. Some parents accompany the process with only short touches (introductory session, evaluation session in the middle of a group, and conclusion and farewell session); some of them prefer entry into a parallel parental process designated solely for them with the group leaders, or with other group leaders who speak the "language"; and some are happy to join a **parent counseling group** that is learning parental remedial (corrective) teaching, parallel to their children.

In each of the options, fundamental therapy principles are maintained: The parents, like their children, need a containing therapeutic environment, but one that also provides knowledge, insights, and tools for coping with the children's disability. Sometimes parents need this because of suffering from a disability themselves; sometimes because of the emotional load that accompanies the very existence of the disability in the family; and in most cases - out of the difficulty of dealing with it on a day-to-day basis. An approach combining a supportive and empathic therapeutic environment with the provision of knowledge and tools and acquisition of the language of parental remedial teaching, gradually creates accommodated environments for the child - that empower the change processes.

CHAPTER THREE

"The Parental Voice" of Parents of Learning & AD(H)D Disabled Children

1.

The "Parental Voice" - Parents' Unique Language

Parenting is a multi-faceted occurrence. It has overt aspects of practical, care-giving behavior alongside covert-psychological aspects. The overt and covert develop simultaneously and affect each other. The constant meeting between them, between the concrete and psychological, that is the "parental voice" (Plotnik, 2007), dealt with in this chapter.

Understanding the "parental voice" requires a "musical ear" and a shared terminology common to all those involved, in order to be able to discern between the covert and overt, between expressive behavior and a concealed intention and motive.

"The parental voice" is a psychological and developmental occurrence that forms between a parent and child over the years the child is reared, and with each child anew. A parent of three children has three different "parental voices." Being one person, from one personal and cultural background, who shares life with another person, the three voices will probably be similar in certain components, but they will also be different from each other, either because of the different ages of the children, but mainly because each child "colors" the parent with colors unique to his or her personality structure and innate characteristics. The infant's temperament, its neurological and physical competence, its external appearance, gender, and later on, other overt traits - these construct an array of influences on the parent. Such an array is formed in a different manner than that of the child's preceding siblings or those who will be born after it.

Learning- attention- and concentration-disabled infants, possessing unique temperament characteristics and specific difficulties as a product of their disability, will probably arouse different voices in their parents compared to their normal siblings.

In most cases, parents speak two languages: the "maturese/ adultese," spoken language, (English, Spanish, French, and more) serving them in the variety of life functions and the "parentese" language. The "parentese" language is seemingly based on the "maturese/adultese" language. This is the same English, Spanish or French, but its meaning is different from "maturese/adultese." The ways of expression used by a parent to communicate with the environment regarding his or her child - with the various therapists, educators, and other parents - is not similar in its psychological essence to a "maturese/adultese" dialogue that would be held between them on any other topic. Many parents sometimes tend to speak "maturese/adultese" when intending to express parental needs, with the (conscious and unconscious) objective of disguising, concealing, and defending against the manifestation of the "parental voice." Many educators and therapists, who are not aware of the existence of the universal "parentese" language, tend to get confused between the two languages and continue speaking in "maturese/adultese" instead of "parentese," with the parents, thus often failing in their mission.

The "parental voice" is born and develops from four focal points of influence, on the continuum between two intersecting axes. The meeting between the four focal points constructs for each parent and each child, a unique "parental voice" and the specific shade in every developmental moment.

The four sources of the "parental voice" construct the psychic-psychological experience and the care-giving-concrete action simultaneously:

1. Developmental aspects in parenthood: a continuous journey between a parent and child - from the fantasy about the parenthood and child to the concrete parenthood and child.

2. Systemic and ecological aspects: "Who does the child belong to?" - the division of duties between the parents and educational and social systems.

3. Inter-generational transference: What have my parents handed down to me and what will I hand down to my children?

4. The parent as an individual: relations and struggles between the three structures of the self - the private self, the professional self, and the parental self.

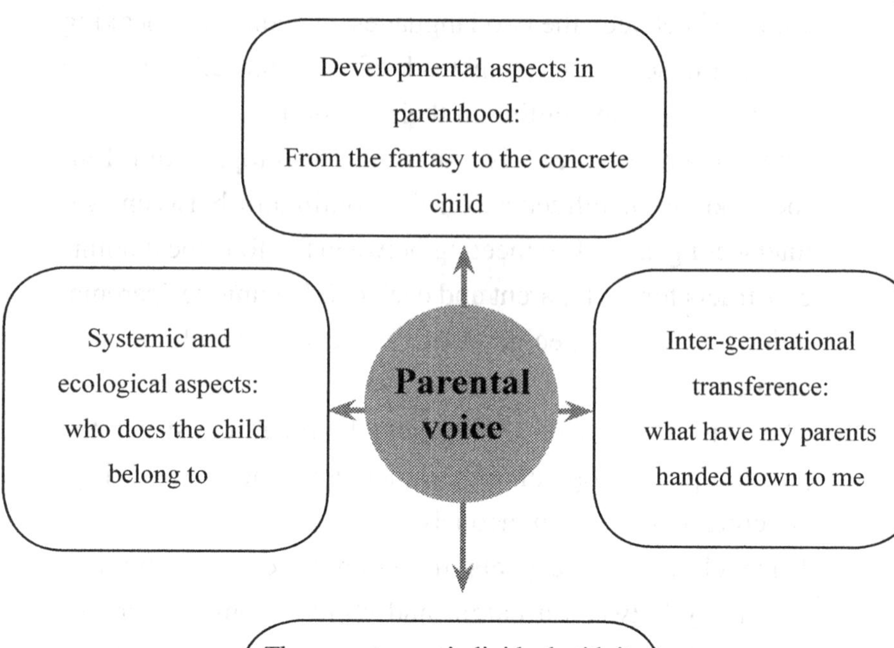

The presence of these four sources of influence in the overt parental act or in the covert "parental voice" varies all the time. Sometimes, an overlap exists between them, sometimes there is a match, and often conflict or concealment relations: One component intensifies in order to disguise the presence of another component.

In the parenting of children with learning- attention- and

concentration-disabilities, the reciprocal relations between the four components are essentially different from those in parenting a normal child. Nevertheless, in every family and in every parent-child relationship there are unique relations, characteristic only of them, without belonging to or resembling others.

2. Parenting Children
With Learning & AD(H)D Disabilities

Children suffering from learning- attention- and concentration-disabilities are seemingly ordinary children. Like all the infants in the world, infants that will be diagnosed as such, have also been born out of a "promise" and a prayer of a shared life with their parents, which is supposed to provide great happiness. Infants are not born with an instruction manual. Specific details about their inner essence are washed out with the placenta and from this moment onward, they and their parents have no choice but to grope their way to each other - to discover mutual characteristics together, to find and develop the unique bond that will accompany them in their shared journey.

When an infant is born, possessing neurological characteristics, which in the future will be defined as a learning- attention- and concentration-disability, it (the infant) "tells the story of its disability" only with functional and behavioral aspects, which in most cases are not perceived by the parents as an indication of its future difficulties. The parent will address the infant over a long time as an ordinary infant, while it sometimes is in need of other parenting. The gap between the overt and covert in the mutual encounter will receive interpretations that are painful for both parties and leave behind a heavy sediment of feelings of guilt, failure, inadequate parenthood, a disappointing child, and more.

This chapter will attempt to describe the formation of the "parental voice" of parents of these children, while addressing the unique processes the parents undergo while being exposed to and coping with their children's disability in different life periods.

The knowledge that in some of the families genetic transference exists, where one parent carries the disability and it is inherited by the child, often arouses additional difficulties and therefore necessitates additional reference.

The "parental voice" in general, and that which is unique to parents of learning- attention- and concentration disabled children, not only necessitates the understanding of the processes, but also their simultaneous translation in to the language of the disability. Just as parents speak the language of "parentese" and not "maturese/adultese," the parents of learning-attention- and concentration-disabled children must learn to speak a unique "parentese" language - the "language of disabilityese." To understand their child and provide assistance, they must acquire an additional language - the language of the disability. A learning-attention- and concentration-disabled child's motives of action and emotion are often different from those of a sibling or peer who does not have the disability, and misunderstanding often leads to error and harm. Therefore, it is necessary that the parent's insights concerning the disability's nature and ways of expression be expanded. The parent must understand how the disability forms a "language of disabilityese," which must be learned.

A parent of a child with learning- attention- and concentration-disabilities is therefore invited to **learn the language of the disability as an extension of parental language**, and from it, construct a unique approach of **"parental – remedial (corrective) teaching."**

"Parental remedial teaching" is a learned "parentese" language that simultaneously provides the parent with knowledge, understanding, and skills, and fits the child's needs according to age and developmental needs. Learning the language and the skills derived from it enables the parent to feel less helpless, less guilty, and more capable of coping with the child's needs at home with the siblings, with the friends outside, and in the school world. Parenting with a remedial teaching approach enables the parent to be an active partner in the change processes undergone by the child in the other focal points of life (pre-school, school, peer group - the gang), and thus contribute to the empowerment of the other interveners, and surround the child with significant adults ("self-objects"), serving as change and strengthening agents.

A. The Parental Work of Mourning

Upon the emergence of the infant into the world, the two parents, especially the mother, are left emptied out for a while. This emptying out, as a psychic experience accompanying the sense of physical emptying out is intended to enable the parents a momentary delay prior to transitioning from a waiting position to the position of being an actual parent. This transition does not occur in one moment, but rather, is spread out over a period - concurrently with the processes of acquaintance with and adjustment to the new infant, and the changing from an adult who is not a parent to a parent, or from a parent of one child to a parent of two, etc.

Prior to its birth and frequently even prior to its conception, every infant carries a "bag of tasks" - the bag constructed and designated for it by its parents, which in most cases is transferred as a set of expectations.

The decision to give birth to a child arouses various expectations in many parents concerning what they expect from the infant, from the interaction between them and their shared life with the infant. In most cases, parenthood is constructed as a response to a basic existential need of continuity and commemoration. By the time one reaches adulthood, every person is aware of one's limited time left on Earth, and most adults seek offspring who will continue their "enterprise" after they pass away. That is why children are born "equipped" with a "bag of tasks" - the decree of continuity established by their parents.

This "bag" is constructed, inter alia, to respond to the parents' needs, secret and overt wishes, and dreams and values concerning what is good and right in the world they live in.

Firstborn children are born with a bag that includes one major task: to provide their parents with the experience of parenthood for the first time, and therefore, their place in the parents' lives is significant and very valuable. Their siblings, born later, receive a bag concerned with "expanding the family" - to meet the need of the firstborn to have siblings - the experience of being a single child is avoided; there are males who are born so there will be a son after one or several daughters and there is a daughter who will be born to provide her parents with the experience of rearing a girl after having several boys. Many children are born for the sake of familial commemoration, filling in the void left by a dear, cherished family member's death; others are born to "compensate" for the loss of a child, or after having given birth to a child with special needs. There are "precious" children who are born to their parents after many long years of waiting.

The bag of wishes is accompanied by a complex psychological set of parental attitudes and expectations, and the need to realize them constructs a varied and rich array of expectations for each child.

In most cases, the birth of parenthood involves the construction of the (conscious or unconscious) fantasy about the newborn's "duty" and "tasks." The parental fantasy increasingly intensifies during the pregnancy period (the stage of preparation for parenthood) and is affected by many additional factors: cultural background, value system, family structure, socio-economic status, the person's personality, professional background, and more. These are joined nowadays by a set of influences from the media - via the world of written literature, and visual and electronic media. The myriad visual influences unconsciously construct our visual conception alongside the more complex life tasks, as they are shaped by the media. All these shape, to some degree, the universal expectation, but also the specific one of each parent in each family.

The initial encounter between a parent and the newborn child is therefore not only accompanied by an experience of emptying out, but also by the beginning of a long journey of parting from the fantasy, from the imagined infant (Refael-Leff, 1993), as constructed in the parent's mind during pregnancy and the preceding period, to befriending and accepting the concrete infant.

The information concerning the future, obtained about the embryo in its mother's womb can surely somewhat moderate the loss of the fantasy in the face of concrete information about the newborn's sex, size, etc., but this early information is still not enough to contain all the parameters by which the fantasy is shaped. Therefore, the need to part from the fantasy and befriend the concrete newborn is still one of the first parental tasks by which the "parental voice" is constructed.

During the first hours, days, and months of shared life, the parents go through a psychological journey, involving parting from the fantasy or parts of it and accepting the concrete child. The more the actual child is similar in its shape and traits to the imagined child, the easier the parents' work of befriending and accepting. The more it is revealed as distant and different, the more difficult, long, and complex the parental psychological work will be. The work of parting from the fantasy and gradual befriending of the concrete child is comparable to the psychological process of work of mourning. The more the actual child is similar to the fantasy child and the fantasy is realized, the shorter, smaller and easier to handle, the work of mourning will be. The larger the gap, the longer - the more difficult, the parent's psychological work will be.

In most cases, learning- and attention-disabled children not only cause their parents to deal with learning a difficult and complex parenthood, but also a difficult and prolonged work of mourning. Moreover, because the psychological process is not labeled as a journey of mourning and the discovery of the signs of the disability is accompanied by difficult, but undiagnosed feelings concerning the child's differentness, the psychological turmoil increases.

A slow-to-warm-up infant or one with a difficult temperament possessing regulation or sensory disorders arouses in its parents ups and downs in the parenting experience. In most cases, the conceptualization of the process of their getting closer and bonding does not include the definition of work of mourning, as actually happens in parents of children born with special needs - needs that are immediately visible and diagnosed (invalidism, disability, an overt syndrome, and more); therefore, the late discovery of parental distress among parents of children with learning- and attention-disabilities contributes to additional distress - such as a feelings of guilt, anxiety, and failure.

The parental work of mourning in the face of the manifestations of the gap between fantasy and the concrete child is not a one-time event in the lives of the parent and child. The more their shared developmental journey continues, the more the parental psychological world will open repeatedly to expectations and fantasies of correction, disappointment vis-a-vis the gap, to renewed stages in the work of mourning and renewed expectation of correction at the next stage. Over the entire course of the infant's development, and mainly toward each new and significant stage, a new fantasy will be constructed and a renewed work of mourning will be evoked - until the moment in which acceptance and reorganization regarding the concrete child occur, i.e., accommodation of parenting and expectations to the child.

| Stages in the Parental Work of Mourning

The parental work of mourning is a long psychological journey with several stages, traveling in quite a structured trajectory: from the receipt of the news through coping with its meaning, to the stage of renewed organization of life, and accommodating the expectations to the child. Every parent goes through the cycle of various stages - sometimes in sequential order and often while skipping stages and returning to them later - and sometimes (in abnormal work of mourning) while staying stuck in a certain stage for a prolonged time.

The "parental voice" is often saturated with mechanisms designed to express the specific stage in the work of mourning the parent is in. While struggling to understand the child and the unique needs - at the peak of the encounter between the parent's work of mourning and the child's needs, on the one hand, and the demands made by therapy and education bodies, on the other - tension and misunderstandings might often arise between the parent and other partners in the child's care. Therefore, familiarity with the work of mourning stages and the ways these are expressed in the "parental voice" is a joint obligation of therapists and educators who deal with these parents. The stages are as follows:

1. The stage of knowledge and shock.
2. The stage of "negative" emotional reactions: anger, aggression, rage.
3. Parental defense mechanisms: denial, projection/ throwing of blame, over-doing, "shopping escapade."
4. The stage of "positive" emotional reactions: crying, sadness, depression and sorrow.
5. The nostalgia stage: "flipping through the photo album"
6. Reorganization stage

Every family walks along the painful path in its unique way, and every parent shifts between being aware and unaware of the private work of mourning. The course of the parental work of mourning is influenced by a varied range of indices such as, whether this is the first child in the family, whether there are other family members suffering from the disability (and mainly whether one of the parents is characterized or diagnosed), the mental resources, familial resources (a support network of the extended family), the economic resources, the resilience of the couple relationship, each parent's private history in withstanding pressure and crisis, previous exceptional events in the family, and more.

It is the encounter between the discovery of the child's difficulties and the current state of the family that will give the coping actions a specific nature. The existence of additional families with children possessing similar difficulties can constitute a support network, as well as the environment's awareness - awareness of and help from educational and therapeutic systems.

Because the identification and treatment of children suffering from learning- attention-and concentration-disabilities is a dynamic process, taking place over at least two decades of the child's life, the families too, are in a process that recurs during various periods of rearing their child. An infant or toddler undergoing preliminary assessment at an early age forms a renewed set of expectations and fantasies concerning the results of early treatments and their effect on that child's continuation of development. The hope that forms - that with the intensiveness of the treatment, the child will reach the next stage of life while being "normal" and devoid of the disability - shatters anew when the parent realizes that the disability has an effect on the next stage as well. In this way, cycles of mourning processes are created, accompanied by processes of coping with and accepting the disability over and over again. In some of these, the awareness is clearer, some take place in more symbolic and covert ways, but they are always there.

1. The Stage of Knowledge and Shock

How do the parents come to know about the existence of the disability? How is it discovered and what is the connection between phenomena while rearing the child and the formal diagnosis? When did the diagnosis take place: during infancy or at later age? What is the disability's severity and what is its extent? The answers to these questions hold the difference in the way the news has been received, understood, internalized, and how the ways of coping with it have been organized.

Because the disability's overt characteristics (as already described in this book) are not immediately associated with its existence; in most cases the neurological disability remains invisible. For the same reason, the manner that formal discovery and diagnosis occurs is many times over more complex and complicated than diagnosing a syndrome that has a clear and visible physical presence (the existence of physiological characteristics and an ability of evaluation by medical parameters.)

Many parents describe their suspicions as soon as early infancy, in the face of an infant characterized by a difficult temperament, biological-regulation difficulties, delays in achievement of developmental (motor, linguistic) milestones, difficulties caused by medical problems - such as chronic ear infections, bronchitis, heightened sensory sensitivity, and more. However, in most cases their appeal for help will not be responded to according to the suspicion. Sometimes the appeal for help will cause them to experience unpleasant guilt ("If you are relaxed he will be relaxed")—

said to parents exhausted from dealing with an infant with a difficult temperament; "After the age of one the problem will work itself out and there will be no difficulty..."—said to parents of a baby with respiratory problems ; "Don't be so hysterical! No baby develops exactly by the book..." —said to a distressed mother who comes for help after having recognized that her child has not yet achieved motor achievements befitting his age; and many other examples. The lack of sufficient knowledge about the relationship between the early characteristics and those that appear at a later age; the achievement of developmental goals that occur in time ranges and not exact times; the absence of measurable and precise parameters for the complicated connection between the disability's early characteristics to characteristics at a later age - all these often enable the professional team accompanying parents to delay the diagnosis and decision, to leave under watch without a clear statement, or to even dismiss parental fears. These reactions enable worried, and sometimes even anxious and exhausted parents to choose deferral, denial, ignoring, and other ways of escape.

Other parents discover the suspicion following an appeal by a worried pre-school teacher who recognizes difficulty or differentness and asks for their help by suggesting a referral for diagnosis and evaluation. Sometimes a pre-school teacher's cautious request is enough to cause the fracture in the family unit. The parents' reactions to the pre-school teacher's appeal are varied and are sometimes characterized by directing anger toward her ("She doesn't know how to be a pre-school teacher..."; "She marked him from the beginning ..."; "She only wants easy children and ours is a little naughty"; "So what if his speech is not understood yet? My sister's son had the same thing and it worked out"). It is now the parents' turn to react to the suspicions. Each one will do this according to the early baggage they carry, even before the pre-school or school teacher has approached them.

When the pre-school teacher's suspicion corresponds with the parent's prolonged suspicions, the parent might be harnessed more easily. Other parents, due to shock and anxiety, will react by ignoring, or set out on an urgent journey of collecting evidence about the pre-school teacher and their child. They all have a common denominator: The initial knowledge breaks the fine balance that has been constructed in the family in general, and around the specific child, in particular. The very existence of an anomaly creates upheaval followed by a variety of reactions, the most common of which is - the reaction of shock - stopping, freezing, wanting not to move - and to wait and see what the day will bring. This pause is one of the most important among parents' reactions, because it enables (although short, but necessary) processing of the gap between the fantasy child and the real child. Surely a certain parting from the fantasy has already been formed at the initial stages of infancy; this has sometimes been a difficult and troubling gap, but knowing now that other people also see and share the sense of the gap is even more shocking. Some parents will pause to take a breath of relief: Finally someone else can see and join the struggle for treating the child's difficulties.

The duration and nature of the shock will be determined by the extent of the early familiarity the parents have today with the disability, its characteristics, the stereotypes they have been exposed to so far, the early attitudes they have developed regarding the disability and ways of treating it.

The shock reaction to the knowledge is a necessary and important reaction - even if it sometimes "robs" one of precious time devoted to turning to diagnosis/treatment, because it enables the parent to construct a maximum defense against the deep upheaval the discovery might evoke. On the other hand, for those who are already in the journey of suspicions, the shock makes room for a short recess and a feeling of "no longer alone" in the struggle. It should be mentioned that despite its importance and prevalence, the shock reaction is not present in the same degree of intensity in different parents. Some of them will skip it now and might return to it at a later stage.

2. The Stage of "Negative" Emotional Reactions (anger, aggression, rage)

Of all the stages - this stage of "negative" emotional reactions is the most present and felt stage in the relations between the parents and the educational and therapeutic environment; it is characterized by misunderstandings and "spoiling" of relations. When parents are blocked from the possibility of directing these emotions outward, they might often direct them toward each other (parent against parent) or toward the child (as "guilty" of the problem).

Even though they are considered to be "negative" reactions - anger, aggression and rage reactions - have a beneficial and important healing element in them; parents should be encouraged to experience these feelings as a promoting factor in the process of adjusting to life with a child possessing a learning- attention- and concentration-disability. When the parent gradually gets out of the sense of shock, a variety of feelings erupt within, focused on the experience of the loss of the fantasy. These feelings need a place to exit and be released - to be ventilated. Expressing anger or aggression has a releasing factor that takes out and discharges pressure and unease (a ventilation mechanism). This mechanism is vital in order to continue coping.

Sometimes anger, rage, and aggression constitute an unconscious way for the parent in pain to express the sense of helplessness vis-a-vis "what has fallen on her or him." In this way, the parent reacts to the understanding that the course of rearing this child will be different from that of the siblings or from the fantasy that has accompanied the child's formation. Moreover, sometimes the expression of these emotions is an attempt to "destroy" the "messenger" - the teacher, diagnostician, and therapist (like in the tale of Snow White, when the mirror tells the stepmother the truth: Her first reaction is to destroy the mirror…), if there is no messenger, then maybe there will be no message.

But more than anything, these emotional reactions express, to the fullest intensity and openly, the pain of the identification and diagnosis, the touching attempt to fight the message (like the little boy who views the thermometer as the source of the illness and therefore refuses to have his temperature taken).

When the teacher/therapist faces these reactions and understands their sources and what they are intended to express, they can serve as a container that contains the pain, a source of empathy for parental pain. Obviously, along with empathy, helping actions are often needed: setting limits to the expression of anger and limiting the parent's behavior to give him/her freedom of expression without causing any actual damage; but with these actions the teacher or therapist has not received any permission to judge the parent, his or her emotions and feelings.

When an encounter with an environment that allows and contains these difficult emotions is prevented from the parent, and the parent locks them up inside, there might be a deterioration in the ability to adjust to the new-found difficulty. Anger and rage are emotions that naturally burst out, like a great torrent of water confined within a mountain and looking for the opening. When the ability to express these feelings and let them out is absent, they burst inward: a parent toward himself/herself, or toward the other parent and/or the child identified with the difficulty. These outbursts are often at the basis of difficult parental-couple arguments and might cause the destruction of the couple relationship and family unit. Sometimes the direction of the parents' anger at each other reflects personal differences in the processes of adjusting to the difficulty diagnosed in the child, and instead of joining forces, the parents might find themselves in another or new battlefront: The couple relationship becomes weakened.

Statistics show that, because of the parenting difficulties among parents of learning-attention- and concentration-disabled children, the rate of divorce and separation is higher than in comparable families without such children. A dangerous opening forms here of the escalation of relations and a difficult feeling of guilt for the child who is identified as the generator of the fracture. When the anger is also directed toward the child himself, a double danger of hurting the child is formed - not only as one who suffers from the disability, but also as the one who has evoked the fracture in the family unit.

In many other families, however, where anger is experienced in a permitted and open manner and properly contained, the opposite process can be identified - the strengthening of the couple relationship and parental unification - a pulling together to treat the child and difficulties. The same crisis, which might cause upheaval in the couple relationship, can strengthen it in other cases - sometimes as a counter-alliance against the treating system and sometimes jointly with it.

Learning- attention- and concentration-disability is a syndrome that requires systemic, multi-area, and multi-disciplinary treatment (combining several experts simultaneously over a prolonged time). Assisting the parents in this process, including at the anger stage, can constitute a unifying familial factor instead of being a focal point that creates splits and increases upheaval.

In situations where the child's disability is characterized by aspects of impulsivity, hyperactivity, or defiant reaction, parental anger might also serve as a parental "force" reaction against the unrest created by the child - a sort of desperate attempt to forcefully calm the child down. However, clinical experience has shown that these power struggles are not beneficial, even though their sources are understood. It is necessary to assist the parent to express anger without directing it directly at the child and the child's disability.

The parent's place as a regulating factor for the child is also derived from the experience of the therapist being a regulating factor for the parent. An entire set of parallel relations exists here: container and contained (Bion, in Symington, 2006), which enable all those involved to express emotions safely, while being protected and contained, and thus releasing psychic energy essential for continuing to cope.

The child "learns" from the parent about ways of coping with the disability. The parent learns from the therapist, the child from the therapist, and so on and so forth.

3. Parental Defense Mechanisms: Denial, Projection/ Throwing of Blame, Over-doing, "Shopping Escapade."

The reaction to the knowledge that slowly permeates into every family unit, concerning their child as one who suffers from a learning- attention- and concentration-disability often arouses a deep inner need in parents to protect themselves and/or their child. This defense entails an attempt to protect the narcissistic parental origin, whereby the child is viewed as a sort of extension and reproduction of the parent (the child as possessing traits that reflect the parent as an ideal person). Therefore, any impairment in the child is experienced as an impairment in the parent. This impairment necessitates a "protective" process that prevents damage to the self-worth, and self-esteem, and enables the maintenance of psychological balance.

The defense mechanisms used by different parents are closely related to their perception of themselves, to their parenthood and the meaning given by them to their child's disability. In addition, such defense mechanisms are also related to the time that has elapsed from the moment of discovery until treatment has started and the prognosis given to previous resources existing in the family, to the manner the parents have "received the news," to their previous knowledge, and more. More than anything, the variety of mechanisms is indicative of the different need to cope with the discovery, and that in each family more than one mechanism is set in motion at any given moment; and that mechanisms sometimes change dynamically as the process of processing and coping occurs.

Attempts to deny the disability are immanently found in the disability's characteristics itself, and are often supported by various parties not identified with the parental and professional systems. The fact that personality traits can be attributed to the child instead of disability characteristics (laziness, disorganization, problems with motivation, behavior problem, improper upbringing etc.) is one of the more prevalent manifestations in the immediate interpretation of the disability and in the attempt to explain the sources of the difficulty as arising from the child's controllable characteristics. All these manifestations are indicative of the difficulty in connecting between the neurological disability, which is invisible, and its external, visible expressions. Often the way of connecting between the overt and covert erroneously passes through educational or clinical interpretations that skip over this essential stage of difficult identification.

When parents take this stand, of attributing the child's behavior to personality traits instead of to the disability characteristics, they might jeopardize their child's mental health, because the latter's difficulties are conceptualized as processes that can be controlled and directed (e.g., lack of motivation). All in all, they only demand of the child to "self-mobilize" to change behavior, and they completely disregard the objective part that cannot be self-controlled and necessitates specific help. The help will provide the child, as well as the parent with disability-accommodated coping methods. The denials might not only complicate the child's self-image ("If you will/want-you will be able"; "If there's a will there's a way"; "If you don't succeed, it's because you don't want"; etc.), but also greatly delay the structuring of the right therapeutic process.

The learning- and attention-disability is still being questioned publicly and is at the heart of the media debate; this only makes matters worse. Many parents are dragged into denial due to irresponsible publications in the media.

Moreover, the difficulty of the diagnosis itself often causes ambiguity, which at certain stages reinforces the denial of the problem at hand - being a permanent structural-brain disorder.

Projection/throwing of blame. This is often a direct continuation of the anger and rage reaction that has not been fully expressed. In its essence, blame projection /throwing is the parent's defensive reaction stemming from a need to search for an external explanation for the appearance of the disability "internally." The threatened parent tries to free self and parenthood from the painful process of "accepting responsibility" for the disability and acknowledging it as a permanent structural factor in their (parents and child) lives. Thus, parents sometimes project/throw the blame onto the educational system, which throws it back onto the parents, and so forth. To the same extent that the chances of improvement and change in the children afflicted with the syndrome necessitate a multi-party intervention, those involved can similarly turn it into a continued story of directing blame - at each other and to rolling the child into prolonged "divorce" experience between the treatment service providers; thus the child might experience the difficulty of all the significant adults to cooperate.

As mentioned, learning- attention- and concentration-disability is a syndrome that often necessitates a multiplicity of treatment service providers. The absence of agreement and good integration between them might create a tense therapeutic and counseling environment, where the service providers fight each other, and thus the child and parents fall between as victims in the war between providers. Therefore, despite being a built-in reaction, blame throwing/projection entails great danger. The parent who experiences blaming by someone else, more than anything, needs help to mobilize and contribute his or her share in the child's treatment. **The acknowledgment that the disability is not caused because of someone, but is innate and ever-present in the child's life, is a necessary condition for mobilization.** Blame throwing/projection often appears as a defense mechanism in the relations between two parents. There are those who search for the source of the disability in the other parent, whether because of the other's genetic background or because of educational disagreement between them."I keep telling her that because of her pity for him and her lenience she is spoiling him…", a father throws/projects blame on the mother. "Had he listened to me and done like me…our child would have been in a much better state. He sets impossible goals for him, bursts out at him whenever he has difficulty, accuses him of laziness and whining...and that's why the child is not even willing to try to cope," is how a mother describes her husband's fault, as she sees it, in worsening their child's difficulties.

The disability includes diverse elements that concern multiple life areas, and therefore also many treatment areas simultaneously. For this reason, many parents mobilize for **over doing** - treating physical, emotional, academic, behavioral and social needs all at once, with the help of a variety of experts and therapists.

The question of what to focus on and what to work on in

each period is purely a professional question; however, many diagnosticians submit the results of the diagnosis to parents, with all the variety of needs and required treatments, without any priority. Consequently, the parent who is now at the beginning of the emotional journey of the work of mourning might find him or herself not only in pain but also confused, and mainly, longing for the immediate treatment that will "eliminate" or greatly reduce the manifestations of the disability and enable the return to the fantasy—that "they will be able to get back the normal child "hiding" behind the disturbing disability.

Sometimes the journey between the multiplicity of treatments is an indication of a sense of panic. It sometimes exposes the parental difficulty to accept and reconcile with the disability's manifestations and the will to "eliminate it." Over-doing sometimes reflects a lack of parental knowledge and/or over-compliance with professional demands. It sometimes even expresses the experience of rejection evoked by the disability, hence the wish to separate the child from the disability. The problem is that the parent, who is pushed into this great deal of doing, quickly runs out of energy and resources. Worse still, the multiplicity of treatments reflects to the child—(negative reflection) how "damaged" he or she is and in need of such massive treatment in the repair "garage."

Therapists who do not confront their professional thinking with this danger and want the maximum for the child in every area, constitute a pushing, uncontrolled influential agent that weakens the parent.

Sometimes over-doing reflects positive intentions on the part of the parents themselves and their willingness for maximum mobilization, but they act without an accompanying authority that enables the construction of priorities. Eventually, the parent is left exhausted and disappointed in the face of over-investment and unsatisfactory results. The construction of treatment tracks necessitates a professional presence to manage the journey of considerations and decisions.

When no professional authority is present as case manager in the child and family's lives, one of the parents sometimes becomes the therapeutic authority. This parent builds the programs, but these are reflective of this parent's wishes and beliefs for accelerating the process and reducing the child's exposure to the environment as possessing a real disability. It should be mentioned that this mechanism, more than the others, often receives exclamations of admiration (enthusiasm and wonder) by various therapists, who do not see the whole picture and might reinforce this difficult and dangerous path. A parent who feels rewarded by therapists who are impressed by him/her, by the great investment and effort made, will have difficulty parting from the fantasy he or she has created - that maximizing the full range of moves could maybe turn back the wheel and restore the "fantasy child" who has been lost during the discovery and diagnosis. Moreover, the over-mobilized parent sometimes replaces the sense of lack of enthusiasm and wonder in relation to the child, with enthusiasm and wonder concerning their devoted parenthood, and then holds on to it as a substitute for the narcissistic injury caused by the child's disability. Over-doing is also a "good" way for those parents who, at the time the disability is discovered, experience a difficult sense of helplessness and anxiety.

The modern age enables one to go on a media journey, in which various therapeutic ideas are available and accessible - sometimes charlatan and irresponsible ones. The post-modern conceptions espousing values such as freedom of occupation, absence of agreements concerning right and wrong in our world, the following of Eastern cultures offering a harmonious world, as it were - etc., create a sense of confusion and overwhelm. This is a present and available basis for the parent to go on a **"shopping escapade"** in search of those treatments and therapists promising quick and absolute treatment of the disability.

Being at the peak of the emotional crisis and distressed by the shattering of the fantasy, parents might fall victim to all kinds of promises and ideas. The parent's regulation mechanisms are inadequate due to the upheaval, which has been, and is still being experienced.

The longing to find a quick way, promising the "disappearance" of the disability from the child and family's lives, is a temptation located deep within the work of mourning. The wish to "get up in the morning" and discover that my child is acting and functioning like a child without the disability - "like all children his age," without complaints, and is not exceptional - is an integral part of the work of mourning. The uncontrolled existence of promises through advertising and the media enables a hazardous and problematic encounter of the parents, searching for such a sort of defense mechanism.

Moreover, the absence of agreement nowadays concerning the supremacy of the world of science as opposed to the world of beliefs; the existence of opinions without the obligation of possessing knowledge as an accepted cultural-moral way; the overt fear of the supremacy of one type of knowing over the next (the need for shattering "holy cows") - these increase confusion and drive people to exercise the "right" to choose and decide. Surely the "shopping escapade" mechanism has already been a present need in the past, in the parental work of mourning, arising from a longing to obtain a new professional opinion that will contradict the findings of the previous painful opinion. However, when the abundance of experts represents contradictions in the ways the disability is understood and treated, and is sometimes based on beliefs and not on proven scientific information, an infrastructure is created, for therapeutic "fashions" marketed and given public relations via available and widespread media. Out of their injured inner worlds, many parents long for an alleviating cure and are exposed to every possible temptation. Often "success stories" in the written and electronic media arouse a sense of missing out and guilt in them, and create a stimulus for joining an endless journey of attempts, to find the "winning truth."

Thus, drug treatment that is often needed for achieving functional change in the child is often attacked. Long and gradual therapy processes are rejected in favor of short-term treatments. Books, articles, and non-professional media coverage encourage following wonder drugs and hazardous treatment methods. The legitimate disagreements between therapeutic approaches and therapists, and the legitimate skepticism existing in professional-scientific literature, only increase the market supply for the "shopping escapade." Thus the child and parent are prevented the opportunity of making the most of therapeutic processes that necessitate sustained consistency to achieve "proven" results.

4. The Stage of "Positive" Emotional Reactions: Crying, Sadness, Depression and Sorrow

Emotional reactions - like sadness, sorrow and sometimes even depression, are labeled as "positive" reactions here, in the face of the positive reverberation they receive from other people parents are surrounded by. By their nature, parents' expressions of sadness and sorrow enable an experience of empathy and sometimes even identification - mainly acceptance, containment and legitimization, which are so missing from many educators and therapists.

These emotional reactions are essential to the parent as a mechanism that enables the simultaneous expression of many emotional discomforts: giving up the fantasy, expression and release (ventilation) of the distress accompanying the loss of the fantasy, the pain in the face of knowing about the difficulties in store for the child and the parent, the ambiguity and fear of the unknown that the future holds, and mainly the continued difficulty in the long and arduous work of change. All these constitute an objective and subjective basis for the pain and sorrow reactions. Moreover, the prolonged effort and great investment by parents who accompany and care for their child, and the moments of frustration and disappointment from the actual difficulties caused by the disability to the child and other family members, make sorrow a permanent and present factor in their lives.

Caring for a child who suffers from the syndrome necessitates prolonged walking along an unpaved, and sometimes, unconventional road, including investing many resources (both psychological and economical) and relinquishing other wants. Having to deal with household members' reactions, especially the child's siblings, who often feel they are growing up in the disability's shadow, and sometimes even directly harmed by it—they are required to learn to make concessions, to show forbearance, to cope with the parents' relatively little involvement in their lives, due to being mobilized to help their sibling suffering from the disability - only increase these emotional reactions.

The expression of pain and sorrow causes a sense of upheaval and distress in many parents: How can one cry over the child and the child's difficulties? What will the others think and say about me? What am I reflecting to my child with my sorrow, i.e., what is my child's experience in the face of my distress - will my child's experience of guilt increase? Doesn't my sadness intensify my child's injury to self-worth and self-image?

For other parents, expressing sadness is a sign of weakness, which they avoid with all their might. There are those who fear a reaction of pity, and those who view the expression of these emotions as an overt and dangerous sign of admitting the existence of the disability and "surrendering" to it.

However, a parent who allows him or herself to express these emotions at the right degree, time, and place, sometimes discovers, surprisingly, that these emotions are liberating and enable benevolent freeing of coping forces arising from the expression of sorrow. Instead of a weakening, a strengthening comes. The parents are often surprised by the mobilization by others (therapists, educators, and family members) who witness the expressions of pain. Moreover, their expression of sorrow makes them more accessible to help than fighting the syndrome and others who speak of it. For the children of these parents too, an important emotional track is opened, enabling them to join the parent in their personal journey of mourning, thereby obtaining coping forces with less disruptive defense mechanisms.

However, sometimes the expression of sorrow increases parents' and family members' experience of shame and inferiority - the admittance that a "malfunction" exists in their lives. The avoidance of expressing these emotions stems from the parents' prolonged attempt to defend themselves and push away the parts within that accept the disability. This inner struggle between acceptance and rejection, between acknowledgment and denial, between pain and disregard, is an integral part of the parental work of mourning and has an essential role in the continuous process.

5. The Nostalgia Stage: "Flipping through the Photo Album"

The stage of flipping through the photo album is well known to us in the process undergone by people who are mourning for a deceased person. In a different and symbolic manner, this stage exists in the lives of parents of children suffering from learning- attention-and concentration-disability. Obviously, the parental work of mourning occurs simultaneously with the continuation of the practical parenting of that same child, therefore its presence in the parents' lives is in a representative, symbolic, and less concrete manner.

The nostalgia stage is sometimes expressed by an attempt to "keep the child" at regular educational settings, without any overt unique action, out of a will to continue feeling like a "regular child." This choice, of course, also stems from additional mourning processes, such as the defense mechanism of denying or disregarding the disability, but it also serves the nostalgic need. We hear an expression of this in the parents' words: "As long as he has friends, we will keep him here. When he will no longer be able to cope and the kids will recognize his differentness, then we will decide..." The feeling that the child's continued belonging to regular settings enables the concealment of the disability, is a prevalent parental conception, psychologically maintained by the nostalgia mechanism too.

Another expression of the nostalgia mechanism is inner immersion into the times of the child's young age and idealization of these, i.e., the time of the pre-discovery and diagnosis of the disability. Another way is empowering the child's talents in which the disability is not present, and presenting them by way of rationalization ("It doesn't matter that he wanders around outside a lot; He's an outdoor boy, and you can learn something there too…"; He's good in computers, and he will be a computer genius, even without studying in an orderly way…"; He is highly musical, and that is where his future will be, so he doesn't have to be bothered with other 'non-important' things now… "; "Many successful people didn't finish school, so what…" and more).

The stories in the media that often expose a disability in the history of successful people, who turned it into an advantage drag many parents to identify with the success story and to momentarily relinquish dealing with the problem. The ability to reconnect with the period of pre-discovery and diagnosis of the disability and from it conduct a mental leap into the child's unique future in the relatively strong areas, provides parents with recess periods. This is an essential stage of a sort of "warrior's rest," which gives strength for the continuation of the difficult, and sometimes exhausting journey.

6. Reorganization Stage

During this quite long stage, the family learns to organize its life, to set orders of priority and modes of action out of the acceptance of the disability as permanently present in their lives. It is not one stable and fixed episode, but a dynamic, changing, and evolving stage in the lives of all concerned.

The acceptance of the disability and ways of coping with it, both by the child and the parents, means learning to live with a degree of ambiguity and vagueness, with the definition of goals in the present, with the assimilation of new parenting patterns—but with constant expectation that change will come in the future.

The child's development and growth set new goals, taking into consideration both the maturation and change processes common to all children, and the accomplishments achieved thanks to interventions, treatments and the child and parents' new approaches. The reorganization stage closes a move each time, but also opens a new move, in which there are constant parts together with varying parts. This is where its power - but also weakness lies - as we will see next.

Parents who accept and assimilate the meaning of the disability and its characteristics in their child's life, are required to adjust to a dynamic life system. Frequent change is typical of any parenthood - children grow up, children are born, economic situations change along with family assets and other resources, parents' needs change, and more. In the same vein, the disability does too; it goes through changes in the ways it is expressed, in the extent of its presence and degree of influence on the child's adjustment. That being thecase, the reorganization stage contains a cyclical process of acceptance and adjustment, together with the construction of a new fantasy for later and renewed coping with the change, dictated by the child's natural growing up and changing, and so forth.

The importance of this stage in the family's life is

primarily in its acceptance followed by adapting unique and accommodated parenting methods (see the chapter "Parenting with Remedial (Corrective) Teaching"). The changes that occur over time in some of the disability's characteristics necessitate reorganization all the time: acquiring new parental habits and characteristics that are accommodated to the disability, age, and developmental needs.

The more the reorganization stage is positively present, and enables beneficial changes, the easier it is for parents to accept changes appearing developmentally and naturally, to re-examine themselves, to cope again with the work of mourning in the face of change in the child and environment, and to correctly arrive at the next organization stage.

A spiral course of ups and downs, forward and backward, is a more accurate description of the familial reality. Sometimes, the scenario does not take place in a uniform and constant sequence, but moves in leaps forward and backward between the various development stages. Parents can be in several stages simultaneously or discover a gap between them in the degree of coping with the disability. At this stage, parents can acquire and establish for themselves disability-accommodated parenting patterns, which will serve them on a regular basis; but concurrently, they must remain flexible and open in anticipation of the changes that are to come and the adjustments required.

Reorganization in the family has several focal points, and each family chooses to focus on that which is relevant to it:

- A different division of roles between the parents compared to the past.
- Retaining the existing division of roles while introducing new ways of realizing the parents' roles.
- Acquiring disability-accommodated parental skills.
- New utilization of all the family resources by a different division between the household members, such as parental time, economic resources, shared and separate habitation, daily schedule, shared and separate ways of recreation, changing contact and attachment patterns between children and parents, mutual help between siblings, the children's share in the running of the household and more. The accommodation of resources and skills is done out of the understanding of the disability in the child's daily life and accepting it in the various areas. Despite the initial investment required for this, an experience of adjustment shared by all household members is created, which frees resources in favor of new tasks later on.

Nevertheless, the pause required for the introduction of new parenting methods is a complex, threatening stage that requires investment. Many families have difficulty reaching these accomplishments at the beginning of the work of mourning because they lack the required knowledge. The work of mourning is a complex familial occurrence, at which each household member moves at his or her own pace; therefore, a lack of fit or uniformity is sometimes created between the various stages taking place within the various family members. The reorganization stage might reach each of the household members at different times, and a few of them will already be at the next stage of the prolonged work of mourning.

B. "The Parental Voice" - Characteristics of Parental Needs

As mentioned, the "parental voice" is the parents' language. The voice of parents of children with learning- attention- and concentration-disabilities is characterized by four specific needs, which have been described and studied by the important psychiatrist Gerald Caplan (Caplan, 1970) when describing the construction of consultation circles for parents and other educators and therapists.

According to Caplan, parents are "subject matter experts." They are experts on their child and his or her needs, but sometimes encounter difficulties necessitating the seeking of consultational help. According to other intervention and treatment approaches, the uniqueness of consultation is in that it acknowledges parents as experts on their child. Therefore, the parents' act of turning to another expert is done based on familiarity with their (the parents') own abilities, and with acknowledgement of their own distress, which for them, disrupts their ability to be good-enough parents for their child.

When a child is evaluated with learning- attention- and concentration-disability, parenthood takes a shaking. When we examine what parents need following the discovery and diagnosis of the child, we witness an ascending series of unique needs usually constructed one over the other. Meeting these needs makes parenthood better.

First and foremost, parents need new professional and parental knowledge, which assists them in knowing and understanding what their child's difficulties are, where these stem from, and how they are connected with the disability's overt and covert phenomena.

According to Caplan, this stage has been termed as the stage of coping with the **lack of knowledge.** Following the reception of knowledge, and the greater its importance becomes, the parents face the following discovery: They **lack skills** that enable them to put knowledge into practice correctly. Later in the journey, when parents are equipped with both knowledge and skills, they experience themselves as having difficulty acting objectively - **lack of objectivity** - toward their child. Even though in its essence, parenthood is not only an objective skill, but rather mainly a subjective attachment, the subjective experience might prevail in the parent. Various emotional reactions from the parent's past and present (experiences termed **intervening themes**) are aroused by the manifestations of the disability; these make it difficult for the parent to experience the child's disability as an event devoid of irrelevant considerations. The manifestations of the disability arouse emotional overwhelm and this overwhelm might create in the parent blindness or impaired interpretation of the child and his or her needs. Therefore, Caplan viewed this stage as a critical stage possessing great significance in the process of work of mourning and achievement of reorganization. The parent's ability to understand the child from more objective aspects will enable the achievement of an important separation between his or her own parental needs and the child's needs. When the separation is achieved, even just at its beginning, many parents might ask themselves whether they are equipped with all the tools and instruments necessary for assisting their child or whether they should turn to extra-familial assistants who will replace them in the contact with the child. This stage is described by Caplan as a **lack of a professional self-image**. The parents feel helpless and insecure in their ability to act in a manner that is different and accommodated to the child, therefore they are willing to put someone else - more professional - in their place.

The psychologically continuous encounter with the parents of children and adolescents diagnosed as suffering from learning- attention- and concentration-disabilities reveals the presence of these four deficiencies in the parents' lives, both in the order documented by Caplan, and in different order.

The need for professional knowledge arises in every parent as early as the first stage of pondering, and intensifies in the face of the findings of evaluations and diagnoses by professionals, with whom the parent has interacted since the beginning of the work of mourning. Professional knowledge provides the parent with information and understanding concerning the disability's character and sources, its unique ways of expression and its influence on the child's functioning and future. The acquisition of knowledge, which nowadays is obtained in diverse ways, enables the parent to better cope, both in getting out of the stage of shock, as well as in the journey against the defense mechanisms of the type of denial, avoidance, over-doing and "shopping escapade." Knowledge is primarily the factor that largely restores the parent's sense of control over his or her own life and the child's life - as opposed to the helplessness felt at the beginning of the journey. Knowledge provides the parent with the connection between the overt and covert parts of the disability, between the visible and invisible, thereby enabling a reorganization of life.

We are witnessing a great extent of chaos related to the topic of knowledge. Knowledge is spread out and uncontrolled in various places - from conversations with the expert through written and electronic media. As a result, many parents find themselves bombarded and overwhelmed by information that is sometimes contradictory, and which results in a return to the feeling of confusion and helplessness. The absence of agreement on the correctness of knowledge, the existence of higher- and lower-quality sources, the possibility of learning alone, without any mediating and assisting professional body - all these might be risky more than useful. It is therefore important that the stage of receiving knowledge will be a first, trust-building step between the parent and the professional expert - not an unregulated encounter between the parent and the abundance of knowledge that is so available nowadays. Sometimes, a parent will go through several contradictory and confusing encounters of knowledge reception - such as reading something on their own, a "shopping escapade" on the Internet, one-day seminars open to the general public, brochures from various organizations - until he or she consolidates and adheres to the good sources of knowledge. There are cases in which, during the journey, the parent will be influenced by public relations of various organizations, and will unknowingly move away from the accommodated understandings to be content with the adaption of weak defense mechanisms. Other parents will acquire the knowledge in stages, according to their advancement in the personal mourning journey and according to the nature of their child's disability (especially if this is visible and disturbs the child or them). These parents will only acquire the complete knowledge later on in the journey.

As mentioned, obtaining knowledge is a necessary but not sufficient condition for the parent's advancement in the adjustment and coping process. To translate this knowledge into accommodated parental skills and behaviors, the parent needs a guiding authority who will help in the acquisition of new skills. The stage of coping with the lack of skills, Caplan claims, constitutes a foundation stone in the change process the parent is to undergo. The parent must conjoin, in practice, new understandings with the daily reality, both practical and emotional. Sometimes the acquisition of skills might cause "over-doing" and a temporary lack of balance in the parents and entire family's lives; However, the acquisition of skills with the assistance of a professional authority might moderate the difficulty through a new division of roles (both between the parents themselves and between the parents and outside elements - education and therapy personnel outside the family); constructing orders of priority; practicing and mastering the new way of coping - thereby strengthening an experience of parental competence versus parental impotence; strengthening functional independence as opposed to dependence and helplessness, or over-reliance on extra-familial sources of strength (which might weaken the parents and fixate difficulties, instead of moderating them by empowering the parent).

Learning- attention- and concentration-disabilities can be maximally treated through the construction of an accommodated life environment, both familial and educational. The growing and coping processes of children suffering from this syndrome are closely related to an accommodated environment. An accommodated environment moderates disabilities, whereas an unaccommodated one might exacerbate them. Therefore, the skill acquisition stage is a critical stage in the achievement of balance and making the parents and child allies in a coping family.

Often the stage of obtaining knowledge and skills leads to the eruption of various emotions in the parent's psyche - mainly those related to past experiences or expectations from self and child regarding the future. Unprocessed and sometimes unconscious, these emotions cause a sort of temporary "blindness" of the parent, for example, the parent's difficulty to disconnect from his or her own distress and focus on the child's needs. The arousal of feelings of rejection, fear of failure, and irregularity originating from the experiences and difficulties that have characterized our childhood and relations with our parents and the environment we grew up in, might negatively influence the parent and his or her reactions to the child. The reaction will not be according to the child's needs but rather, according to the parent's difficult feelings. These emotional experiences are termed "intervening themes" by Caplan, and they describe a type of unconscious and unprocessed emotional overwhelm associated with our past, which arises in us in the face of our children. Each parent has his or her own themes. However, when the parent faces the child and the child's needs, there is increased danger that these themes will intensify and influence the parent's functioning.

Current cultural and social approaches, as well as accepted beliefs and orders of priority, can also contribute to the intensification of intervening themes in a parent's life. The fear of diagnosis as causing labeling weakens parental discretion, because it causes the parent's blindness to seeing that the child's irregular functioning is even more cause for labeling. The need for receiving assistance can also arouse themes- themes pertaining to motivation; dependence versus independence; the child and/or parent being judged by the environment as "undisciplined and not disciplining"; "a problem of boundaries/limits"; of "making efforts"; parental past experience with arousing situations with regard to the current situation, the genetic component and more—all these can be sources of the intervening theme. The danger in the theme is that it poses difficulty for the parent to examine the child's needs cleanly, and involves the needs of others in a manner that is unaccommodated to the child.

Lately, articles and news items have been published about types of family violence, children abused by their parents, and the like, and these might cause parents to hesitate and to fear adopting new, accommodated ways of parental involvement. The fantasies drawing on the conception of a permissive and democratic parental ideal might pose difficulty for the parent to change direction when encountering the barrier of the disability. The dissonance between this external theme and reality is not at all simple for many parents.

Parents who succeed in reaching the identification and understanding of the sources of blindness and weakening are still subject to the danger of weakening for another reason: **lack of a professional self-image**. The accelerated variation today in the division of roles between the family unit and educational and therapeutic environments - issues of "the child's rights" versus the needs derived from the child's age and disability, the need for adopting innovative parental approaches - all these might cause parents to "give up" - a willingness to relinquish their involvement in favor of introducing foreign therapists and educators into their lives. They are willing to view them as a more efficient extension of their unaccommodated parenthood; however, therapy methods that prefer direct work with the child and that leave the parents out of the educational and therapeutic contract might leave the parent with an experience of lack of professional self-image and pose difficultly in implementing the stages already achieved.

Many therapeutic modalities customary nowadays, such as coaching, individual therapy focused on the child, individual remedial teaching in academic subjects and skills leave many parents behind. They view themselves as lacking ability to increase their involvement in their child's life, due to the unique needs that are unknown-inaccessible to them. It is therefore very important to search for any possible way of integrating the parent into the unique practice, to prevent the weakening and staying behind, even in those cases where treatment by an expert is required.

C. Parenting with a "Remedial (Corrective) Teaching" Approach

Parental understanding of the "disabilityse" language their child "speaks" and "acts," is the key to gradual achievement of mastery of the language and translating it in practice to the daily language of the house. The language of the disability is present in the disabled child/teenager's adjustment process, and should be present in the parallel process of parental adjustment. Adopting the language, understanding its meaning and making an accommodated interpretation will lead to the acquisition of relevant parental skills. Nevertheless, there is no doubt that often, parental emotional involvement is mixed in with the new knowledge, thus promoting or delaying the parent's ability to act according to new understandings.

Parenting with a remedial (corrective) teaching approach

requires similar skills to those required from teachers and other education and therapy personnel, who engage in instilling social skills with a remedial teaching approach. Both parents and professionals are required to make practical interventions into the sequence of events within the child's natural life environment. Their language or mode of action is similar, even if it is put into practice in different territories and other situations. Moreover, the possible cooperation between the different adults, "speaking" and "acting" in exactly the same language, might bring about an intensification of the change, both in the child and parents, and mainly in the relations between them.

1. Protective Parental Presence

As mentioned, children with learning- attention- and concentration-disability usually have difficulty restraining, regulating, or planning their actions with respect to a desired goal. This is manifested in daily life and in the sequence of actions of life at home. The parents, of course, witness this reality.

When neurological competence is impaired or not efficient enough, according to the depth of the damage, an external element is required, that will "work" in the child's service while the child is obligated to meet daily demands. This element is the parent, who is required to be present throughout each situation, and with his or her presence, provide a response for missing functions.

The principles of protective parental presence:

- The very presence of the parent provides an experience of protection and focusing.

- The presence of the parent enables parental intervention in "real-time" or prior to this (see Chapter 2: Social Remedial Teaching) and "on the go" correction of impulsive or other mistakes the child might make.

- The adult's presence can retain the child's focus and bring him or her back whenever attention slips away.

- A protective presence ensures a " verbal intervention" the child lacks due to the verbal disability and to difficulties in the "inner language"—instead of the child's "behavioral language."

- A protective presence exposes the child to a benevolent "self-object." The latter's intensive, regulated, and accommodated presence facilitates the transmuting internalization, thereby enabling coping with all the child's memory and internalization difficulties.

- A "protective presence" does not mean that the parent "sticks" to the child and prevents the latter from doing things by himself or herself, but rather, the parent is present in the room and follows at a distance, returns and gets closer as necessary, and moves away as much as possible, but always on protection alert to return and intervene before the storm erupts or the next failure arises. Here also, as in social remedial teaching, the present parent serves as a linking figure between teaching and its execution, as well as a temporary substitute until the child succeeds in internalizing the parent as an inner memory, and acts with accommodated behavior by means of memory-evoking cues.

- The ability to be present - but not to intervene

unnecessarily - is the complicated part of the assistance. The achievement of the ability to be present necessitates the parent to practice, and receive training on one hand, and show restraint and withstand emotional frustration on the other. The protected child often feels pressurized, threatened or "not free" to act with the spontaneity typical of the disability, and directs rage against the protecting parent. Sometimes the child will reject the parent and arouse a difficult parental reaction, without the parent realizing that this is the child's test balloon. "Go away!" the child will say to the parent - but in fact, paradoxically ask: "Don't go away, and show me you are not frightened by me and are going because I've made you go away, but staying and proving to me persistence, a tolerance for frustration, and emotional caring" (see the concluding Chapter: "A Dictionary of Colloquial Disabiltyse").

- This ability not only necessitates practice and withstanding the emotional difficulty, but also being available and making oneself available for this specific purpose over substantial parts of the child's activity time. Many times a claim arises by parents that time is an unrealistic resource in their life load (as well as among pre-school or school teachers dealing with this issue). Tracking the shared life with a learning and concentration-disabled child shows the opposite is true: the more the adult is missing, not present, or unavailable (for justified reasons of load, being divided between many other needs and more), the more the child will find his or her own techniques for "dragging" the adult to him or her. Being dragged takes up nearly the same time required for protective presence, and it is done under less beneficial conditions - as the adult's reaction, and not by one's initiative, out of anger over the time that has disrupted and improper behavior, instead of directing and containing emotional regulation of the child.

The time of pretense in which the adult is dragged into following the child's upset, is no less than the time required for initiated protective presence, but its quality and benefit are lower and its contribution to instilling the desired interaction pattern in the child is less.

- In addition, parental presence not only reserves the initiative to the parent, but also illustrates the parent's hierarchy and authority to the child. The initiating parent is the director/manager. When the parent is dragged by the child, the experience is of an absence of authority.

To summarize, time measurements done in many families that have taken this initiative, show:

a. Protective presence time is no greater than the time required for after-the-fact corrective presence.

b. The quality of initiative is immensely better than that of the reaction.

c. The child's positive learning ability becomes much higher.

Therefore, with time and constant repetition, the child

begins using the adult's cues and the need for the intensive parental presence no longer exists.

2. Constructing a Family Routine

To facilitate the present, protective parental involvement, a parent would do well to make a point of constructing a daily schedule and fixed life routine. This will ease functional demands from the child on several levels:

a. A routine serves as an effective substitute for biological clock disruptions in many children with learning- attention- and concentration-disability.

b. A routine and regularity create an expected and predictable focal point of order in the children's lives. This makes it easier for them in the face of the ambiguity and vagueness caused by the disability. Transitions between situations and action improve, and the functional norm becomes engrained in the various memory functions. Thus the routine creates an entire setting or framework based on prediction and cues.

c. As a fixed and recurring demand in the child's life, routine also contributes to an increase in the level of independence and autonomy, which the child with the disabilities lacks. The more the course of the day is clear and predictable, the less the child needs the protective parental presence.

d. When some new demand enters the child's fixed life order, he or she becomes more autonomous (able to do things independently without the parent). So more time and room become available for them, to extend the reciprocal relations in the areas of enjoyment and connection, or for introducing additional demands made of the child according to the Priorities Principle, presented by R. Greene in his book (**The Explosive Child**, 1998).

3. Advance Preparation

Advance preparation is a key principle in parenting with a remedial (corrective) teaching approach. As in social remedial (corrective) teaching, it deals with the present and protective adult's ability to act in advance for the purpose of prevention. The adult must assist the child in choosing, deciding, and preparing **before the fact**. In this manner, advance preparation constructs the knowing prior to an outcome, prepares the child for what lies ahead, mobilizes the child's resources for the required task, and focuses the child on it.

Advance preparation is done verbally, and is said to the child close in time, or some time prior to the action or occurrence. Much advance preparation in a variety of situations, places, and people is required, so that a generalizing principle be formed in the child with the disability - from all the details - but when the child is drilled in this approach countless times, it slowly becomes the child's own work strategy and is adopted as a work tool in adjusting to various situations in life.

Advance preparation additionally serves the child as a preparatory means toward transition or change situations - encountered with many difficulties by the child with a disability. The difficulties stem from a tendency to perseveration (repetitiveness), from difficulty in getting organized for a new situation, and from emotional difficulty (such as withstanding frustration). An unplanned transition increases the child's sense of lack of control and helplessness, the experience of emotional deprivation, and therefore—also the tendency to defiance and insubordination. When a transitional situation is prepared for in advance, by guidance and short notice, this enables the child to have timeout for parting and getting organized, thus the child's sense of self-control and ability to manage the transition autonomously is strengthened. Advanced preparation, then, not only constructs for the child the plan that is so lacking, but also enables preparation time, required due to the lack of flexibility.

4. Mediation and Verbalization

Adopting **the mediating approach** as an effective tool in the interaction between parent and child, enables the parent to provide the child with two-fold assistance in each situation: First, it focuses the child on the important stimulus, prioritizes the main point over the secondary one, and assists the child in selecting the important one, i.e., assists in focusing on it, and avoiding increased and disruptive distractedness. Second, the mediating approach assists in constructing the accommodated reaction and correcting ways of its expression.

Regular intervention by way of mediation "constructs" for the child a gradual ability of self-mediation; it provides the child consciously and repetitively with an approach to mediating various life and learning situations, hence it becomes a remedial teaching technique for an adaptive life. The more mediation is present and repeats itself in various life situations, the more the child gains twice - accommodated behavior now and another layer of learning future self-mediation in new and other situations.

Verbalization is an expansion of mediation through spoken language. As described in the chapter on social remedial teaching, the power of this approach is that it provides the child with ways of verbal expression instead of behavioral expression.

The "language of the disability" is expressed by the child as behavior - mainly at those moments when emotional arousal increases; and because many situations in family life have a potential for high emotional involvement, they lead the child to situations of verbal helplessness, followed by a behavioral, disability-related reaction.

A parent who uses verbalization in the interaction with a child assists the child on several levels:

- First, the parent enables the child to acknowledge the emotions bursting out through behavior. Together they name the emotion, thereby creating an overt and agreed-upon framework for discourse between them.

- Verbalization, then, creates an experience of acknowledgment of the child's emotions and legitimization given by the parent for these emotions. The parent's ability to act, while recognizing the feeling, but protecting and preventing the behavior, forms in the child a sense of being protected. "I understand that you are mad because I asked you to collect the dirty clothes;

you are allowed to be mad, but you are not allowed to kick"; or "Your feeling that you are always deprived is understood, but I am telling you I won't be lenient with you about..." Verbalization enables the called-for separation between the emotion and ways of expression, and moreover, provides the possibility of expressing the emotion only in ways accepted by the family norms: "You feel I'm demanding too much from you; you are allowed to tell me that, but you are not allowed to curse me." Mediation has the power to make the child aware, at an earlier stage, of emotions that might appear when confronted by a certain situation. Mediation and verbalization of emotions sometimes create preparation for, and illumination of the future situation and construct a safer world for the child; and if the parent remains in a position of protective presence, this intensifies the experience of protected guidance: "The school bus will arrive in five minutes, and you need to get organized and leave now - even if this irritates you and you don't want miss another round on the computer... "

5. Monitoring

The parent as a present monitor while the child is active - while performing or preparing for a task - expands the child's areas of confidence and illuminates the accommodated path of action.

The existence of the parent who is present as a monitor makes the parent an external element that brings the child back to the focal point and enables correction whenever the child must get back on the correct track. The parent provides the child with real-time cues concerning the deviation and its correction. The parent's absence from this role might repeatedly expose the child to the frustration of discovering an outcome after the fact, instead of the satisfaction of thinking and planning before, or during the fact.

By means of monitoring, as a prolonged overseeing presence, the child acquires successes in real time. In addition, the child learns to use the strategy that has been transferred from outside inward, from the adult into the child's inner world, through transmuting internalization. An overseeing adult with a significant relationship creates a **double defense:** both here and now, as well as learning self-monitoring for the future.

The parent as a monitor is, above all, a concrete figure that sends out a message of involvement, sympathy, and caring. The concrete figure generates an opportunity for enthusiastic reflection in those cases the child has reached the marked destination, providing opportunities for repairing the damaged self-worth. By contrast, the parent's absence might cause the child to fail, to be taken back to situations of lack of wonder and enthusiasm associated with him or her, and to damage the self-image repeatedly.

6. Feedback and Correction

The circle of relating that develops between the child and parent in situations of parenthood with remedial teaching is dynamic and variable. A child who receives parental presence that also serves as a positive "self-object," will attain transmuting internalization with respect to functioning and construction of a positive self-image. The child will enjoy satisfying moments of enthusiasm alongside correction and control actions. With time, the child needs the concrete presence less and less, and can start relying on the diverse internalization constructed within. Through one of the strong channels, the child will be able to retrieve the inner parental presence when the time comes and be assisted by it as an element that independently directs in the child's moves.

For the process to gain power and momentum, the learning child needs continued reinforcement and guidance. This is enabled by the feedback cycle that forms between the child and parent. To a great extent, this stage can be viewed as a reconstruction of an earlier move that forms between parents and children in the period of constructing Separation and Individuation. Margret Mahler (1975) emphasizes the child's need at this stage to move away from and get closer to the adult through the inner "fueling" of the presence (Rapprochement). The young child, who has just recently established motor abilities that carry it some distance away from the parent, is momentarily frightened by the discovery of being alone in the world, because the inner parent schema has not yet been established well enough to serve as a reassuring source. Out of the fright, the child runs back to the parent, clings physically (holds onto the edges of the clothing or on to the body) or psychologically (with a glance, eye contact, or a word); "refuels" himself or herself with the parent's concrete and calming presence; gains an exalted moment of the parent's "wonder and enthusiasm" (a fueling reflection: "You run so nicely…"; "Well done for stopping on time…"; and more); internalizes the parent and the wonder and enthusiasm - and so, being refueled - can continue onward.

The learning- attention- and concentration-disabled child sometimes finds him or herself moving away and becoming frightened, but not finding a way to return to the parent. The child reacts with panic, or is forced to stop because of a forbidding, unenthusiastic parental demand, ("Stop running so fast! It's dangerous…How many times have I told you that if you carry on running like this, I won't go out for a walk with you…"), and remains without an ability of transmuting internalization. Therefore the child will lack the parental presence and will be left with a negative self-worth.

The rectification of the situation is possible with the aid of the corrective feedback cycle. By the parent's initiative, the child who has dared to start acting on his or her own, gains approving and enthusiastic feedback or feedback that is accommodated (to the child) and directed toward change. In this manner, the child simultaneously gains a variety of self-experiences, making reactions more flexible according to the circumstances, the continued protection of the adult and the construction of positive and autonomous self-worth based on protected experiencing. Gradually the circles of autonomous distance will enlarge, the child's self-reactions will become more numerous and will be retained through corrective feedback.

7. Sorting and Choosing

The multiplicity of tasks and the parent's involvement in the disabled child's life often necessitate sorting and choosing processes. In his book *The Explosive Child* (1998), R. Greene points to the necessary principles for the survival of the parent and child during the construction and implementation stages of intervention plans. The many difficulties in daily reality impose a double responsibility on the parent - to decide among the myriad demands - but no less important - which demands are to be handled at the expense of others at any moment, and which are now negligible? There are no compromises in the face of the main point; there are no demands in the face of the rest. Focused renunciation teaches the child not only what the most important thing is, but also about the right to rest and stumble in areas that are secondary in importance at any moment.

Non-sorting and non-choosing during the intervention jeopardize both parent and child. They are in for a harsh reality of life, full of tension and conflicts, a reality with many negative reflections that reinforce the child's experience of guilt and shame, feeling of helplessness and the forgoing of the experience of positive self-worth. Focusing invites successes, positive reflections, followed by the repair of self-worth.

The encounter between the successful child and the parent, who mirrors the success to the child, increases the opportunities for joy- and satisfaction-arousing meetings and for repairing the emotional shade in parent-child relations. "Pouncing" on all life areas at once ensures failure and hopeless relations.

Parenting with a remedial teaching approach obligates the parent to put an emphasis on the most important thing and focus on it, until the child is led to the establishment of achievements. Achievements that have been assimilated and stabilized in the child's life routine serve as a basis for the next changes, which are also carefully chosen, while discriminating between the main and secondary points, and so forth.

A present parent who chooses the most important thing, regularly presents it to the child by means of advance preparation, mediation, and verbalization, and reacts to change dynamically by giving feedback and correction - is the one who, together with the child, experiences the gradual change that slowly expands into additional areas of functioning and to future goal achievement.

Appendix

Dictionary of

"Colloquial Disabilityse"

or "What Do You Mean When

You Say No..."

Along the book's chapters a new language emerges - the language of the disability. In most cases, it concerns the overt expressions of the covert disability. Sometimes it is a "behavioral language," sometimes it is the "language of the hands," and many times it is a short verbal message stemming from lingual disability or from difficulties in organizing the overt expression and the inner language.

The overt behavior expressed in the "language of the disability" conveys a message that is different from what one thinks - different from the interpretation attributed to this behavior. Examples of the erroneous interpretation: violent instead of explosive, wild instead of lacking regulation, shy instead of possessing an attention deficit disorder that harms social initiative, and more. The spoken or behaving disability-related language requires a disability-accommodated interpretation, which is often the exact opposite of the original educational interpretation.

The absence of overt physical characteristic signs of the disability, and the constant need to bridge the gap between what is overtly expressed and the covert motive obligates the care- giving/intervening adult (parent, teacher, therapist) to develop a disability-adapted listening. They must be familiar with the dictionary and its meanings for their actions to be effective and to prevent additional harm to the child or teenager with the disability.

The collection of expressions presented next has no pretense of encompassing all possibilities. It has been born out of my continuous multi-year encounter with children, adolescents, parents and education and therapy personnel, and it this that has enabled me to present this preliminary collection to the reader. Many good professionals and parents have encountered additional examples and they are invited to expand and enrich their "private dictionary" for their own sake and for the sake of others.

The guiding principle for choosing the expressions is first and foremost their degree of prevalence in the familial, educational, and therapeutic fields, and afterward - the extent of the gap between the disability-related intention and the erroneous educational and therapeutic interpretations. It should be remembered however, that also among children and adolescents with disabilities, there are normative developmental "moments," accompanied by statements having an open and direct intention, as found in the rest of their peers. Adults should, then, show sensitivity and ability to discern.

Understanding the language of the disability enables

the adult who is present in the child or teenager's life, to more accurately and suitably accommodate the patterns of "functional remedial teaching" laid out in the chapters of this book.

The majority of expressions appearing here come up in encounters between the child or teenager with the disability, and the adult, who tries to lead them to functioning that is accommodated to the situation, age, culture, context, or environment. Most of the expressions are seemingly associated with a "negative" or "non-compliant" and / or "avoidant" messages, but the vast majority express disability-related distress, anxiety about another failure, and feelings of guilt and shame. Therefore, when the child receives a renewed understanding, i.e., "accommodated interpretation" (reframing) of messages (even if these too get a reaction of negation and rejection at the first moment), the child simultaneously achieves many things:

a. For the first time, the child might feel understood with his or her reverse messages and even almost "transparent" in their intentions, which are sometimes not even obvious to the child himself.

b. The child might finally gain expressions of support and empathy for his or her painful or stormy emotions, exposed through the words/and or actions by which the real intention is hidden.

c. The most important achievement of all - for the first time, the child will realize that a correct understanding of their language of disability does not lead the adult to concede the demand.

As the entries in this dictionary will show, renunciation is not a renunciation of the demand from the child, but rather **giving up on the child and his or her strengths and abilities.** Therefore the child who has momentarily gained the "victory" of renunciation might feel a sense of loss and damage to self-worth or worse still, abandoned - –because of being given up on and that others can do without him or her. Therefore, a correct disability-related interpretation necessitates the continuation of making the demand within safety limits/boundaries, but without blaming and negating the child and behavior, and mainly without attributing malicious intentions to the child's action and words.

Even if this limit/boundary setting seemingly receives an overt "negative" reaction by the child - angry, rejecting, non-compliant - it is actually a special type of "expressing thanks" on the part of the child - thank you for the fact that you, the parent or teacher, are protecting me, caring for my wellbeing, for not giving up on me, and believing in my abilities.

By nature, children seldom express thanks for a "protecting" parent (not even in a bar/bat-mitzvah party or wedding party) - but in the type of children under discussion (with these disabilities), the very accomplishment of the change in functioning *is* the expression of gratitude felt toward the adult, who speaks, and acts according to their disability-related language.

This understanding of the messages ought to be internalized in the "protecting" parent or teacher's emotions and thoughts, and should implant an active mini-translator for "colloquial disabilityse" in one's ear. This mini-translator will enable them, at any difficult moment, to correctly translate the disability-related situation, and to act from the understanding of the language, and not from a standpoint that judges overt behavior - that hindering behavior which is many times interpreted as deliberate, conscious, motivated by malice or intention to harm, instead of part of a disability-related vulnerability.

1. "Don't Want"

Many times the demands directed at the child are responded to with this reaction. It is very easy to be wrong and suspect the child of responding to the demand with non-compliance and defiance out of conscious intention; however in the language of the disability, the negative response is actually a mechanism expressive of the child's difficulties: The demand is difficult for me, or it's hard for me to transition from the thing I am immersed in (a computer game, watching television) to a new situation (transition situations), or I am afraid of performing the demand lest I fail again.

In most cases the child concerned is one who, deep down inside, very much wants to comply with the demand, but does not know how to prepare for it (impaired self-organization), or has difficulty gaining composure for it (frustration threshold problem), or is afraid of it (fear of failure), or is "testing" the demanding adult's intentions ("Do you really mean it?; Will you be strong and confident enough to make demands of me all the way?").

Being lenient with the child will give rise to an additional failure and shattering of the child's self-worth ("Demands are being taken off of me, meaning that my abilities are not being acknowledged, I am being considered little, weak, messed-up, and more), especially when the difficulties in self-management and in prediction of consequences produce worsening distress situations. The mistaken adult renounces and removes a demand, whereas the child or teenager interprets this with reverse psychology: "You attribute no importance to me; for you, I don't deserve any effort, you are externalizing my exceptionality."

2. "Leave Me Alone" or "Get Off My Back"

The insistence of an adult in "protective presence" that the child perform a task often produces momentary escalation of the child's reactions in the style of, "Leave me alone," or "Get off my back." However, these statements are, in essence, a provocative challenging of the adult: Is he or she really intending to demand of me, meaning acknowledging my value and abilities, or will he or she actually leave me and get off my back (separation anxiety)?

This is often the test of the protective parental or teacher's presence. Leaving the child seemingly means complying with the overt request, but actually, it means expressing to the child the non-importance attributed to him or her - externalizing the child's exceptionality to the point of rejection (I am leaving him or her because they are not deserving of the effort).

"Leave me alone" in colloquial disabilityse, almost always

means, "Don't leave me"; "Keep demanding from me"; "Don't get off my back," because I have already had my share of abandonments and concessions.

3. "Get Lost"/"Go Away"

Another expression that might be heard in the relationship between the child or adolescent and the present and protecting adult, is "Get lost" or "Go away." When the child feels that there is no intention of renouncing the demand made of him or her, and accepting their (seeming) non-compliance, or when the child's difficulty to get organized and meet the task is not yielded to, the child tries a last act of despair: "Get lost" or "Go away." This is the most difficult test of all, because the child is seemingly rejecting the adult, but is actually expressing the fear of the possibility of being rejected or abandoned himself or herself. Therefore "get lost is a desperate, and simultaneously challenging call: "Don't go away, stay with me until I make it."

In this case, the problem is the sense of insult felt by a parent, teacher, or therapist; The adult, who sustains the "get lost," feels hurt and insulted by the rejection the child is demonstrating toward them - and therefore has difficulty identifying the child's own fear of being rejected and abandoned by the adult.

4. "I Can't" or "I Don't Know" or "I Can't by Myself"

In expressions of the type, "I can't," a covert message is hidden, requesting from the adult the chance and conditions to actually meet the ability. These expressions stem from a continuous experience of failure and inferiority, in the shadow of which children with learning- attention-and concentration-disabilities grow up. They serve as the child's immediate reaction in the face of a task that at first seems beyond his abilities, and the child is not confident enough to carry it out properly. These are expressions of fear of failure, an experience of helplessness, and mainly an expression of commencement difficulties, so typical of this group of children.

To change this painful experience, the intervening adult ought to react in a completely different manner from what is heard, and say: "You are afraid you won't be able"… or "we'll start together, and then you carry on" (commencement). Sometimes these sentences express a real difficulty in the disability, preventing the child from performing a transfer from one task that has been successful, to a new task, which at the first moment is perceived as different because it is not completely identical (lack of flexibility). The performance of the transfer by the adult - deconstructing it and emphasizing the similar points to what has already been done - can give rise to the experience of ability and daring to try.

The fear of trying and failing again and the sense of lack of ability that constantly overwhelms these children and adolescents, many times cause them to give up in advance, because giving up is an action that is under control: "I am not doing because I don't want" ; "When I want (sometime…someday…) I may be able"; "I can't" is an expression of fear, therefore support accompanied by demanding, deconstruction into elements and gradual execution (remedial teaching) enable the child to slowly discover the experience of capability.

5. "I Feel like Dying" or "I'll Commit Suicide" or "I'll Kill Myself and Then You'll Have Some Quiet from Me."

These expressions "I feel like dying; I'll commit suicide; I'll kill myself..." are among the most difficult and worrying in the environment of a child with the disability. They (justifiably) arouse real concern for the child's wellbeing - anxiety about the child's suicidal ideation or acts. They act as a boomerang against the child.

Discerning when this is the language of the disability and when these statements have real intention is not at all simple and necessitates careful discretion, including sometimes consulting with authorized mental health professionals. Nonetheless, in quite a large portion of cases these are cries for help that do not have a worrying element of suicidal tendencies, but rather, a verbal difficulty conveying the scope of (temporary or continuous) emotional distress, coupled by learning from experience about what such statements cause in adults and how they are influenced by them. In a substantial portion of cases, these statements are the child's will to "kill" his or her disability rather than him or herself - to remove it from one's life. In other cases (or simultaneously with the above-mentioned interpretation), the child is conducting a "test" for the adults - to determine to what extent they are willing to continue fighting over him or her or give up and leave him or alone, subject to distress.

Another possibility expressed in the language of the disability is the child's awareness of the distress and harm caused by the disability to those close and dear to him or her (parents, siblings) and a sense of guilt over the prolonged hurt caused; the child wants what is good for them, i.e., to free others of his or her disruptive presence.

However, in most cases, these sentences gradually become a learned process in the child as a result of adult reactions: The present and witnessing adult immediately removes any demand from the child. The former is weakened due to the fright aroused by such sentences (due to the concern for the child and child's intactness) and lets go of the demand to make things easier for the child, only relating to the distress. Having learned the reaction pattern, the child uses these statements as a mechanism to move functional demands away from him or her, to be let off the hook, and reduce demands. However the anxious adult's responsiveness acts in a counterproductive manner: The child who is "freed" from demands experiences a reflection of weakness, lack of value and lack of ability, which only increases distress.

There is no one correct, all-encompassing way to react to this distress in children, however, the key principle in responding to the disability-related language must include the following elements:

a. Declaration of increased protection and presence: I will not let you harm yourself; I will protect you even more.

b. Empathy and emotional support: I hear and understand the magnitude of the distress you feel toward yourself and those surrounding you; I am aware of what the disability evokes in you, how tired, angry, and sad you are over your disability and the disruptions caused by it.

c. Clear demand: I am not giving up on you, not letting you off the hook, and I will assist you in meeting demands, because they will minimize the distress, as you also experience the beginning of success.

This combined array of reactions, simultaneous with a quick and deep examination of the sources and intensity of the distress in the child or adolescent, will prevent or reduce the possible damage caused to the child due to the helplessness of the adult who is "blackmailed" with suicidal threats, yet will enable giving real help at the same time with the disability-related treatment (referral to a mental health professional as necessary).

6. "I'll Run Away" or "I'm Out of Here", or "I'm Leaving" (in the middle of an activity)

These actions and expressions above, "I'll run away; I'm out of here; I'm leaving" among children and adolescents are common - mainly as a defense mechanism against the experience of rejection they have many times. Often, difficulties of social learning disabilities create a reality of social rejection and loneliness, however when the opportunity to become part of an activity is created, there is also terrible anxiety that forms, accompanied by great tension: "When will I be moved away"; "When will my behavior and reactions again make others unwilling to continue being in contact with me." The threat of, or actually running away "gives" "protection" to the child with the disability: "I will go (I am in control, seemingly, even out of "choice") before being removed. I will determine the time I move away, and will not remain in a state of tension and ambiguity about when I will be removed by them."

Moreover, the continued experience of rejection creates tension and ambiguity in the child, which is a source of difficulty in itself; and if these are also joined by the anxiety about losing or failure (in a game, in a task), the moving away defends "twice": The child both leaves from his or her "own will," as well as avoids the emotional overwhelm that can be caused by losing or failing.

Another motive for this pattern being chosen among these children and adolescents is related to difficulties in persistence and continuity. Often the beginning of an activity is accompanied by an intense thrill, to which the child is drawn, but the continuation of the activity requires investment of forces of persistence and continuous action, with less excitement. These situations arouse difficulty (mainly due to the attention deficit) and premature quitting is an expression of persistence difficulties and the search for new stimuli and thrill.

Another facet of these statements is directly turned toward the adults present. Often the threats of escape and leaving also express a testing of the adult, and their willingness to insist the child and the child's presence in the activity. Escaping or the threat of it is a "loyalty test" for the protecting adult.

Another motive for escaping or threatening with escape is associated with the overt, painful meaning of escape, the will to escape from the continued difficulty and the desperate search for the quiet and refuge from the encounter with the distress.

However, when escaping becomes a regular defensive habit, getting out of it is more and more difficult. Every act of escape distances the child from daring and mobilizing the mental strength for coping with the difficulty. Escaping weakens the child emotionally and weakens the child's coping forces. The role of the adult who understands the language of "disabilityse" is to prevent the child from this action. The adult must assist the child to stay and complete the task, while demonstrating empathy for the distress reflected by this statement/act. The emotional support, combined with limits of maintaining continued action, this time as well, gradually generate the required change.

7. "What Do you Want From Me?"

This sentence ("What do you want from me?") is one of the common distancing sentences that children tend to throw at the adult out of a desperate attempt to move the task, currently experienced as very difficult, away from themselves. At the same time, this statement also entails the conveying of a disability-related message: "How is it possible that you want something from me at all? Am I still worth something to you?" This statement, of course, is expressive of the continued damage to the self-worth. Sometimes this sentence can express another dictum in "Disabilityse": "Why me?" which means: Why am I always the one to blame? I haven't done anything, but again and again I feel the experience of victimhood resulting from me and my disability being constantly blamed. The sentence contains two contradictory messages - amazement from the fact that I am still wanted and something is expected of me, alongside the experience of victimhood - I am always blamed for something.

Only a disability-related interpretation in each of these two directions can keep the adult "wanting something from the child," alongside helping to stop the unwanted behavior for which the child is blamed. The problem is that sometimes the music (intonation) with which the sentence, "What do want from me?" is said is experienced by the adult as a type of disrespect and/or insolence, arouses anger at the child, and blinds the adult from the possibility of understanding the anxiety and victimhood.

8. "It's Difficult for Me" " or "I'm beat"

Both expressions "It's difficult for me" and "I'm beat" express the child's experience of distress, the prolonged fatigue, from the sequence of difficulties they are required to cope with. It is difficult to understand how much a sequence of seemingly simple daily actions and tasks constitutes focal points of difficulty and struggle for the child or adolescent with learning- attention- and concentration disabilities. Often, a regretful misunderstanding of the child by the adult makes the latter irritated: "What's so difficult for you?... All I asked you to do was... What's this tiredness?" In addition, often this is an experience of fatigue and difficulty originating from the physical weakness of a child with biological clock regulation difficulties, making him or her sleep little at night (because of difficulties in falling asleep and falling asleep late) and having difficulty getting up (fatigue mixed with transition difficulties and impaired self-organization). Many times, these children walk around in a chronic state of fatigue, therefore alongside the psychological-mental difficulty, there is also objective, physical fatigue.

The ways to handle this feeling of mental and physical fatigue are complex, but in any case, they must not include concrete acceptance of the request; as such acceptance means additional harm to the child and added distress - a sort of confirmation of the sense of weakness and inability (a negative reflection by a self-object who is significant to the child.)

Therefore, here too, the path to change necessitates an understanding of the sources of weakness, while attempting to provide a solution for the physical aspect (how to alleviate the sleeping/falling asleep problem) and giving partial "organizing," and deconstructing help, in order to mobilize the child's forces for action. Doing something, even partially, immediately constitutes a type of positive reflection for the child, concerning the overcoming, reliance on his or her own strengths, vitality, and ability to do things.

9. "Later" or "Just Now" or "Soon"

As described many times in this book, the concept of time as a component of a person's life constitutes a significant disability-related focal point of difficulty.

For the child, the deferral sentences of "later" or "soon"

express a chronic problem with understanding the concept of time (how much time is "later"?). Additionally, the attempt of the child or adolescent with the disability to postpone a difficult, burdensome or threatening task indicates another way to escape the difficulty.

With a neurological reality, where impairments in executive function exist, actions and statements of deferral are bound to lead to prolonged procrastination (("later," means "after tomorrow " - an indefinite and unlimited time…).

When the child's attempt to postpone an action is accepted, thanks to the promise that the child actually intends, with all seriousness, to do the thing later, this means the demand will be forgotten (due to the disability) and the child will, time and time again, face shattering experiences of failure, lack of credibility, and irresponsibility because of not doing. Sometimes a frightening recall of not having done something will arrive a moment too late, after the time set for doing has passed. For example, recalling the school bus ride when seeing the bus pass by you, or recalling a test only when arriving at class, without having prepared, of course, because when mom reminded you yesterday, you said: " later," and now you have awoken to discover that "later" did not arrive.

The shattering in the face of not doing something constitutes a recurring source of damage to self-worth and exposure to feelings of guilt and nullity. These feelings themselves constitute a burdensome and emotional addition that arouses self-anger and/or pity.

Therefore, help in such situations of procrastination obliges the protecting adult to meet the conditions of "remedial teaching": advance preparation for the demand, protective presence for the transition from inactivity to activity, or from stopping one type of activity to starting another, requiring verbalization and mediation or continuous monitoring with feedback until the longed-for completion. A repeated reaction of this type will form experiences of success (proven results of execution) in the child, an experience of capability, a reduction in the sense of being the disrupter who does not do and does not belong, and mainly, equip the child with a self-toolbox of how things are done. In this way, the child will gain combined help - both the desired action in the present, as well as the construction of a toolbox of how and when things are to be done in the future.

10. "I'm Not Coming In" or "I'm Not Coming," or " I'm Not Participating"

These sentences in the language of the disability usually reflect the fear of joining an activity that is associated with failure or rejection anxiety. It is the child's attempt to prevent participation in activities he or she is not sure of his or her ability to accomplish, or that these activities might put the child into conflict situations with the environment. Therefore the child often attempts to avoid them in advance as a defense mechanism.

In addition, as in the previous examples, these expressions reflect a type of test for the significant other facing the child. "Will you really renounce me and go without me?;

Will the event also take place without my presence?" When there is no understanding or awareness of the disability-related language, the child remains abandoned to loneliness, whereas the others, like family members or classmates, are at the peak of their shared activity.

This non-compliance often expresses a sense of deep injury to self-worth, an experience of failure, and a will to avoid it. To the adult, it reflects the need for recreating conditions for success. When conditions for success are constructed again and again, we see, in a moving and recurring manner, that the child is nourished by them and this enables the gradual raising of demands.

Thus, for example, a child who refuses to enter a lesson, is expressing the sense of being disconnected, the lack of belonging, and lack of understanding of what is happening in the lesson. This experience is among the difficult ones for the child: "I didn't get in" means "I have spared myself the sense of humiliation that occurs there."

These sentences also express the weakening of the child's coping forces and being in a state of a decreasing frustration threshold. In order to mobilize the child, a standard that is accommodated to the abilities and strengths at this moment should be set, thereby constructing a success environment that will enable refueling of coping forces.

11. Curse Expressions of any Type, Language, or Genre

In emotional turmoil, situations of anger, explosion and rage, the expressive tools of children with a disability become even poorer or more "base." The more emotional overwhelm increases, the more their tongue often becomes heavy and cumbersome. The ability to retrieve and organize adapted expression in situations of overwhelm is extremely difficult for them. In addition, these harsh expressions also entail an attempt to powerfully express the defensive aggression they are overwhelmed by in the face of injury and failure. The curse is an easily retrievable and expressible lingual pattern; it is powerful and accurate compared with the intensity of the anger, it sends out aggression of a child who feels attacked, as well as a will to destroy the other (regressive thinking to the magical language of ages three to four.)

The more the educational and cultural environment serves as role model, it enriches these easy ways of expression (linguistically-communicatively), thus the accessibility and availability of these become easy and quick and they serve as an easy, disability-related solution for the child or adolescent.

The absence of regulation and restraint forces, a low frustration threshold, impulsivity, and verbal disability join together to cause the child to prefer the curse expression to any other more complex way, the one that in the sense of society's norms, is correct.

How should we behave in relation to the child in this case? Any adherence to the trivial interpretation of insolence or inappropriate behavior of the child - and moreover - feeling insulted by the child - is dangerous and hindering. Precisely at this stormy moment, the child needs help that combines three elements simultaneously:

Reflection/reflecting the emotional turmoil = I understand you are very mad...
Setting safety limits = but you are not allowed to use such expressions.
Replacement by and verbalization of a norms-adapted alternative = you are allowed to tell me you are mad at me, that you disagree with me, that you are angry about the demand I have made from you.
This integrated approach, as a part of functional remedial teaching, will enable the adult to avoid actions that do not contribute to the solution of the disability problem, and only adhere to the issue of behavior. It will mainly enable the setting of limits with support and understanding and constructing alternatives or a bypass for the disability. It should be emphasized: Like in many other intervention plans, this practice requires repetition and consistency, even before the beginning of a change is accomplished.

12. "I've Had It" or "I've Reached My Breaking Point"
The constant need to cope with the disability in various areas of life and over prolonged periods often causes a sense of fracture in the learning- and attention-disabled child or teenager's life. It is a common situation in important periods of their lives.
The cry of distress, "I've reached my breaking point" reflects in "colloquial Disabilityse" the sense of collapse (which is usually temporary), the difficulty to go on coping, and mainly, the request for help to treat the fracture. Like a fracture in the body, a fracture of psychological forces often

necessitates using discretion: How much time-out can and should be provided to the child in order to recuperate and regain energy? Under which conditions should the time-out be given (with partial functioning and in which areas?). Can the demands be continued in a more moderate manner to build a training program ("gym") for strengthening the coping forces, or for the renewed construction of successes? And all this - fitted to the depth and extent of the fracture and the child's level of vitality and strengths.

13. "I Hate You"

This painful exclamation toward another mainly expresses the experience of the child's self-hatred and/or hatred for the disability. The sometimes continuous sense of lack of worth arouses a painful experience of self-hatred, and it this which children tend, at peak moments, to project on to the significant other (self-object) in their proximity.

With this harsh expression the child poses question marks before the adult: "How can you love me when I have difficulty loving myself?" or "Will you fall into the trap and reject me or will you go on feeling close and caring toward me?"

Sometimes, directing the hate is part of emotional turmoil and being overwhelmed (see Section 11 concerning the curses), and it is actually directed against the demand and not against the demander. The adult is identified with the task, but the anger is mainly directed toward the task itself. Encountering regulation difficulties and lingual disability, the emotional overwhelm arouses in the child the need to sound this exclamation out of the personal focal points of pain. One should not miss the distress within the exclamation and attribute a trivial interpretation to this statement that seemingly concerns the nature of the relations between the child and close environment. The opposite is true: The child who directs this desperate exclamation is not only in distress and asking for help, but also tends to direct the request for help only toward the person who is trusted and whose love is trusted, the person who is less likely to retaliate painfully.

14. Going Physically Wild on an Object, Child, or Adult: Breaking Things, Throwing them, Smashing or Using Blows, Kicks, and Bites

The phenomenon of violence and vandalism in society in general is today at the center of public discourse, particularly violence among children and teenagers. The reasons for the increase in these phenomena are complex and multiple, and their increasing spread among children and teenagers is indeed worrisome; however, even in this troubling reality, one must not confuse violence for its own sake and the expressions of the disability that resemble violence. Seemingly, the practical and overt consequence is similar and even identical and in any case, dangerous. The need to restrain, stop, and mainly prevent these manifestations is critical to the continued wellbeing and existence of every human society. However, when disability-related motives are concerned, a unique understanding and disability-accommodated interventional reaction is needed.

Sending away and punishing children and adolescents with learning-attention-and concentration-disabilities are hardly effective at all for prevention of the phenomenon. In most cases they are the key to recurring manifestation of the phenomenon, although sometimes in other places, where the punisher is not adequately aware of the continued existence of the violent and vandalistic behavior.

Sending away and punishing children with disabilities joins a sequence of actions that are experienced by them as a negative reflection, which is not regulating and effective, but rather, contributes to the next event, that might happen in the absence of correct handling, and increases the child or teenager's emotional distress.

Handling with the disability-related language here necessitates strict adherence to the five principles of "social remedial teaching" (see page 190). **Protective presence** will significantly reduce both the prevalence as well as the intensity of the phenomenon. It will not only protect society, but also the child from self - from the unregulated impulses, from the severe frustration problem, and mainly from the lack of a toolbox for handling anger in legitimate ways and without harming others.

In situations where the child possessing the disability is not protected by the adult and the child's unregulated aggression has burst out and destroyed, "the moment after the storm" always comes, when the child calms down and discovers, "after the fact," the magnitude of the damage caused. Under conditions of normal moral development, typical of many children and adolescents with learning-attention- and concentration-disabilities, this discovery will arouse a new emotional overwhelm of pangs of guilt and a bad conscience. Constant exposure to difficult experiences such as these might sometimes end in deep emotional injury to the point of depression and acute damage to self-image.

To prevent the exacerbation of the child's emotional injury and the recurring existence of disability-related events, characterized by unregulated behaviors, a multi-system combination of social)-remedial (corrective) teaching is needed, with individual assistance for each child according to their needs (psychotherapy, medical treatment, and more).

15. "I'm Bored"

This expression ("I'm bored") reflects aspects of the disability related to organization difficulties of self-engagement, to the constant need for intense and short-term stimulation, to the difficulty fitting into an activity environment, to an experience of emptiness due to an inefficient working memory, and sometimes also to the danger of the encounter with feelings of pain and sadness in the absence of intense external stimulation.

"I'm bored" does not mean that the child is criticizing the environment that is poor in means and stimuli for self-activation, and does not entail a concrete request to construct an external plan of thrills (as some of the parents tend to do sometimes to avoid these expressions of distress). Actually, the child expects the adult's help in gradual construction of self-organization, in planning leisure time, in commencing and continuing activities. The adult should assist the child to find, from within, areas of interest and an organizational ability to put them into practice. All this, with intervention in the social aspects of the disability are needed to prevent an experience of loneliness.

16. "I'm not Feeling Well: My Head & Stomach are Sore; I'm tired, I'm hungry"

Psychosomatic sensations are often an exact expression of the child being in stressful situations. Many times, these sensations reflect the child's momentary or ongoing distress level in the face of functional demands, activity locations, or certain areas. The sensation of distress is real and authentic, and in most cases its content symbolically reflects the child's focal point of difficulty.

One should be careful in these situations in light of the existence of a real physical problem, such as an illness; therefore the recurring pattern of these phenomena primarily necessitates safe responsiveness of a medical inquiry.

Only when it has been proven that the distress is associated with the mind and not the body, i.e., with stress resulting from the disability, it can be treated with functional-remedial (corrective) teaching.

17. "I'm Not Connected With Them" or "I'm Not Your Friend"

The topic of socialization friendship is a focal point of distress from the social aspect of the disability. The expression of these sentences often reflects the child or teenager's will to distance himself or herself from a group of children or adolescents - to leave pre-emptively before being sent away or rejected.

When the child directs this cry toward a group of children, this restores, for a brief moment, the sense of control over his or her life. It is not I who is being sent away but rather, I am the one who is moving away; It is not I who am unwanted, but rather, it I don't want; however, deep inside, the child experiences the pain of being sent away and rejected and is longing for help that will give a chance to get closer and connect.

A mediating adult can enable connective experiencing that will gradually create the opportunity so longed for by the child or adolescent.

18. Disruptive and Harassing Actions, Directed at a Child or Adult who is in the Middle of an Activity or Game

The will to join an existing activity often arouses distress and difficulty in the child with the disability. Not knowing how to manage this type of appeal (non-verbal learning disability, lingual learning disability, social disability, and more (see Chapter 2, which deals with social remedial teaching) causes the child to shift to a way of a behavioral appeal.

This behavior is often experienced by the other, who is not familiar with the disability-related language, as a kind of interruption or harassment, and it immediately arouses rejection and refusal. Thus the child with the disability finds him or herself in a reality where there are "self-fulfilling expectations" - the fear of rejection and not knowing how make an appeal have led to a disability-related act, which has brought on rejection from which the child was so afraid. The first step toward the longed-for change can be done by adults who are "social remedial (corrective) teaching teachers" and who are present in the place. They will act with the child to avoid the difficulty (by a social-remedial teaching move) and simultaneously interpret the meaning of the annoying act for the other person.

19. Verbal or Physical Teasing/ Provocation

Acts of provocation/teasing are seemingly typical of many children suffering from the syndrome. Sometimes it is not an intentional provocation, but rather a disability-related monotonous action, due to the attention deficit disorder, and the child performs it almost without being aware of its existence e.g., hums while performing a task, whistles softly, taps on the table with the hands or taps with the feet while listening to a lesson, or while waiting next to the dining table, or when the family is watching television, and so on.

Another type of provocation - a deliberate action done silently and covertly - is intended to "turn on" the other, whether as a defense mechanism against the assumed aggression of the other person, or as a mechanism to prevent a lesson or other unwanted activity.

These actions are concerned with a rest and ventilation on the one hand, and the organization of sustained attention on the other, without any awareness of the extent of their disturbance to the other and without an ability to control them.

This provocation/teasing sometimes expresses the difficulty in addressing a parent, teacher or friend, due to the absence of addressing norms and adapted verbal organization for the appeal. In these cases, the provocation is a way of getting the other person's attention to the child's existence and wants from him or her.

Among children suffering from sensory regulation difficulties, the relentless touching of the other person - the seeming physical provocation - expresses abnormal sensory needs, difficulties in controlling physical-motor planning, and/or impaired spatial orientation. Therefore the child reaches friction without having intended to harm the other and out of blindness to the meaning of touch from the other's point of view.

Regulation difficulties are also often the reason for the recurring appearance of an annoying action due to lack of regulation, such as over-talkativeness, repeated touching, and hyper-activity.

The different and varied sources of behavior necessitate intervention in two foci: on one hand, raising the child's awareness to one's actions, while giving an accommodated interpretation of the reasons, with speech that is devoid of judgment; and developing solutions accommodated to the child's needs, which moderate the degree of harm and harassment to the other, on the other hand

Understanding the child's language of disability, whose expressions vary as the spoken language changes according to the zeitgeist and become varied with the subtleties of current slang, is the key to the adoption of a remedial and beneficial disability language by parents, teachers, educators and anyone who has children's best interests in mind.

REFERENCES

Ainsworth, M.D.S. (1963). "The Development of Infant–Mother Interaction among the Ganda." *Determinates of Infant Behavior*. Vol. 2, (ed.) B.S. Foss, pp. 67-112. Wiley, NY.

Ainswroth, M.D.S. & Bowlby, J. (1991). "An Ethological Approach to Personal Development." *American Psychologist*, 46: 333-341.

Anthony, E.J. & Benedek, T. (1970). *Parenthood, its Psychology and Psychopathology*, Jason Aronson Inc, NJ & London.

Amir, N., Rapin, I. & Branski, D. (1991). *Pediatric Neurology: Behavior and Cognition of the Child with Brain Dysfunction*, Karger, Basel

Barkley, R.A. (1997). *ADHD and the Nature of Self Control*. The Guilford Press, NY. & London.

Barkley, R.A.; Murphy, K.R. & Fischer, M. (2008). *ADHD in Adults*. The Guilford Press, NY & London.

Baron-Cohen, S.L. & Frith, V. (1985). "Does The Autistic Child have a Theory of Mind?" *Cognition*, 21: 37-46.

Baron-Cohen, S.L. (1990). "Autism: A Specific Cognitive Disorder of Mind Blindness," *International Journal of Psychiatry*, 2: 81-90.

Biderman, C. (2007). The Efficiency of Therapeutic Intervention of "Activity-Group" among ADHD Children. (In Hebrew). *Thesis of M.A, School for L.D*, Haifa University.

Blank, S. & Fuchs-Shabtai, O. (2004). *Good Parents*. (In Hebrew). Kinneret, Zmora-Bitan, Dvir – Publishing House Ltd., Or Yehuda.

Bonshtein, U. & Wientraub, Z. (2006). Very Low Weight Neonatal's Mental Development and its Relevance to Psychotherapy. (In Hebrew). *Sihot – Dialogue. Israel Journal of Psychotherapy*, 11/1: 70-78.

Bergman, Z. & Cohen, E. (1994). *The Family – In Search of Equilibrium*. (In Hebrew), Am Oved Publishers Ltd, Tel Aviv.

Blos, P. (1982). The Modern Psychoanalytic Interpretation Of Adolescence. In: Muuse, R.E. Theories of Adolescence. Random House Inc. New York.

Bowllby, J. (1958). "The Nature of a Child's Tie to His Mother," *International Journal of Psychoanalysis*, 39: 73-350.

Bronfenbrenner, U. (1979). *The Ecology of Human Development: Experiments by Nature and Design*, Harvard University Press.

Bronfenbrenner, U. (1986). "Ecology of the Family as a Context for Human Development," *Development Psychology*, 22: 723-742.

Brown, T.E. (2000)."Attention Deficit Disorders and Comorbidities" *Children, Adolescents & Adults*, American Psychiatric Press Inc., Washington & London.

Brown, T.E. (2005). *Attention Deficit Disorder*, Yale University Press: Health & Wellness, New Haven & London.

Byrnes, J.P. (2001). *Minds, Brains and Learning*, Guilford Press. NY.

Caplan, G. (1970). *The Theory and Practice of Mental Health Consultation*, Basic Books, NY.

Einat, A. & Einat, T. (2006). *Accusation Script: Learning Disabilities, Truancy and Deliquency.* (In Hebrew). Hakibbutz Hameuchad, Tel Aviv.

Erikson, E.H. (1951). *Childhood and Society*, W.W.Norton. NY.

Fonagy, P. (2001). *Attachment Theory and Psychoanalysis*, Other Press, NY.

Fonagy, P., Gergely, G., Jurist, E.L. & Target, M. (2002). *Affect Regulation, Mentalization, and Development of the Self*, Karnac. London & NY.

Freud, A. (1966). *Normality and Pathology in Childhood, Assessment of Development*, International Press. New York

Freud, S. (1982). Psychoanalytic Theory of Adolescence. In: Muus. R.E. Theories of Adolescence. Random House. Inc. N.Y

Frith, U. (1989). *Autism: Explaining the Enigma.* Oxford: Basil Blackwell Ltd

Green, R.W. (1998). The Explosive Child. *A New Approach for Understanding and Parenting Easily Frustrated, "Chronically Inflexible" Children,* Guilford Publications, Inc. NY.

Greenspan, S.I. (1992). "Infancy and Early Childhood: The Practice of Clinical Assessment and Intervention with Emotional and Developmental Challenges," International Universities Press, Inc., Madison, CT.

Greenspan, S.I. & Wieder, S. (1993). "Regulatory Disorder" In: Zeanah C.H. (ed.) *Handbook of Infant Mental Health,* Guilford Press, NY.

Greenspan, S.I. & Wieder, S. (1995). *The Child with Special Needs*, Da Capo Press Cambridge, Massachusetts.

Greenspan, S.I. Chair (1994). *Diagnostic Classification: 0-3: Diagnostic Classification of Mental Health and Developmental Disorders of Infancy and Early Childhood*, Arlington, VA: ZERO TO THREE, National Center for Clinical Infant Programs.

Greenspan, S.I. (1998). *The Growth of the Mind and the Endangered Origins of Intelligence*, Preseus Books, MA.

Gross-Tsur, V. Shalev, R. (1995). "Developmental Right Hemisphere Syndrome: Clinical Spectrum of the Non-Verbal Learning Disabilities," *Journal of Learning Disabilities*, 28: 80-86.

Hagai, I. (2005). *My Special Child* (In Hebrew), Modan Publishing House. Ben-Shemen.

Hallowell, E.M. , Ratey, J.J. (2004*). Delivered from Distraction. Getting the Most Out of Life with Attention Deficit Disorder*, Ballantine Books, NY.

Hulme. C. & Snowling. M. (1997). *Dyslexia: Biology, Cognition and Intervention*, Whurr Publishers Ltd. London.

Klein, M. (2002). *Selected Writings.* (In Hebrew), Bookworm Publishers, Tel Aviv.

Klein, P. S. (1986). *More Smart Kids, Modification Cognitive Ability in Early Childhood.* (In Hebrew) Bar Ilan University Press,

Klein, P.S. (2000). *Babies, Infants, Parents and Care Givers.* (In Hebrew), Reches, Even Yehuda.

Kohut, H. (1977). *The Restoration of the Self,* International Universities Press Inc., Madison, CT.

Kohut, H. (1979). "Four Basic Concepts in Self Psychology". In: Ornsien, P. (ed.), *The Search of the Self: Selective Writings of Heinz Kohut*, Vol. 4. NY.

Kranowitz, C.K. (2005) . *The Out-of-Sync Child*, Penguin Group, Inc. NY

Lavoie, R. (2005). *It's So Much Work to Be Your Friend*, Touchstone, Simon & Schuster. NY.

LeDoux, J. (1996). *The Emotional Brain*, A TOUCHSTONE Book. NY.

Levine, M.D., (1987). *Developmental Variation and Leaning Disorders*, Educators Publishing Service, Inc., Cambridge & Toronto.

Mahler, M.S., Pine, F. & Bergman, A. (1975). *The Psychological Birth of the Human Infant: Symbiosis and Individuation.* Basic Books, NY.

Moss, D.M. (1989). *Shelley the Hyperactive Turtle*, Woodbine House, MD.

Muuss, R.E. (1982). *Theories of Adolescence*, Random House. Inc., N.Y

Nofar-Yishai, K. & Chen, M. (2006). *Special Kids (ADHD and L.D) and Their Interaction with School by the Theory of the Self*. (In Hebrew), Hebrew Psychological Net, Pardes Hana

Ogden, H.T., (1990) *The Matrix of the Mind*, Aronson, Jason Inc., Washington.

Oppenheimer, A. (1998). *Heinz Kohut.* Presses Universitaires de France, Paris

Osterweil, Z.O. (1995) *Open Solutions.* (In Hebrew), Schocken Publishing, Tel Aviv.

Piaget, J. & Inhalder, B. (1969). *The Psychology of the Child*, Basic Books, N.Y.

Piontelli, A. (1992*). From Fetus to Child. An Observational and Psychoanalytic Study*, Routledge/ Tavistock, London and NY.

Plotnik, R. (2003). *Both of Us Together and Each of Us Apart* . (In Hebrew), Yesod, Hollon.

Plotnik, R. (2007). *The Voice of Parenthood*. (In Hebrew), In: Cohen, E (ed.) *The Parenthood Experience: Relation, Coping and Development*, Ach, Kiryat Byalik.

Rapheal-Leff, J. (1993*). Pregnancy – The Inside Story*, Aronson, Jason Inc. Northvale, New Jersey, London.

Rapoport, J.L. & Ismond, D.R. (1996). *DSM-IV: Training Guide for Diagnosis of Childhood Disorders*, Brunner/ Mazel, Philadelphia, PA.

Segal, H. (1989). *Klein*, Other Press, LLC., NY

Solmas, M. & Trunbull, O. (2003). *The Brain and the Inner World. An Introduction to the Neuroscience of Subjective Experience*, Other Press, LLC., NY

Spencer, T., Biederman, J. & Wilens, T. (1998). "Growth Deficit in Children with Attention Deficit Hyperactivity Disorder." *Pediatrics*. 102 (2 Pt3): 501-506.

Spitz, R.A. (1965). *The First Year of Life*, International Universities Press, NY.

Stern, D.N. (1985). *The Interpersonal World of the Infant: A View from Psychoanalysis and Developmental Psychology*, Basic Books, NY.

Stern, D.N. (1995) *The Motherhood Constellation: A Unified View of Parent-infant Psychology*, Basic Books, NY.

Stern, D.N., Bruchweiler-Stern, N. & Freeland, A. (1998). *The Birth of a Mother,* Basic Books, NY.

Strenger, C. (2005). The Psychoanalysis of Contemporary Identities (In Hebrew). Am Oved Publishers Ltd. Tel Aviv.

Symington, J. & Symington, N. (1996). *The Clinical Thinking of Wilfred Bion,* Routledge. London and NY.

Thomas, A., Chess, S. & Birch, H.G. (1970). "The Origins of Personality," *Scientific American*, 223: 4-102.

Tuckman, A. (2007). *Iterative Treatment for Adult ADHD*, New Harbingr Publications, Inc.Okland.

Tyano, S. & Manor, I. (2001). *Living with Attention Deficit and Hyperactivity Disorder.* (In Hebrew), Tel Aviv University Press, Tel Aviv.

Winnicott, D. W. (1988). *Babies and Their Mothers*, De Capo Press. Cambridge, Massachusetts.

Winnicott, D. W. (1998). *The Child, the Family and the Outside World*, De Capo Press. Cambridge, Massachusetts.